In Search Of...

A Millennial Message of Hope in Turbulent Times

by

Alistair Smith

Centaine Publications

In Search Of...
A Millennial Message of Hope in Turbulent Times
by
Alistair Smith

Published 2000
Copyright © 1999 Alistair Smith

03 02 01 00   0 9 8 7 6 5 4 3 2 1

Published by
CENTAINE PUBLICATIONS

US Office:
33418 Furrow Court,
Wildomar, CA 92595

Canadian Office:
PO Box 79036
Hull, Quebec J8Y 6V2

alistair.smith@sympatico.ca

Cover photograph by Brandi Lepore

The names of some of the individuals in this book have been changed to protect their privacy.

ISBN: 1-929769-23-7
Printed in the United States of America

Table of Contents

Dedication

To My Parents, from whom I ask for forgiveness for the pain, the heartache and the anxiety I caused them as I grew up, and after I should have already grown up. They gave their all, and did the best they could. I ask them to rejoice in the joy of their son's newfound love, freedom and peace.

To My Children. As you grow up and travel your own journey of life, may I be able to offer you a guiding hand, a caring hug and a receptive ear. I wish you well in your own pursuit of love, freedom and peace, and may I refrain from placing any expectations on you other than your absolute happiness.

Acknowledgments

Many people have helped me on my journey, and to all of them I offer my deepest and most sincere thanks, in particular, Belinda and Sasha, the two women who shared my early struggles. May the pain they endured lead to a deeper understanding of love, and may their journey from here be more joyous.

To my brother and sister, for their love and support.

To my friends Robin, Karen, Gerard and, of course, Ashoka, who guided me on the way.

To Sabrina, who will always have a place in my heart.

And to two wonderful people who entered my life after the story in this book closes. To my friend, James Twyman, for his inspiration and encouragement, and to Janine, my lover, best friend, wife, teacher and spiritual companion, for simply being who she is.

And finally, to Tony Stubbs, my editor and book designer for crafting this beautiful volume.

Foreword

I vividly remember the first time I met Alistair. In the summer of 1998, I was leading a retreat in Assisi, Italy, once the home of St. Francis, one of the greatest sages the Western world has ever known. At Rome airport, I met the fifteen or so people with whom I would spend the next week, and they welcomed me, drew me in, and touched something deep inside. I was immediately struck by the intensity in Alistair's eyes, and wondered, who is this strange Australian who's suddenly fallen into my life? I hugged him, just as I did with the others, and thought about the adventure that lay ahead. But those eyes stayed in my mind, still focused on my soul.

After we'd arrived in Assisi and settled into our rooms, Alistair asked if he could speak with me for a moment. He said that ever since reading *Emissary of Light*, he knew he had to meet me. There are so many parallels, he said, between my journey and his own, and he hoped he would get the chance to share them with me. I promised that we would talk, and then walked away. I wasn't trying to put him off or say what I knew he wanted to hear. I knew that it was important and we'd get the chance. There was something wonderful and refreshing about him, and if he really was like me, then I hoped to find out how.

In retrospect, I understand what it was, and this same quality fills the book you're about to read. I have always said that people find it easy to identify with me because I'm so ordinary. I'm no different from anyone else, and that realization has filled me in a way I never expected. We live in a time of empowerment, of looking within to find the answers, of realizing that *we* are the answer we seek. In the past, we've often picked teachers who were different from us in one way or another—a simple egoic trick to make the guru "more" and us "less." But the fact that "ordinary" people are now springing into the light, into experiences that were once reserved for mystics or highly initiated spiritual practitioners, means that we all have permission. We all have what it takes to be enlightened right now, simply because it's the truth, no matter how ordinary we think we are.

Alistair is an ordinary man; this is his power, and this is how he and I are the same. Yet he has done something that we are all called to do. He has dissolved the boundaries and the walls that were keeping him from the experience of love, and broken into a boundless reality that reflects the truth within him, not the illusion. He has used the ordinary experiences of his life to do it, and that, I believe, is what the spiritual path is all about. It's not so much about achieving fantastic, supernatural powers, but choosing love every moment of every day, especially when those around us would rather choose conflict over peace. Alistair's journey shows us that *life* is the testing ground, that the truth is within us, and that mastery is achieved by looking into the eyes of one another and seeing the truth. It is so simple, and yet we often make it so hard.

Alistair's experiences are certainly inspiring, and the importance of the material should not be overlooked. His journey is for us all, for we are all the same in these things.

This is a fine, well-written book, one that has the power to change lives, and I am grateful to have the chance to share in Alistair's journey. And by the way, he was right. We are very much the same.

James F. Twyman, author of *Emissary of Light*

Preface

I'm at the peak of my life and my world is collapsing around me.

I'm successful. I've fought all the way, and have it all—a six-figure income, a successful marriage, a child and another on the way. We own our own four-bedroom home outright, no mortgage. My career is stellar. I'm in the fast lane, flying up the corporate ladder and have just been promoted to state-wide manager.

Oh, not everyone likes me, but they sure as hell respect me. I'm good at what I do and usually win in confrontation because I'm rarely wrong. I've done it all on my own, after all, that's what life is about. I've learned that you can't afford to rely on others. You can rely only on yourself , and stand on your own two feet.

As for God, who needs Him? All that nonsense is for weaklings, for those who can't hack it in the real world. They're not strong enough to face life's realities on their own, so they cling to their God. But I don't need to believe in such a lie; I'm doing just fine on my own. Besides, there's simply no scientific proof of God.

So, here I am, king of the world, until the unthinkable happens! It begins quietly and slowly and, at first, I can push it away, but it grows in volume until it's screaming. There's no doubt about it; a message is coming from somewhere inside of me, from somewhere so deep, somewhere that can't be real.

The message? "It's all a lie!"

"What's a lie?" I ask.

"Your life. It's all a big lie! Your life is false. Just look at yourself. Are you blind!"

I try to push the irritating voice away, but it won't quit. Instead it gets louder, stronger, and unmistakable. As it gets louder, I begin to panic and try to protect everything I've built around me. Help me, someone! Won't anyone help me?

But there's nobody there for me, no one to turn to because the only things I believe in are myself and my life's accomplishments. Yet this damned voice tells that even my life is a lie, that it's false, that everything I stand for is meaningless.

I'm 36, broken, lost, freefalling, alone in my own darkness, and in pain. Not physical pain, but a deep inner pain. After years of being driven by arrogance and self-centeredness, some part of me is in revolt, fighting back, unwilling to stand by and watch as I career headlong down a path of self-destruction.

Oh, to a casual observer, I seem to be cruising in the fast lane, but my inner world is in turmoil as some unknown part of me sabotages my happiness, not that I've ever been genuinely happy. Yet nobody knows, because, frankly, who would I tell? My wife? My family? No, I shut them all out long ago. And what would I tell them, anyway? I'm having a midlife crisis. I don't think so, but what the hell *is* going on?

I see three options: (1) Deny the feeling and try to live in as much material abundance as I can; (2) Suffer in silence, darkness and loneliness; or (3) Get to the bottom of what's going on, face the truth, acknowledge the superficiality of my life, and do something about it.

My first choice is (1) since it beats suffering (which I hate), and who wants to admit that his life is a lie. So I throw myself into my work, and life is good for a while, but then the darkness and loneliness return, followed by that damned voice, stronger than ever. "It's all a lie. Nothing's changed. Look at yourself. Your life is false. It's all a lie!"

This time, I can't ignore the voice and the physical symptoms that accompany it. I lost sight of the truth long ago, and have no tools with which to even face the truth. In fact, I really have no idea who Alistair Smith *really* is, buried as he is, like a hapless skier under an avalanche.

This is one person's story of the search for his real self, a search for the truth, a story of realizing the emptiness of a superficial life, and the journey from inner darkness to light. It's also a story of searching for love—first unsuccessfully in other people, and then a higher source, and through that, of learning to love myself rather than constantly punish myself, learning to love myself, not for *what I am* and my meaningless achievements, but for *who I am*, complete with all the imperfections.

This is not a book about psychological theory. Nor is it a book about a particular spiritual path, although it certainly brings in psychology and spirituality. Neither do I hold it up as a blueprint for anyone else. No, it's simply the story of an ordinary person, just like you, who lost his way in life and fought back to meaning. May it inspire you to look at your own life and start your journey to the light within.

This book is akin to field notes, much like an explorer would write. However, the territory being explored is the human condition. As such, I encountered new concepts and terms, and have defined them as I saw them at that point in the journey. One concept, however, is so crucial that it deserves special mention here: the concept of God. Of all the concepts, this gave me the greatest concern. Its evolving definition also reveals the growth made along the way.

I began my journey with something close to the acceptance of the word God in our society—the remote, judgmental being that Christianity portrays—something I rejected out of hand. So where am I now?

I perceive the existence of a "true me," the essence of who I am, my spirit, my soul, or what some term "the higher self." This "me" exists in a continuum of consciousness, at one end of which is what I term "my human," my body, my emotions, and my thoughts. My soul has taken on my human to enable it to manifest its truth on Earth, and to experience what it needs to. At the other end of the spectrum is "universal consciousness," or what I call God.

My soul/spirit came from pure universal consciousness, and will, at some unimaginable point in the future, merge back with it. In the meantime, my spirit/soul is caught in a struggle. In one corner is my human—who sees himself through the ego as separate from others, and who therefore seeks to control and possess them to make himself feel safe and worthwhile. In the other corner is universal consciousness, which is total harmony and oneness.

In terms of reincarnation, my spirit/soul has, and will continue to, manifest many "humans" in order to explore the fullness of the human condition and grow towards fully conscious awareness of being part of universal consciousness.

My mission in writing this and future books is to focus on the transformation from the old ego-bound human to the new boundless human, living in the harmony and oneness that manifests when we know we are an intimate part of universal consciousness.

It has become apparent to me that my life is going according to a plan being orchestrated by a higher power, and that there is a great plan, of which we are all part. After listening to a tape by Carolyn Myss, it occurred to me that, "We should treat life like a mystery novel in which we each play a character, and God is the writer."

However, to say that it is our higher self that is the writer, implies to me that that we can control our lives totally through our own power. But what about the higher selves of all the other humans? They also have plans, so how do their plans interact with ours? How can the synchronicity that we see so much at play occur unless all the higher selves are linked in some common consciousness? Yes, our higher selves are very much at play in our lives, but to me there is a vaster consciousness—one to which each of our higher selves is connected—that controls the game. This is what I refer to as God, although I was not aware of this when my journey began.

The question of taking personal responsibility for our lives is another classic question I have grappled with. Many people in my life have thrown this curve at me. Many sources tell us that we create our own reality and must take responsibility for our own lives. However, to me, this has connotations of ego, of the "human" trying to take responsibility for the bigger picture, trying to manipulate things so that we get what we think is right for us.

Yes, I believe that I have total responsibility for my life, but that my responsibility is to listen to what God, universal consciousness, call it what you like, wants me to do. In other words, if I'm a player in a football team, then higher consciousness is the coach. My job is to align myself with the other members of the team so that we do what the coach wants us to do, albeit colored by each player's own flair and creativity. If I take it upon myself to define the game plan, then all is lost.

Do these instructions come from my higher self or from God? I don't know enough about either to answer that categorically. However, I believe my higher self, spirit, or soul, is intimately connected to the larger consciousness, or God, receives messages from that source, and passes them on to my human for implementation. The extent to which I am a spiritual person, then, is a function of how well I listen to the messages, and how easily I can sublimate my own ego needs to them. Easier said than done, eh!

Part One • Ego Meltdown

The Journey Starts

MARCH 16, 1992, and my second child will be born today. My other creation—my company's biggest bid ever, a $200 million proposal to build Sydney Airport's third runway—is due tomorrow, and must be finished tonight.

I think to myself, everything is under control. My staff will work all night and Belinda's mother has arrived to look after our four-year-old daughter. I plan to go to the hospital with my wife, and return to the office after the birth. The delivery will be by C-section due to problems with delivering our first child, so it will be over by noon and she'll be "out of it" for the rest of the day. I'll be back at work by mid-afternoon.

The delivery goes according to plan, except for the pain Belinda feels. No one warned us that it would be agony. It's a boy; we call him Paul. Everything seems okay, so I return to the office. It should be a day of celebration—a proud father spending the day with the people he loves, celebrating the birth of a beautiful boy—but that doesn't happen. No, it's back to the office to put the finishing touches to our airport bid. What a buzz if we win this one. As we leave the office at three the next morning, I'm so proud of my staff, for their dedication. Everything's under control, and we feel we have the winning bid, so I drive home early that morning dreaming of success.

A few days later, my wife is moved to a private hospital in Sydney's North Shore. I arrive with a bottle of wine to celebrate but she's far from happy. "Alistair, where do your priorities really lie? What's more important to you, your family or some airport runway? I'm not sure I can survive in this marriage."

Naturally, I resent her words because I'm doing it all for them anyway, but I smile and say, "Look, you know how busy I've been, but I'll really try to make changes, okay."

Why can't she understand? Why can't she see how hard it is for me? I'm doing my best, in the only way I know how, but I'm caught in a trap, torn between my work and my family. I love the excitement of being in Sydney and fully immersed in my work. But I know I'm not giving my family what they need in other ways. Why can't Belinda see the strain I'm under, and be more supportive, rather than always trying to change me? She always makes it my fault! I'm the real victim here, and people are always trying to change me, always trying to make me into what they want me to be rather than just let me be me. Why is it always me that has to change? Why can't other people give a little?

A few weeks later, I have to drive to Newcastle for the day, a trip of about 200 kilometers. On the way, I have car trouble and while it's being fixed, I end up spending time in a house owned by an elderly man. The house overlooks one of the many beautiful ocean inlets in the area, and I'm forced to sit down on his patio and relax for a few hours—a rare thing for me. I'm overwhelmed by the peace of the place, and feel as though I'm in a different world. The peace of that house touches something inside me, and all the way home, I think that there must be more to life. I guess that this something inside me, whatever it is, is trying to send me a message, but I have no idea what. Once back home, however, I'm able to push its disquieting message away and blast on with my usual fast-paced life.

Around this time, things rapidly begin to deteriorate at work. After we lost the airport job, the usual internal company politics flare up, and I hear through the grapevine that my job is in danger. On impulse one morning, I pick up the newspaper and casually look through the job ads. I'm not really looking, but one ad jumps out at me with the South Australian Gas Company, an Adelaide utility company. This piques my interest since we own a house in Adelaide and it's where my wife calls home. Our decision to move to Sydney a year earlier was really my decision in order to further my career, a decision, in all honesty, that I pretty much imposed on my unwilling family.

This job also appeals since being in Adelaide would make life easier for me, not because I have friends there, but because I would feel under less pressure from my wife and kids. I reason that if I move back to Adelaide, then I've done my part and can focus more on work.

I apply, and two weeks later, my employer announces that the office I manage will be closed, and we'll all soon be laid off. My office includes a group of specialists in cleaning up contaminated sites. They decide they want to stay together if at all possible, and I agree to lead them. After a week of frantic phone calls and interviews, a company from Perth, on the other side of the country, expresses interest in employing our entire team and establishing a new office in Sydney. Before flying to Perth to meet them, I call the company in Adelaide to check on my application and learn that I've been short-listed.

In Perth, also where I grew up and where my parents and brother live, I meet with the company's managing director, whom I know personally. The meeting goes well and he agrees to everything we've asked for. I should be overjoyed, but oddly I feel miserable and leave the interview feeling as though I've just signed my own death warrant. It's more than mere apprehension; it's a gut-wrenching desolation, as if I'm being screamed at from inside, telling me not to accept the position. But, I tell myself, I'm also representing three other people and must consider them, too.

I have dinner with my brother and parents, but just can't get involved in the conversation. I feel physically sick, and the inner turmoil increases, as if my insides are being torn apart. I hope the feelings will go away, but if anything, they intensify. I simply don't understand what's happening, so I invent a whole slew of reasons for why I feel so bad, and push it out of my mind.

A few days later, the team and I accept the assignment with the Perth company. Hours later, the Gas Company recruitment agent calls to ask me to come to Adelaide for an interview. I tell him he's too late but he won't take no for an answer. The interview goes well and two weeks later, I'm offered a job in Adelaide. However, I'm already committed to staying in Sydney despite my family's unhappiness. So now I'm pulled in two.

On the one hand, the Adelaide offer is simply too good to refuse, so I know I have to accept it. I owe it to my family to accept it, not just because it's a move back to Adelaide, but because of the stability of working for a public utility. It would mean that the itinerant life of construction work is over. But there's another reason I have to accept it: it just feels right. I have a strong inner feeling that this job is meant to be, compared with the dread I felt over the job with the Perth company.

On the other hand, it isn't that simple. I feel bad about leaving the Perth company, having so recently joined them. Secondly, I'm worried about what will happen to my team members, who have also joined me. I worry about what everyone will think of me, and once again, I feel physically sick with anxiety. I'm torn between other people's expectations of me, or worse, my own perception of their expectations. Yet I want to do what's right for my family.

I think long and hard about what seems to be a contradiction. On the one hand, I'm admittedly controlling, self-centered, and generally driven by what's best for me. But on the other hand, I care about how others feel and what I think they expect of me. I know that I can't satisfy both. My wife thinks I'm failing to meet my family obligations, which only serves to make the situation worse. She jokingly refers to my work as the "other woman," yet that soon takes on a far more serious tone. I feel she's judging me, and it brings up a deep guilt that I try not to acknowledge.

I finally summon the courage to tell the company I'm leaving. My misgivings prove groundless; my boss fully understands the family situation and assures me that he will keep the other team members on. With a great sigh of relief, I wonder why I'd worried so much? Had I created all the problems in my own head?

We move to Adelaide in October, 1992, and I step off the plane at Adelaide with hope in my heart, hope for a new start, a new job, less stress, and my wife back in her home town and in our own house. By changing my external environment, I hope that the deep sense of unease that has begun to plague me will be calmed, and that I'll find a quick fix to my inner turmoil.

The change of pace is a Godsend for me personally. In the construction industry, where I've spent nearly all of my working life, the focus is always on getting the job done. People issues are low on the list of priorities, unless they're likely to cause an industrial dispute. At the Gas Company, it's very different. People who see themselves as employees-for-life focus more on their long term development than on getting the job done. But given time, I'll change all that.

My boss, Robert, is around 6 feet 6 inches tall, and several years older than me. He separated from his wife a few years earlier and I discover he has a passion for personal development. I soon find myself being challenged by him to explore what's happening in my life. Our personalities are uncomfortably similar, and I get the feeling he knows exactly what's going on in my head, even when I don't.

Along the way, I encounter Fenn, an internal human relations consultant, and a woman of significant intuition and insight. She sums me up in about five minutes and takes it upon herself to change me. With an uncanny insight into people, Fenn tells me what I must do to adapt to the organization's culture. I listen to her advice because a few incidents have already shown me that people skills are definitely not my strong point, and my bull-in-a-china-shop style is not winning any popularity contests.

One of our first joint initiatives is to set up a team to implement internal changes within my division. I establish a group of four young people with energy and enthusiasm, who are assigned to research workplace changes. They, together with Fenn, will assist me to drive the changes that are obviously needed if the company is to survive in the increasingly competitive market. I was hired for my "atta boy" approach, and feel that I'm doing all the right things, so while I outwardly support the team, and indeed hand-pick its members, my hidden agenda is really to use it more as a tool to change the corporate culture to something I'm more familiar with, and to change the attitudes of the managers reporting to me and their subordinates.

One day early in 1993, I'm sitting in my office feeling pretty good about my first three months' accomplishments, when two team members, Robin and Julie, come to see me. Robin is a Field Supervisor and Julie is coordinator of the Drawing Office. Both have high energy and I selected them because of this, as well as their willingness to look at things from a different perspective. Neither are they bashful about saying what they think. In fact, what they have to say takes my breath away.

"Look, Alistair, we think you're a good manager as far as that goes, but you don't know how to manage change at all. Unless you change how you communicate and unless you make a real commitment to change yourself, then there's no point in us doing anything. We might as well disband the team."

What a shock! These people, hand-picked by me, are attacking me and challenging who I am. What gives them the right? Here's the very team I put together to change others telling me that first of all I have to change myself. Normally, I would bite their heads off, but I'm dumbstruck, and they simply turn around and leave, message delivered.

Christ, this starts me thinking. Sure, I'm having problems with some employees, but I'm trying to change them for their own good. However, they're resisting me, and in turn trying to change me to fit in with what they want because they don't have the guts to deal with me the way I am. And, of course, when things go wrong, it's just this damn company, with its "touchy-feely" attitudes that people matter more than productivity.

But why, I ask myself, would Robin and Julie feel impelled to raise this matter so directly. I respect their openness and honesty, and know that telling me that *I'm* the major problem must have taken a lot of courage, so I'm not going to dismiss it out of hand.

As I drive home that night, I reflect on my habit of trying to change others. I wish I could talk to Belinda about this, but I've lost the ability to do that. So I ask others for feedback, something I've never done before. I tell Fenn and the team that I need help, and ask them to tell me when I'm not doing the right thing. Robert is a great help in this area. He's very much into team-building and pushes me to explore my relationship with others at work and what it means for myself. Maybe his life will provide me with a few pointers that will help me to discover who I really am. If I am to go through some changes, maybe even a major metamorphosis, perhaps I've landed in exactly the right place.

On the home front, my children are growing up. I try to be there for them whenever I can, but admit that I'm never really present emotionally. In my own way, I love them dearly and want to give my best to them, but I just don't know how. My thoughts are always elsewhere. My daughter has been diagnosed with Attention Deficit Disorder (ADD), which will later be enlarged to include Aspberger's Syndrome (higher functioning autism). Getting involved in the ADD Association keeps Belinda and I both busy and compensates for the emptiness in our relationship. The ADD movement provides a common focus and something to talk about. We both firmly believe we're doing the right thing by being involved, but in my truthful moments, I know I'm driven more by a desire for personal success than anything else. Also, to make up for the lack of joy in my life, I busy myself with construction projects around the house.

Hovering on the edge of my denial is the awareness that even though I'll talk to people about most anything, I can't talk about my real feelings, not even to Belinda. In fact, I've lost the ability to talk to anyone about my *real* feelings. Sure, I can talk easily and openly to people about feelings, as along they're positive or non-threatening, or opinions or judgements of others. I am totally unable, however, to talk about anything I feel is threatening or could reveal my insecurities or vulnerabilities. Hell, I can't even talk to myself about them, and hastily suppress any uncomfortable feelings, refusing to acknowledge their existence.

The more unhappy and lonely I feel, the busier I keep myself. However, my rising stress level leads to chronic muscle spasms in my neck and jaw. My neck often goes into a spasm, and the muscles form a knot about the size of a golf ball. It feels like my neck and the back of my head are being squeezed in a large vise. Sometimes, it's so bad that I can't move my neck more than a few degrees. The spasms last for weeks at a time, and the slightest increase in stress triggers one.

My jaw spasms so badly one day, the pain so great that I can't eat, and so in desperation I make an appointment with Heather, a local doctor who recently moved to the area. She immediately strikes me as a friendly, helpful woman.

"My jaw is so sore that I can't eat anything which needs chewing, and I can't stop grinding my teeth together," I tell her as I sit down.

She looks at my swollen left jaw. "My God, Alistair, this is serious. You must do something about your stress level."

"I can't help it. I just have so much pressure on my plate. I handle it pretty well, but every now and then, it spills over."

She gives me a puzzled look but decides not to pursue that line of conversation. "I'll give you some Valium this time, but remember, it's only a stopgap, not a long term solution."

"What's actually happening to me? Why is my jaw like this?"

"Well, the human body has a point at which it goes into distress and lets you know that things are not right. This distress manifests itself in different ways in everybody, but the neck and jaw are both common stress points. Some stress in life is normal, but a continuous elevated level causes the body to go into spasm."

"So my stress level is pretty high?" I ask, already knowing the answer.

"Yes, in your case, your normal stress level seems to be so high that the merest increase in stress triggers a spasm, and it just keeps building on itself. And it isn't going to get any better on its own."

One Saturday, Belinda is planning to go out for the afternoon. My frustration level has built up and I feel agitated as we do the weekly shopping. My daughter throws a mild tantrum and I explode at her. I pick her up and push her back into the car seat, into which she refuses to go. As I strap the seat belt tightly around her, my stream of language lets her know exactly what I think about her behavior.

Just as stress builds up in the earth's crust and releases violently in an earthquake, mine has built up, and I've been able to suppress it, at least until now. My poor daughter just happens to be in the wrong place at the wrong time and triggers a release of pent-up stress that's out of all proportion to her minor tantrum.

Months and years of trying to control my frustration and pain through suppression rather than expression, fall away and I lose control, my words erupting in a torrent that must terrify the little girl they are directed at. Belinda reacts to my outburst by canceling her afternoon plans and refusing to go out, claiming that she no longer trusts me to be around the children. She is clearly upset and the way she speaks makes me feel that I'm responsible for, once more, ruining her weekend. This burns me up inside even more, and I resent her for it, so I unleash my anger on her, too.

Later, once I calm down, I see that she's not really to blame. She, too, is only reacting and trying to protect the children in her own way, and in any case, I don't think she has any idea how to deal with me. Anger was rarely expressed in her family and she simply doesn't know how to confront it. I know she needs a good dose of love and understanding, but we've both lost the ability to dispense even a small amount of that special commodity to each other. Instead, we try to manage our own fear and vulnerability by controlling each other.

One day in particular, I'm feeling pretty good about myself until I come home and my mood disintegrates around me. I walk in the door and immediately get into a row with the kids. They just want to be with their Dad, just want to be given some love, and I just want to left alone.

I'm struggling so much with myself that I've nothing left to give to those in my life, and for the first time in my marriage, I'm faced with the fact that I don't want to be there. I sit on my bed and cry, and cry. I don't know what else to do. I feel crushed by the pressures of the world, as though I've spent my whole life doing things for other people, and that now, I don't even have a life left. There's only a deep, aching emptiness, a black, hollow pit of despair. But I have no idea what to do or where to turn.

After my first performance appraisal with Robert, I linger in his office, desperate to talk to someone. I don't know how to start the conversation so I blurt out few words and as I do, I open up like a dam bursting. "I feel so much pain for my children, it breaks my heart. They just want their dad to love them, to give them even a little part of himself. Is that too much to ask? I want so much to be a good dad. I love my children, and in many ways I would do anything for them. But the cold hard truth is that I do very little for them. I'm so caught up fighting the world that I've nothing to give them."

"Who are you really fighting?" he asks, with compassion in his voice. "It's not easy, I know. But so much of our pain is driven by guilt, and this only makes it worse."

"Belinda thinks I'm self-centered and selfish, that everything I do is for me, but the truth is I spend my whole life doing things for other people."

" I don't believe you're doing everything for other people. People like you and I don't do that. We do things because we want to. We can consciously choose to do things for other people because it makes us feel good."

"What do you mean?" I ask suspiciously, not liking what he's saying.

"It seems to me that you're being driven by fear. You have to prove yourself all the time, as if you're fighting the world. But who are you really fighting? To you, everything has to be flat out, has to be the best. Maybe you should look at spending time with your children as an achievement rather than a chore."

I put my head in my hands and slump on his desk. "I don't know," I mumble through my fingers. "I just feel such frustration. There's no light in my life."

"You know, I used to feel like that. What I realized was that I didn't have an effective release mechanism. So I turned my frustration inwards at myself until it was eating at me like a cancer. When we don't release our anger, it builds until it erupts out of all proportion, often over silly little things."

He's right, I think. This is what happens with my children. "I can see what you're saying. I do this with my children and then I feel really bad. Then I torture myself for taking my anger out on them."

"Yeah, I hear what you're saying. But that only makes it worse. It ties in with what I was saying earlier. Your self-persecution further adds to a sense of worthlessness. I think you need to take a good hard look at yourself, my friend. You can't keep on fighting the world to prove yourself on the one hand and yet persecute yourself on the other. You're on a vicious cycle to self-destruction and personality meltdown."

No one has ever spoken to me like this before and I'm not sure how to respond. All I can say is, "But what can I do?"

"You've got to stop being afraid to look honestly at yourself. And you've got to stop blaming others. Stand up to your fears. Perhaps you should go to a counselor."

The hell I will, I think. I'm not crazy and certainly don't need to see a shrink. But as I reflect on his words, I'm even more confused. Part of me wants to get angry with him. What's all this talk about fear? I don't want to hear about my fear. I'm not afraid of anything. But am I? Deep down, I know he's right, but I'm damned if I'll acknowledge it.

To show Robert just how wrong he is, I throw myself into work with renewed vigor, making myself busier than ever. I'm certainly not going to admit to myself that my life is as barren as the toxic dumps I used to clean up.

Internal Change Agent

ONE DAY FENN pops into my office. "Good morning, Alistair," she chirps in her usual friendly voice. "I want to talk to you about a new program the company has just initiated." "Oh no, not the latest human relations fad."

"Well, I don't think so. It's an Employee Assistance Program, where employees can go for counseling. It's free and totally confidential. I think a few of your employees could benefit from it. Perhaps you can let them all know about it and encourage them to go."

She looks at me with the oddest pleading expression, and as she leaves my office, I have a feeling she's talking about me. Has Robert been talking to her? Shit, I don't need to see a counselor. There's nothing wrong with me. I'm the last person who needs to see a shrink. But why, I wonder, are Robert and Fenn trying to help me? Do they think I need help? Am I really being honest with myself? Okay, maybe not totally. What the hell, I've nothing to lose, so I make an appointment.

Debbie is the epitome of sweetness. Sharp too; it takes her only seconds to figure out that I'm over-stressed, taking on too much, and have no time to myself. "You need to learn to relax," she suggests.

I laugh, "You've got to be joking. Me, relax?"

"Well, we could try hypnotherapy."

I look skeptical, so she adds, "It's nothing like you see on television. In a hypnotic state, your mind is able to accept positive messages rather than immediately taking a critical, negative position. You're totally aware of what I'm saying and can pull yourself out of trance if you're uncomfortable with anything I say."

"Okay, it can't hurt," I agree, cautiously.

11

The next week I go back for my first hypnotherapy session. Debbie says, "So, make yourself comfortable." Then she talks to me in a soft, soothing tone until I'm in a deeply relaxed state. I go into relaxation easily, which surprises me. She shows me how I can slow my body down and relax my muscles. The tension just pours from me and I feel like a wet rag. Maybe there's hope after all, I think as I come out of the session feeling as though I'm floating. My voice is softer and slower. All week, I look forward to my next session but I'm in for a shock! In her soft, soothing voice, Debbie says, "Lie back and relax. Now, I want you to remember a time when you were really happy. When you do, just raise your left hand."

I'm stuck. I simply can't remember ever being really happy. I try hard to recall a time when I was really happy, but I can't. I start to panic as my mind darts over the years of my marriage, and back over earlier relationships to my college years, but there's nothing there. Oh, I recall being satisfied at having achieved something, but that's different. It usually involved winning, being heralded as being the best, or getting acknowledged by my superiors. I simply can't remember ever being happy, so Debbie closes the session and gives me a relaxation tape to listen to.

I know I have to do something and fast, but I've no idea what. I continue with the sessions for a while, and religiously listen to the tape, but more often than not, it simply puts me to sleep. Over time, however, I find myself feeling calmer and able to reduce the amount of wine I habitually drink every night to deaden my despair.

Based on the success of the relaxation tape, I buy a visualization tape that requires me to imagine I'm in a scene that the narrator talks me through. When I first use the tape, I have some strange experiences, as though it's too powerful for me. I stop using it because the intense anger that wells up scares me. After a few weeks, however, I find that I can handle the feelings, and soon, I'm comfortable with it, but although it helps me reduce stress and feel calmer, I'm still no happier with my life.

One night, I'm driving to an ADD committee meeting. The group is having problems and is on the verge of collapsing, so I expect the meeting will be difficult. I feel myself tightening up, but suddenly, my whole body comes alive as massive currents of energy course through me. However, it's negative, angry energy, not positive, and I know that I must not go into the meeting like this.

After sitting in the parking lot for ten minutes, I'm finally calm enough to be among other people, albeit scared out of my wits at what just happened.

At previous meetings, I've successfully managed to stay calm and not dominate the proceedings, but tonight, I feel possessed, and despite my best efforts, can't help but be negative and critical. A couple of times, I have to get up and leave the room on the pretence of going to the bathroom.

A few days later, I'm in another session with Debbie and I tell her about the meeting experience. "What's happening?" I ask.

"Well, it seems like you just went back to your old self for the evening. Probably that's how your nervous system used to feel all the time, but you never realized it because your system was used to it. But the relaxation has calmed your body down and now, when you return to your old state, you really notice it."

"I'm not sure I understand."

"It's like the boy who lives in a big city, and then he moves to a quiet country town. He gets used to the slower pace of life, so when he returns to the city, everything seems so fast, and he wonders how he could have lived like that. But he never noticed it when he lived there because he was used to it. Your body is like that. The nervous system is like the roads and highways. Through relaxation, you've slowed down the flow of your nervous energy, so when you go back to the crazy, frenetic pace, you really notice it."

"Okay, I understand." After a moment's reflection, I add, "Debbie, how did I ever live like that?"

"Many people do, but it can't last for ever. Something always has to give."

Not long afterwards, we're on a family vacation in Melbourne, staying in a trailer. Four of us in a small trailer in the middle of winter isn't the easiest environment, and to stay calm, I listen to my relaxation tape two or three times a day. This alone tells me just how far I've come on my journey. I've become acutely aware of how negatively I used to view the world, and how easily I got frustrated and lashed out at my family.

While this awareness is a positive step, I know that it's still far from satisfactory. I'm simply suppressing my anger and controlling it through relaxation. I need to transform the negative forces inside me so that I can be free to enjoy life without constantly being on guard. But how?

I measure the success of the vacation not in terms of how much fun everyone is having, but by how well I am managing my anger. And ironically, I'm now even unhappier than before because I'm far more aware of my problems, but there's still no solution in sight.

The drive back from Melbourne is difficult. It's raining heavily but I insist on doing the driving the whole way. I'm feeling pretty good, but as we pull into our driveway, I'm hit by a tidal wave of negativity. A powerful force surges up from deep within me and out through every cell, reminding me of when I was about ten years old, and would wake up in terror as a huge black cloud enveloped and consumed me. It feels just the same, and my body goes so crazy that I'm scared, really scared.

I need to get away, so I tell everyone that I'll unpack the car alone, and then go to the store. The truth is that I'm terrified at the prospect of getting angry with the children, who are grumpy after a nine-hour drive. The trip to the store is a disaster, and I bitch and moan at the checkout clerk. I know I'm being a royal pain-in-the-neck, but I'm powerless to stop. Maybe I've been on guard for too long, stuffing my emotions during the vacation, and now that I can relax, it's just pouring out. So I get on my own case, and chew myself out for letting my negativity get the better of me. Out in the parking lot, I cringe at the way I treated the folks in the store, but this just makes things worse.

Things are no better when I get back home. My mother-in-law, who's been housesitting for us, says to my wife, "Alistair doesn't seem to smile as much, now that he's doing all this relaxation stuff."

Now, my mother-in-law is very dear to me. She is a devoted Christian in the true sense of the word, unlike those who think that because they go to church on Sunday, they're somehow more godly or superior to the rest of us. That too few Christians truly follow the teachings of Jesus turned me long ago against organized religion, but my mother-in-law is one of those rare exceptions. Even so, anything that isn't endorsed by her church is deemed "New Age" and therefore not to be trusted, including my relaxation and hypnotherapy practices.

Her comment strikes a nerve. First, it's absolutely true, and second, it shows me that I'm actually making progress, funny as that may sound. I'm not smiling as much for two reasons. First, I'm now aware of just how dominating and intimidating I can be, and how extreme my mood swings are. I use relaxation to smooth my emotions, so not only am I less abrupt and aggressive, but I smile and joke a lot less. Of course, taking the spontaneity out of life is not smart, but until I develop confidence in my ability to control myself, it's essential.

Secondly, and more important, I'm slowly getting more in touch with myself, and realizing just how messed up my life is, how lost I am and how false my life is. I derive no happiness from it, but although I imagine that there's much more to life than I'm able to receive, or to give, I really have no idea what is it, or how to tap into it.

I have no one I can talk to, because there's nobody who I trust with my dark secret. It's too scary to talk to the people in my life about how I feel, and in any case, I don't even know how I feel. All I know is that it's all wrong. I'm alone and lost, very lost, and very scared.

Finally, however, the fear of not confronting my demons is becoming greater than the fear of having a showdown with them. I know that I must look deep into myself and face the reality of who I am and where I am, but do I have the strength to do that? Yes, I've mastered the art of proving that I'm okay, that I'm a good and worthwhile human being, but to whom am I trying to prove it? The only person who really needs to know is me; no one else really gives a damn.

At this point, I hit another roadblock. To give up my act of being okay, I need somewhere else to move to. I know I'm not secure enough as a person to strike out into no-man's land, trusting that I'll end up somewhere better. I don't have a God to put my faith in, only myself. Yes, I can sense that there's a part of me desperately trying to send me SOS messages but its voice is drowned out by my need to control—what some would call my dominant ego—and I've no idea how to stop it.

My misery is now compounded by the recognition of myself for what I am, and I spiral down into self-recrimination. No wonder I suppress my feelings. No wonder I don't know how to love. No wonder I can't give anything of myself. I'm just an empty shell, mechanically going about my duties in the outer world, but unable to function inwardly, unable to deal with emotions and feelings, and unable to give. I'm a taker, a user, whose actions are driven solely by "what's in it for me."

The people around me have no idea just how bad things are. How can they possibly know when even I don't know? I'm still figuring it all out. I don't show anybody what's going on inside, not even myself. All they see is an empty shell, an outer exterior, an arrogant and over-confident, self-centered person, who has life pretty good, and seems to get his own way most of the time. But surely that's not who I really am? Surely there's something more worthwhile deep inside.

While this is going on, I continue to make progress at work. I accept that I have to change my management style and how I interact with people. Ironically, the changes I make at work drag me forward in the rest of my life. And as "fate" would have it, a woman comes into my life who turns everything upside down. I need to hire two graduate engineers, and Fenn and I set up a rigorous interview process for the short-listed candidates that involves interacting with a number of managers. Sasha comes through with flying colors, and is the only person we're interested in hiring.

Although Sasha is attractive, sexy even, I label myself "married" and deny any physical attraction she might hold for me. Therefore, the intense inner excitement I feel when she accepts the job takes me completely by surprise. Anticipation and joy bubble up like springwater from somewhere deep in the earth, unlike anything I recall feeling before. Where is this coming from, I wonder.

Sasha is an interesting and challenging person, quick-thinking and analytical, but at the same time unusually intuitive about how people are thinking. She is an intriguing blend of maturity (older than her years) and girlish vulnerability. She holds strong opinions and is forthright in her criticism when managers, including me, fail to live up to her expectations.

At this time, most utility companies are exploring outsourcing, in which contractors replace employees. I feel this is a cop-out, an admission that someone else can motivate and manage people better than we can, so I launch a three-year program to change the culture of the employees. I have already made major strides, but Sasha accelerates that progress and promises to be a new source of challenge and growth in my life. She enjoys confronting me, and one day, storms into my office, demanding, "What are you really trying to do here? Do you really know what your motives are?"

Taken aback by her accusatory tone, my initial response is hostile and negative, but I admire her courage to do this. Also, I have to admit that it's a good question because I can't answer it.

Old grievances come to a head in the management team of which I am a member. During a meeting, I make an offhand, cutting remark and one of the other members comes unglued. "Who the hell do you think you are? All you can do is sit there with your smug high-and-mighty attitude and pour scorn on the rest of us. Well, I've got news for you. I'm sick and tired of your arrogance."

In the stunned silence, Robert adjourns the meeting to allow everyone to cool down.

That evening, I replay the incident over and over in my head, and realize that I have to change more rapidly. I must find a way to defuse the hostility that's built up against me. A year earlier, I'd have ripped the other guy's head off for not been able to accept that I was right. So I'm pleased that, for once, I haven't blamed others for being wrong, and can take some of the responsibility, but I guess there's still room for improvement.

The next morning, I contact all the other members of our team and ask for honest feedback on how they perceive me and how I come across to them. Well, to their credit, they give it to me, all right. Right between the eyes. Listening to their views without making disparaging rebuttals is agonizing and takes all my strength. But I asked for feedback, so I must just listen and then ask what I can do differently to make their life more pleasant.

After these painful meetings, I talk to Robert. "Well done. It takes guts to ask people for their honest opinion."

"You have no idea how hard it was not to retaliate and tell them what I thought of them."

"Oh, I suspect I have a pretty good idea. So what did you find out?"

"Apart from Paul, they all seem to find me intimidating."

"So why do you think that is?"

"Well, Paul and I really respect each other, but if I'm honest, I don't have enough respect for other people's ability and I guess that comes across."

"Hole in one! You and Paul have similar strengths. My impression is that you judge people based on your own strengths, and from your own perspective. Because your strengths are very strong, when other people aren't as strong in those areas, you don't value them. This certainly comes across in the way you talk to them. They feel judged and unworthy. You have to admit it, you can be pretty challenging. Even I feel it."

"I guess you're right. I've never looked at it like that. So what can I do about it?"

"You need to recognize that everyone is different. We all have different skills and strengths. Try to value others based on what *they're* good at, and not what *you* consider important. You may surprise yourself and even learn something."

I leave Robert's office knowing he's right, so for lunch, I drive to a nearby park to think. Maybe I'm not perfect. Maybe I do need to stop blaming others for not having my strengths, and instead, start appreciating them for what they *do* have. Well, I think, at least I'm making progress in one area of my life, and its only taken 36 years. Obviously I have a lot of catching up to do.

Being forced to face such unattractive aspects about myself is painful emotionally, but I'm determined to keep going, and notice my work environment steadily improving. I come to rely on Sasha's challenges, which constantly force me to examine myself. As a result, I'm getting on better with people and enjoying life more.

I'm making little progress on the home front, however. Belinda and I have a "working partnership" in which we raise the children and run the house, each with our well-defined roles. We also work together in the ADD movement, trying to raise awareness within government, schools, and medical circles. We don't fight because the relationship simply doesn't have enough intensity for that. I treat Belinda politely, and with deep respect, but something's missing, something significant.

Unlike work, where the walls I'd erected are gradually coming down because people help me and challenge me, Belinda still wants more than I can give. While I really want to succeed in the workplace, I'm just not that invested in my marriage any more. Since I don't know how to make it work, I end up not caring, and I build even more walls to stop her getting close to me.

This very subject comes up during my next session with Debbie when she asks, "You seem to be doing really well at work, but what's happening at home?"

I'm reluctant to discuss my marriage, even with Debbie, but I know I can't keep avoiding it and I blurt out, "Belinda keeps trying to change me, to make me the way she wants, someone who fits her image of how I should be."

Debbie looks at me with unusual intensity. "Are you sure you're not being too hard on her. Perhaps she's trying to help you for your own good?"

I don't want to even look at this, but Debbie just looks at me serenely, waiting for me to speak. "Perhaps you're right," I begin slowly. "I always say I'm willing to change, but deep down, I resist becoming who she wants me to be, because I'll lose a part of myself. If I change to suit her, I'll lose the essence of who I am."

"You didn't really answer the question, Alistair. Is she really trying to change you for her own selfish reasons? Are you really happy with who you are? Don't you want to change?"

"Well no, I guess I'm not happy. And yes, I do want to change. But ... oh, damn it ... I don't know."

Debbie continues, "Okay, so maybe I can't convince you that Belinda might only be trying to help you for your own good. You know, life is like an onion. The outer skin stops the smell escaping, but once you peel off that first layer, the smell is exposed and your eyes begin to sting. The only way to deal with this whole situation is to peel off all the layers, one by one. So perhaps you don't like what you see now that you've peeled off the first layer. What you see will sting your eyes, just like the onion, and you may be tempted to bandage the onion back up and try to get back to normal."

She's right and I know it. "But I'm scared of what's happening, especially facing the way I really am," I confess.

"It takes courage, I'll admit, but if you want to make progress, you'll have to face your fears one day."

Deep down I know she's right, and as I leave her office, I know a voice is coming from deep within, has gained a foothold and isn't going to shut up without a fight. But I'm not ready to listen to it yet.

By this time Belinda, faced with my implacable, ongoing resistance to change, eventually loses heart and gives up. Our marriage becomes an entrenched battle, albeit a subconscious one, in which we each strive to control each other psychologically using our own respective tactics, either improvised or picked up from others.

Part of me wants to accept what Debbie has said and open up to Belinda about how I feel (or don't feel). But because she's more adept emotionally, such exposure is simply too risky and I'm not going to take the chance. Belinda tries to talk to me about my being walled off from her, but every time she does, I manage to stonewall her. There's no way I'm going to confront the monsters lurking deep within, so it's better to shut her out, put life on auto-pilot, and immerse myself in work. Of course, I feel sorry for the children, forced to grow up with a father who's not really present, but there's nothing I can do about that.

For Christmas 1993, we head for Perth and my family—always guaranteed to be a difficult experience for two reasons. First, my deep lack of self-worth made for painful childhood, teenage, and university memories—half of my life that I'd prefer to forget. In Adelaide, I can pretend it never happened, but back here, all the old unworthiness is up in my face, something I hardly need right now.

When I lived in Perth, my need to be recognized meant I had to win at everything. I yearned so often for my father to simply tell me he loved me or that he was proud of me, but he never did. He would boast to other people about his "number one son," and how well I was doing, but never to my face, perhaps because he felt I was already too arrogant. I really needed someone to clip me around the ears when I overstepped boundaries, a role model to show me what it meant to be a man. But, in the absence of that, I did the only thing I knew how. I fought harder and harder to prove myself, to satisfy my thirst to be acknowledged, and to stifle my hunger for self-worth.

Whenever we go back to Perth, my family invariably carps about my past and how I haven't changed much. "Still the same old Alistair." They simply don't realize how those remarks hurt by dredging up the old unworthiness. In the past, I would brush them off, but in the midst of what I'm going through, they are mortal wounds.

The second problem is that Belinda used to enjoy a really good relationship with my family at the start, but for some reason, it deteriorated after the birth of our first child. As a result, I feel torn between my family and my wife. She further alienates herself from my family by trying to protect me, taking my side in any hostilities.

For survival, I fall back on suppression, avoiding any topics likely to lead to conflict, such as playing cards, having more than a couple of drinks, or discussing any sensitive topics. However, this Christmas is particularly bad. My tension level is high, and my neck is in constant spasm. I spend several hours a day lying down listening to relaxation tapes and trying to ease the knot in my neck. Outwardly the ten days appear to go smoothly—none of the usual fights—but that's because I'm busily forestalling any inflammatory situations.

I leave Perth in the depths of despair, but even so, can't discuss it with any of my family. Even if I could find the courage to broach the topic, I couldn't express my feelings clearly enough to get through to them. On my return to work, I confide in Sasha that I've lost my family forever, and don't think I'll ever visit Perth again. Once more, I just want to run, run from the pain of my past and the old hurts that cause me to view myself so negatively.

While in Perth, I'd visited an old, dear, trusted friend who I've known for over twenty years. He calls me later back in Adelaide, worried that I'm headed for a nervous breakdown. He's not too far off. I can feel all the pressures inside me coming together and pushing me into overload. So, in Perth, without the distraction of work, I knew I was right on the edge of losing it. But I dismiss his warnings and throw myself back into work, anything to fill in the gaps and burn off excess mental and emotional energy.

I plunge more deeply into the ADD movement, when I know I should be asking myself questions such as, "What am I *really* here for?" ADD helps justify my existence. Having a daughter diagnosed with the condition and battling a non-responsive establishment drives both Belinda and I to take up the fight even more vigorously. I know what I'm doing but can't help it; as long as I'm busy fighting external battles, I can put off facing my demons.

The original ADD group has fallen apart and I see an opportunity to fill the resulting gaping hole. So, in mid-1994, I prepare a strategic plan and constitution to form a new group, and send it out to interested people for comment.

Children with ADD are treated with amphetamines to control the condition, but these cannot be prescribed once the child reaches eighteen. One of the mothers in the ADD movement, Sandra, has two sons on the medication who are approaching eighteen, so the loss of their medication will soon cast their lives into chaos. I offer to help Sandra in her lone battle against the Government, and we plan a strategy and write letters to the Health Minister, the Health Commission and the Medical Board. After several months, countless phone calls, and many meetings, the Head of the Health Commission authorizes the limited use of the medication by adults.

Elated at the news, I leap in the air with joy, jumping about like a child. I'm happy, profoundly happy. Joy wells up within me, and for the first time, I know what Debbie meant when she asked me to remember a time that I was really happy. Then something occurs to me: This is probably the first time I've done something to help someone else with no personal agenda. Am I being rewarded for helping another? Is this the feeling of satisfaction spiritual people talk about when they're doing what they call "God's work"?

By October 1994, the new ADD group (called PLAD for People Living with Attention Disorders) is ready to launch. I continue to make progress, and Robert knows exactly how to push the right buttons to impel me forward. However, on the home front, Belinda and I continue to co-exist without the spark that could re-ignite our relationship and let us climb out of our respective isolation.

Where Did My Marriage Go?

I T'S OCTOBER 1994, and my life is going crazy. As we've often done before, we rent a cabin at a vacation farm for a weekend. We arrive on the Friday afternoon, settle in and spend an uneventful evening. However, the next day, with nothing to do except reflect, something disturbing happens. I go into some kind of trance, as if I'm at the movies, watching myself and my family on the screen. A voice within asks me, "What are you doing here? Get out! Get out!"

I've been married for over ten years, and have remained faithful except for my work as "the other woman." I've never consciously contemplated leaving Belinda, but obviously the idea is lurking in some dark corner of my mind. At first, I think it's just a temporary aberration that will pass, but it doesn't. That afternoon, while horseback riding, my clarity of vision peaks and I know that my life is about to take a sudden change in direction. My sense of being in the wrong place grows and I have more "movie" experiences. By Sunday night, I can't keep my feelings to myself. The pressure has built up and I must release it before I explode. It's time to confront Belinda.

"I'm in real trouble," I tell her. "I don't even know if I love you any more. I need some emotional space. I want to move into the spare room for a while until I sort out how I feel."

Belinda is nonplussed and stares blankly at me, as I continue. "Also, I want to spend some time with Sasha to help me work through some stuff, as she's the only person I can talk to about this."

At the mention of Sasha, Belinda blows her top. "Either you love me or you don't. And if you think I'm going to let you go off and spend time with some other woman, then you're dead wrong."

"But Sasha's only a friend, the only friend I have," I explain weakly.

"I don't believe that for a second," she spits back.

I'm taken aback, but not surprised, given our lack of communication about anything important. It's taken a major crisis to force me to speak up, and coming out of the blue like this, my announcement has taken her completely by surprise. If ever Belinda and I needed to treat each other with tenderness, love and understanding, it's now, but then if our relationship had been tender and loving, we wouldn't even be having this argument.

I hardly sleep that night, and back at work the next day, I tell Sasha about my confrontation with Belinda. She advises, "You'd be crazy to leave Belinda. Stay with her and try to work through this. Look, my marriage fell apart a few months ago, and I'm still going through the leaving process. It can get really messy."

On the Wednesday night, Belinda returns from tennis as I'm preparing a speech to present to my staff the next day. My feelings of isolation and emptiness have increased to the point where I'm close to panic. I realize that I've been an idiot for remaining silent for so long, but now I feel like the floodgates of a dam holding back a swollen river; once the gates are open, the water rushes out in a torrent of confusion.

In bed that night, I confront Belinda once more, "My feelings haven't changed since Sunday."

She replies acidly, "Well, you'd better sort yourself out. Perhaps you should write a poem."

I used to write poetry when I was younger but even now, after so long, I find that the cryptic nature of the words allows me to express threatening feelings more openly than ordinary words. From three until five in the morning, I write seven pages that express exactly how I feel, leaving little doubt about what I must do next. As I leave for work, I hand Belinda the poem. A few hours later, she calls me in tears. "We need to talk. Pick me up at my mother's this afternoon," she says and hangs up.

I know she's right, but part of me also knows it's too late for talk. Anyway, she made me crystallize my feelings in that poem, so some of the blame for our marriage being over must rest with her.

I'm shaken after her call, though, and worse, in half an hour, I'm supposed to deliver that presentation to my staff about the future direction of our department. It might be important to them, but in my current state, I don't give a damn. In a panic, I call in Sasha, and tell her, "Let everyone know the presentation is cancelled."

"No way. You can't do that. It's too late; you're just going to have to go through with it."

For the next thirty minutes, Sasha talks me down from my panic so that I can make the presentation. The next couple of hours are among the most difficult I can remember. Someone comments afterwards, "You used pauses very effectively." What I don't let on is that the pauses weren't planned at all, but me trying to fight back tears.

Belinda has taken our son to her mother's house and I pick her up from there. We drive to a nearby beach and sit in the car overlooking the water. She seems to be struggling for words, trying to understand the situation. On the surface, she's calm and composed, but tears are just beneath the façade and her voice trembles, so I help her out with a suggestion. "Look, I'm flying to Brisbane next Monday, so why don't I move out for a few days to have some space and think about what I should do."

As she nods a tearful assent, it strikes me how unreal this seems. Less than a week ago, there were no outward signs of our marriage being in trouble, and now we're talking about how to end it. What's happening, I ask myself. Part of me wants to reach out, hold her, and say, "Let's just go back in time and forget about the last week," but another part of me wants to run. And right now, the stone-faced runner is in control. We drive back to her mother's house, and as Belinda gets out of the car, she asks, "What will you do until Monday?"

"I'll call you," I say, tersely.

Once back at the office, I call one of my employees. His wife died a year earlier and he lives on his own. He's delighted to have some company over the weekend, so I arrange to move in with him. However, I make a lousy houseguest. All weekend, my mind cycles through the options, but in my heart, I know the die was cast when I wrote that poem. Belinda and I have several phone conversations over the weekend, and I try to find something consoling to say, but the words she wants to hear just aren't there. So she bounces between, "I'll do anything to have you back," and "I don't care if I ever see you again."

We agree that I'll tell her my plans when I get back from Brisbane next Wednesday but I suspect she already knows.

Belinda is waiting up for me. The scene is surreal as we sit in the lounge under lights that are too bright, and politely sip tea. I've never drunk tea before, and had my first cup ever earlier that day in Brisbane. She comments, "It's ironic that I've tried to get you to drink tea for ten years, and you start on the very day you're leaving me. You *are* leaving, I take it?"

"I'm leaving."

"I figured as much. I'm going to call my parents and ask them to come over. Then you should call your parents in Perth."

When I break the news to my parents, their first reaction is, predictably, "How can you do this to the children?"

"It's just something I've got to do," I say resolutely, more for my sake than theirs. But their icy reception is nothing compared to facing Belinda's parents. Her father looks as though he'd like to kill me slowly and painfully. Her mother, bless her heart, looks at me with a sad but sympathetic half-smile, and gives me a huge hug, as if to say, "I understand," which I'm sure she doesn't. But it's not her way to see the negative in anyone. It's all I can do to stop from bursting into tears in her arms. As we break off the hug, I suddenly realize that I should have gone to her for help long ago. She certainly gave me plenty of openings, but now it's too late. I can't stay here, so I turn and walk out on my wife, her parents, and my children.

Telling the children is something I'm dreading. The next day after work, I drive to what was once my home, and I never want to relive that encounter again. My two-year-old son simply doesn't understand, and in any case, he hardly knows me, but my daughter freaks out. I'm tearing up inside, and it takes all my self-control to suppress the pain and not start crying with her.

So my marriage is over! No fights, no arguments, no drawn out sniping back-and-forth, just a quick, clean death. Part of me is freaking at what I've just done. *Have you lost it totally? You're always so conservative and cautious, and work everything out to the last detail, but you've just blown it big time. You've no idea where you're going to stay. You don't have the money to start over. You haven't even thought through what it means for the children. What the hell are you doing?*

Watched by my wife, her pale face blotched red from crying, and with my daughter in tears on my lap, the enormity of what I've done crashes in on me. "It's not too late," says a tiny voice. "Shut up! I'll drown if I stay here," I retort. "I simply can't stay in this situation. And working through my own stuff is just too hard. I've been trying to change forever and gotten nowhere. And if Belinda hasn't been able to reach me in the past, the future doesn't look any brighter. It's time to run!"

I say goodbye to my children, but as I drive away from the house I once called home, I realize I have nowhere to go. I haven't even thought about my next move. I don't have a friend in Adelaide who I can stay with. They're all Belinda's friends. Except for Sasha. I stop at a call box and catch her before she leaves work. She offers to let me stay at her place until I find my own.

As I unpack my few meager things, I'm aware of the dangers of being under the same roof, and I clarify, "Look, I'm just moving in as a friend, okay, and it needs to stay that way, at least until I sort myself out." Sasha agrees vehemently that that's how it should be. Too vehemently, and I wonder if perhaps we aren't just deluding ourselves.

We drive to work in separate cars the following morning, and I throw myself into mundane tasks to dull the pain. Late afternoon, Robert stops by my office to ask me a question, and the look on my face says it all.

"What the hell's wrong with you."

Without warning, tears roll down my cheeks. The proud man, who eschews emotions lest they disrupt his eternal quest for achievement, brought to his knees by the desolation of his own life. My outer defenses are ripped apart and my vulnerabilities spill out like the intestines of an eviscerated animal. Too drained to push the flopping intestines back into their armored cage, all I can do is cry.

Having been through this himself, Robert does the only appropriate thing. He takes me gently by the elbow and says, "Come on, we're going for a beer."

As the third glass of Fosters slips down, the questions flow from my tortured heart. "How could I let it happen like this? If I ever had any feelings at all, then they've been surgically removed. Waiting at the airport on the way back from Brisbane, I tried to make myself cry over leaving my children, but I felt nothing. I love them for God's sake, but I seem to be in emotional paralysis."

As I say these words, the memory of my daughter's wracking sobs overwhelms me in a nauseous tidal wave of guilt. "And it all seems so unreal," I blubber. "Belinda acts as if it's inevitable, and just wants to get it over with as soon as possible. I mean, I've never been in this situation before, and I don't know what to expect. But surely we should have tried to talk it out, maybe even let some emotions fly. But there was nothing, just a clinical extinction of ten years together."

I pause, and look at Robert through tear-glazed eyes, but he appears to be deep in thought. Then he clears his throat, and begins, choosing his words carefully. "You may not like what I am going to say, Alistair, but I've been where you are and what you need now is honesty, not sympathy. Put yourself in Belinda's position. She knows you, and let's face it, once you've made up your mind on something, there's little point in trying to change it. She's probably resigned herself to you leaving and now just wants to minimize her pain. Also, remember that she'll be feeling protective towards the children."

"What do you mean?"

"She won't let her own feelings out while your children are going through their grief, because she'll be focused on protecting them."

My head drops as another wave of guilt picks up my heart and crashes it against the rocks of my failed life. I didn't support her when we were married, and now it's all falling on her shoulders again. What a miserable, self-centered louse I am, leaving her to carry the full burden of dealing with our children.

Robert senses the plunge in my emotions and continues quickly. "Look, there's no easy way to end a marriage. Don't be too hard on yourself. I took a year to end mine because I didn't have the strength to put my wife through the pain. But, in the end, I hurt her more. You're both going through a really bad time now, but in many ways a quick, clean break is easier."

"Did it have to be this way? Did I have to leave Belinda?"

"That's an unfair question. I still haven't come to terms with that one myself. In a way, it seems that nothing's changed for me. I still have to work through my own stuff. Changing your partner doesn't save you from dealing with your own fears."

As I raise another glass to my lips, I wonder if that's what I've done. Have I simply run from my own fears? From the pain in the empty shell I call my life? Maybe, if I hadn't been so obsessed with myself, I could have opened up to Belinda. But then, that's not who I am. So now I'm running. But from what? To what? And who the hell am I anyway?

Part 2 • Spirit Emerges

A Time Of Change

S ASHA AND I arrive back at her house about the same time. The Fosters have left me vulnerable, and when I hug her, the inevitable happens. We're both licking our respective emotional wounds, like each other a lot, and need support. Our bodies respond and silence any threads of commonsense. The hug becomes a prolonged kiss, and we tear each other's clothes off. Standing naked, our hands and mouths hungrily explore each other's bodies, and I carry her to her bedroom, where our lovemaking is passionate, driven by our respective needs.

Afterwards, the little voice starts in on me. "This is a mistake. You both need time on your own to grieve for your marriages and get to know yourselves again." But I'm simply not strong enough. We both know that we should talk about what just happened, but neither of us is willing to broach the topic.

Not only does Sasha report to me, but also she's become my unofficial personal assistant, and we're working together on some sensitive and important matters. So, for the next two days, we live the lie, driving to work in separate cars, and when with other people, treating each other as we've always done. However, I'm determined that all the work we've invested in building trust within the division is not put in jeopardy, and I know that it's only a matter of time, so after we've been together for three days, I call a staff meeting.

"I think you should all know that Sasha and I have started a personal relationship, and we're now living together. We'll do our best not to let that affect our working relationships, and how we deal with you, but if you see a conflict, I want you to feel able to raise any concerns you might have."

On the surface, we receive tremendous support for being so open, but deep down, we both sense the scrutiny that our as-yet unformed relationship comes under. We both feel we're being forced to expose our relationship to the public spotlight too early, but there seems no other way.

The next three months go by quickly. Without lawyers and courts, Belinda and I arrange our divorce settlement, decide custody terms, and negotiate alimony and child payments. Apart from Belinda's occasional barbs, and my guilt-driven retorts, it's all so civilized, which I take to mean that deep down, we both knew long ago that our marriage was over, and we'd both done a lot of the grieving before the actual separation. Even so, negotiating politely with the woman who shared my bed for over ten years is surreal, as if it's not really happening and a giant river over which I have no control is sweeping me along.

As my marriage formally ends, I'm juggling two different worlds at the same time. On the one hand, Sasha and I are hopelessly in love and are becoming increasingly dependent on each other. Deep down, I know we should be taking things easy, but I tell myself that, as a couple, we're different and that it's meant to be. Being with her feels right and comfortable. We like doing the same things and both give gladly to each other. And, oh, how sweet are the periods of euphoria when we escape to a world of our own and immerse ourselves in the sweet aroma of love. Our goals are so aligned, and we talk into the small hours about all the things we'll do in the future.

On the other hand, I'm beginning to encounter the fallout from my marriage, as unpleasant feelings bubble to the surface, especially guilt. Why, I ask myself, if I've let go of my responsibilities towards Belinda, do I still have that nagging feeling that I'm not being truthful with myself, that there's still work to be done. That blasted inner voice. Why doesn't it leave me alone to get on with my life?

At one level, Sasha and I have a wonderful relationship, yet I know deep in my heart that I'm holding back from her by not talking about my innermost fears. Yet, despite the love I feel for her, or perhaps because of it, I can't expose her to my monsters. The wounds are still too painful, and I'm afraid that talking about my life with Belinda and the children will spoil the beauty of what I have with Sasha.

So in a sense, I live a double life. I'm in love and feel a rich sense of belonging with my new partner, yet the pain and guilt over leaving my children bubble beneath the surface like molten lava. Whenever they try to erupt, I clamp the lid down tightly, and push them back down inside.

Another new burden is the loss of the financial security I once enjoyed. The payments to Belinda and my share of the household costs with Sasha leave little to spare. I lie awake in bed, long after Sasha has gone to sleep, crying inside. My guts feel like the clothes in a tumble drier, churning around inside me. I'm in far more pain than I dare let Sasha, or anyone else, know. I hurt to core of every cell, and every thought and emotion is shrouded in a black cloud. But not knowing what to do, I suppress it all as I've always done, and live with the self-recrimination of being an abject failure. I can't do anything right, except hurt people, of course. Shit, I'd probably even screw up suicide. So, each night, with images of self-demolition looming up from the depths of my mind, I drift off into a fitful sleep.

As the months roll by, I define a new relationship with my children. Belinda used to make all the day-to-day decisions regarding them, with my involvement limited to the occasional weekend outing. I never really took responsibility, but now the kids are with me every other weekend, for 48 hours straight, during which time, I'm solely responsible for them. I have to decide what they wear, what they eat, and what we do. When they're with me, I must focus on them intently. So ironically, our relationship is now much closer. Also, my lower level of frustration and increased overall happiness help me be more tolerant of their demands. Yet I'm still torn between my love for them and my guilt over what I've done to them.

The relationship with my children is having unexpected fallout. From the outset, Sasha and I agreed that having children of our own is not in our plans, so I didn't think I had to worry about that one. After about three months, however, she begins to give signals that she may be having second thoughts, and tension creeps in to our lives. Apparently, the fact that I spend quality time with my children is waving a security flag for her.

One night, out of the blue, Sasha suddenly blurts out, "It's all right for you. You already have your own children."

"But they can be yours as well," I respond, really put on the spot by her outburst.

"Not with *her* manipulating them."

"Why is it such a big deal? I thought we'd already agreed you didn't want children?"

"That was when I thought your children could be ours, but it isn't going to happen. She'll never let that happen."

The depth of Sasha's resentment towards Belinda takes me by surprise. She continues raging, "You already have children, someone to love you. But I don't have anyone."

As the tears roll down her cheeks, I move towards her, saying, "What about me? I love you."

"You don't even love me enough to have children," she sobs, and storms into the bedroom, slamming the door behind her.

Shit, now she's putting conditions on the strength of my love. Christ, I didn't realize how insecure she is. I thought she had her act together, but this little display tells me that her sense of self-worth is as screwed up as mine. For the first time in our relationship, I wonder what I've gotten myself into, and get concerned for the future.

The problem is that I still want to keep what's beautiful about our relationship, and the thought of it ever changing bothers me. But this thing over having children shows me how dependent I've become on Sasha for my social activities as well as my emotional support. I'm scared of slipping into the same old pattern, and just want to run for freedom. Sasha's growing need for love and the belief that having children will fill it make me want to go off and live on my own, yet I can't because I need her. So, once again, I'm trapped. I need to break away, but haven't got the balls to go out on my own. Not yet, anyway.

Between Sasha and my children, work is taking a back seat. I've started working reasonable hours and not bringing a full briefcase home every night. The company is in the middle of a restructuring, and everyone at work feels the general lack of direction, so I'm not alone. Sasha still reports to me while we wait for the restructure to happen, as Robert doesn't want to change things until the new organization structure is announced. But that also means that any domestic tension follows me to work.

Every weekend I have the kids, I'm caught in a tug-of-war between Sasha and Belinda. Why can't they leave me alone to do what I want? I only want to do the right thing, and I'm trying hard to please them both, but neither will recognize the other's point of view, so I can't win. All I want to do is keep both women happy, but both think that I'm doing everything to please the other. Why can't they see that I'm trying to find a solution that will keep everyone happy?

When I pick the kids up and drop them off, Belinda manages to say exactly the right thing to twist the knife of guilt deeper into my guts. I come to dread those moments when her barbs stab at the very core of my guilt. Is the gnawing anguish and torment some form of punishment for what I've done?

So much for walking away from my obligations to Belinda and hiding behind the divorce papers. All it takes is a snide little "If you really cared for the children ..." and I feel the knife twisting. What if she's right? What if I just don't care enough? With that thought, my self-esteem takes another nosedive.

To make matters worse, the last thing I need when I get home after dropping the kids off is Sasha hitting me with a tirade, "I always have to fight for my love against *her!*" The 'her' is spat out with a vehemence that shatters the intimacy built up over the weekend. "She's using the children to keep a hold over you."

I try my best to keep the peace and manage the conflict, but now and then, it's too much and I explode and lay down the law. "Jesus Christ, they're my flesh and blood, and I have obligations to them. Trust me, Belinda is no threat to you, so give me a break."

Sasha erupts in a vehement, spiteful attack on Belinda. "She's just a slut, living off your money and having it easy."

"Oh, yeah, Belinda's living the life of luxury on easy street," I spit back, dripping sarcasm. "Look, Sasha, you're not helping me at all. I'm trying to rebuild a working relationship with the mother of my children. Cut me some slack, will you? I'm going for a walk."

Out in the fresh evening air, I'm chilled to realize that I'm beginning to lose respect for Sasha and her paranoia over Belinda.

Despite these Sunday night flash points, Sasha and I experience some exquisite times together. Free of the external forces in our lives, we "escape" to our own world and enjoy some truly intimate and tender moments, talking about how wonderful it would be if we could leave everything behind and elope to a world of bliss. We often take the bike path along the creek near our house, and in the setting sun, sit under a willow tree watching the ducks playfully splashing in the water. Sasha loves these moments. Her ex-husband wasn't the outdoor type, so having a guy who'll share the things she loves fills her heart with joy.

The long summer evenings allow us to explore nature together, free from the smothering clutches of the daily grind of life. Returning home, we shower together before enjoying a bottle of white wine, followed by passionate love-making, often on the living room sofa when the desire comes up too suddenly for us to make it to the bedroom.

But in the morning, reality sets back in and something catches us in a spiral that drags us down. Why is our love so fragile that it can't withstand the buffeting of everyday life? What happened to the dreams I had when our relationship started?

Over time, we find ourselves take opposite positions, protecting our delicate feelings. Slowly, the magical times slip away as our deepest fears creep out into the relationship more and more, and we look for each other to provide the solution. Day by day, I feel my energy being drained and my desire to run increases.

Despite the reality checks that test our love, Sasha is good for me. She challenges me to cast aside the conservative cage I confine my life to. She enrolls us in guitar lessons, which is a real challenge for me because I've never played a musical instrument in my life and my lack of musical talent is legendary in my family. Surprisingly, I find that I'm not all that bad and pick up the basics easily. It's enjoyable for a change to do something I'm not good at. I've always resisted trying something new unless I knew I'd be good at it—my childhood fear of failure or of being made to look silly. But instead, not having to meet anyone's expectations is refreshing and freeing.

We're both becoming increasingly interested in personal growth, but Sasha seems more interested in my growth, feeling her life will be more satisfying if I can resolve some of the problems she considers I still have with Belinda. My interest in personal growth leads me to self-help books, including *Manhood* by Steve Biddulph. When I read the chapter on father-son relationships, I cry openly. "Oh dad, I don't even know you."

I'm hit by the realization of just how important my relationship with my father is, and the loss in not having the relationship I want, and I feel a great urge to make peace with him. I lament to myself, *"Dad, all I ever wanted was to make you proud of me, for you to tell me you thought I was good. I worked so hard to please you, but this only seemed to make you more distant. You seemed to feel that you had to cut me down, so I would be less arrogant. Oh, how I miss you, Oh, how I missed you all those years when I was busy fighting myself, when I needed you to take a position and show me the way forward, rather than letting me work it out for myself."*

With greater clarity than at any time in my life, I feel the veils of falsity falling from around me, and find myself looking at a frightened, vulnerable, little boy. As if in a trance, I gaze into the person I really am. As I wipe the tears away, I feel the truth of my life being exposed, like a tumor revealed by the surgeon's scalpel. It calls me inwards, to confront it, and I feel scared. As I look at the image in the mirror, I know I'm still living the lie I fashioned all those years ago, and I know I have to find the truth. But I don't like the fragments of myself that I've exposed and am afraid of what I'll discover as I peel away further layers of falsehood and pretence. But, I know I must, otherwise, I'm doomed to spend the rest of my life in the cage I feel increasingly closing around me. Surely there must be more.

Not knowing where to start, I sit down and write my father a letter, a really personal letter:

"Dear Dad,

It's been a long time since I wrote you a letter. In fact, this is probably the first one. It's an understatement to say that a lot's changed in my life recently and when that happens it causes you to reflect. I'm reading a book at the moment called Manhood *by an Australian psychologist. There's a chapter in it called 'You and Your Father.' I've included the chapter with this letter and I'd desperately like you to read it, Dad. I want you to know that I cried several times while I was reading it and I felt the pain that is echoed in the pages.*

Many times over the last 15 years or so, I've felt that I desperately wanted a father I could respect, and how desperately I wanted my Dad to tell me he was proud of me. You know, I can't remember you ever saying you were proud of me. It's so easy to be critical of your parents when you're young, and it's not till you become one yourself that you realize what a bloody difficult job it is, and how much you owe to your parents.

I realized about six months ago that I wasn't contributing to my children's upbringing. Sure I provided, and I was always 'there' when they needed me, but I was never really there at all - not in mind and heart. It's different now - better - but I still have a long way to go. I want the chance to be a real dad to my children and not just the typical dad of the 1990s.

Dad, if you and I are honest about it, we haven't had a relationship since I was about 12 or 15 years old. That's no one's fault, and I certainly don't blame you at all. We were both victims of our circumstances, and the stereotypes we fitted into. But I really miss those years. I needed your strength and guidance more than I would ever have admitted before today. And I know you're a strong person, because you bred me and I didn't get all my strength from Mum. But like me, I sense you're very vulnerable and have insecurities - so do I.

Dad, I love you, but I don't know you. You gave so much of your life to get us children to where we are - you should be proud of that. But we have given so very little back. I want to get to know you, Dad. I want to know about your childhood, how you felt when you married mum, why you came to Australia - the real reason that I've never known, how your self-esteem suffered when you lost your job, and what burning ambitions you had but were never able to achieve.

I love you, Dad, and I'm sorry we have missed so many years, but it's never too late to be a father and son for each other, is it?

As I write out the address on the envelope to send the letter, something doesn't feel right. "Surely dad isn't ready to receive a letter like this. Surely it will upset him. And in any case, I've probably gained the benefit I needed from writing it." So, I stuff the letter in a drawer, unsent.

It's early 1995 and, after six months with Sasha, my financial situation is really getting to me, yet I won't admit it to her. Although I tell her I don't care about money and it can't buy happiness, it occupies my thoughts more than it should. I feel I've been cheated by life. For years, I've worked long hours, and earned tons of money, but at age 37, what have I got to show for it?

I left most of the household things with Belinda, and from the start, that created tension. I arrived at Sasha's with just a few personal things, so everything in the house is hers, and whenever she suggests that I buy something for the house, I always seem to find an excuse. One afternoon, she confronts me, "You don't care about me at all do you? You give her so much money, yet when I want you to spend a few lousy dollars on some new bed sheets, you find excuses."

"It's not the money," I snap back. "I give Belinda only what I have to under the law. You can have the bloody money and go and buy the goddamn sheets yourself."

"No, I want you to show some interest in us and go and buy something yourself."

"Look, I've got better things to do with my money. Spending it on myself isn't a priority."

"Nothing about our future is a priority to you, is it? You want all the good times but you don't want to make a commitment."

The argument degenerates, but I know she's scored a direct hit on a nerve. I *am* afraid to make a commitment, of being chained to a future not of my own making. I don't know where this fear is coming from, but I can't deny it, and I feel like running again.

I'm someone who has to rationalize things in my mind before I can accept them. In a way, I envy people who simply accept things the way they are. So, to rationalize the financial benefits of the divorce, I prepare a before-and-after balance sheet. Because I now see wealth as about more than money, I try to estimate the value of happiness. While this helps me to focus on the good things, but I know inside it's not the real answer.

LIFE'S BALANCE SHEET	1994	1995
Financial	119*	88
Relationship	3	33
Happiness	5	35
Personal Freedom	5	45
Relationship with Children	15	20
Relaxation level	8	20
Self Esteem	4	20
TOTAL ASSETS	**159**	**261**

* 50 % of total financial assets of family.

No sooner do I find solace in my increased wealth, than Sasha pursues me with greater passion on the issue of commitment. "Look, when *are* we going to start a family? I want my own children, and if you want a future with me, then I guess that will make you their father."

"Look, you talk so much about your career and how you won't give up work, so why do you want children?"

"Your problem, Alistair," she retorts angrily, "is that you think everything will be the same as it was with her. But it wouldn't be like that."

"That's not it at all," I evade. "I just don't think you're really cut out for children, after everything you said at the start of our relationship. I think you want them for the wrong reasons."

Oops. Not a smart thing to say. The floodgates open. "You didn't even love her, but you gave her two children and a house. And now you say you love me, and you won't give me either. I just want to be loved. Is that too much to ask for? I just want you to show you love me by making a commitment."

She falls apart, tears pouring like a monsoon rain, desperately searching for my arms to comfort her, and my words to nurture her dreams of happiness. But I'm not there, caught up instead in my own struggle for survival, in my own need to be free and breathe free. I do not want this, I scream internally.

Less than nine months after coming together in a blaze of passion, our insecurities bring us to a counselor. Debbie has left on maternity leave and we're directed to a specialist in relationships. Michelle is a few years younger than me, an attractive woman with long golden hair and striking eyes. From the outset, she's direct and I instantly like her. Sasha doesn't share my positive feelings and I wonder how long she'll keep seeing Michelle. Perhaps she's threatened by Michelle's poise and confidence, or maybe her insecurity makes her sensitive to the subtle attraction she knows I feel for our new counselor.

Our relationship has become like a roller-coaster ride, exhilarating at times, then plunging to the depths before the next crescendo. When Sasha plummets to the depth of despair, I crash with her, but she rebounds within a day, leaving me to struggle back up alone, often just in time for the next crash.

When Sasha's mood swings are triggered by interactions between myself and Belinda or the children, and she looks to me for support, I can't help because I'm part of the problem. The thing that bugs me is that, when she gets really upset and I offer her lots of different solutions, we end up fighting. Why does she tell me her problems if she doesn't want me to solve them? I get angry, which upsets her even more, and because I hate to see her upset, I plummet into a deep emotional chasm, which takes me days to climb back from.

In September 1995, my parents arrive for a visit. From the outset, tensions run high. Not only is it the first time Mum gets to meet Sasha, but when she sees Sasha with the children, emotions fly like hand-grenades, and I'm trapped in the middle trying to catch them before they explode. Managing everyone's guilt and anxieties wears me down.

One evening, out alone for a walk on the creek bank, I confide in a wise, old tree, "I just can't put up with much more of this stress. In the past few weeks, I've had to support my partner, my daughter, my ex-wife, and my mother. But who'll support me? I'm expected to be so strong all the bloody time."

Mum and Sasha bring things to a head in a blazing argument, which Sasha ends by announcing that she's moving out. I've had enough and just don't care any more. But it isn't that simple. I sense that Sasha doesn't want to go. Instead, she wants me to take her in my arms, tell her I love her and that everything will be wonderful for ever. But I can't do that. In fact, I no longer believe it. Yet at the same time, I'm not ready to let her go.

Once more, I'm wracked by conflict. Whenever I decide to end the relationship, I invariably change my mind. In a quiet moment, I reflect on my previous relationships, searching for a way out of the confusion. In the four significant relationships before Belinda, I was the one who was left. Despite the pain of rejection, I didn't have to make the decision to leave. The first long term relationship I ended was my marriage and I admit that I handled it abysmally and still feel enormous guilt over never giving it a chance once I'd decided it was over. I clinically extinguished it, unable to find any compassion in my heart for Belinda. So with Sasha, I want to do it properly.

I'm also plagued with a fear of being alone, and dread making the decision to leave. I would much prefer Sasha to leave so I wouldn't have to feel responsible. Then I could wallow in the familiar territory of self-pity. At least that's one monster I know well.

While I'm in this pensive mood, I ask myself, why not be really honest. Clearly I have so many problems that maybe I should start being honest with myself. As I begin to peal away the layers of self-deceit, I see that, at least, I'm taking responsibility for the relationship. Sasha finds Michelle too threatening and has stopped coming with me. She seems stuck in her insecurities and blames me for everything, but I, on the other hand, feel that I'm opening up to an understanding of why I react the way I do.

One morning, Michelle is giving me a hard time, challenging me to see the truth. "So how would you describe the status of your relationship now, Alistair?"

Shit, I think to myself. Why does she have to ask such damned difficult questions? Why can't she just make me feel that everything's all right, or just tell me what to do? But that's not her style, so I sigh and prepare to dig deep and be honest with myself. "This being honest with yourself isn't much fun. I hope there's a pot of gold at the end of the rainbow." She smiles but remains silent.

"Okay," I admit. "I know I have to do it all myself."

After some thought, I resign myself to telling Michelle how I really feel. "It's like we're oscillating back and forth. I reach out to her, but every time we get close, I run away again. I want the relationship, but don't want to make a commitment. I need to have an escape hatch, and I keep talking about living on my own, to emphasize to Sasha that, at some stage, I will go and find myself."

"I find this strange," Michelle says, looking at me with a bemused expression. "You always have the option of going off on your own, so why do you need to keep reinforcing it?"

"Yes, I know, but somehow I just don't get it."

The session is over, and as I leave, I say, "I'm glad you're in my life at the moment, to help me see the truth."

"You need someone who's been on the same journey. Counselors can take you only as far as they've gone themselves, otherwise it becomes too threatening for them."

Michelle appears to be so confident in herself that I suspect she can take me a long way. Like me, she's a perfectionist, and we've developed a close understanding. She's very direct with me rather than tiptoeing around saying nice things. I see her as more of a friend than a counselor, so at least there's one woman in my life whom I don't have to fight with.

After the session, I need to go for a run—running helps to empty my mind and allows me to see things clearly—so rather than return to the office, I drive home and run along the bank of the creek. As I run, a mounting sense of apprehension rises within me, and suddenly the cause seems so obvious that I gasp and ask myself why I didn't see this before. It's simply that I fear my own lack of inner strength. I don't trust myself enough to make the right decision when the time comes. I'm afraid I'll end up agreeing to marry Sasha and have children just to please her, so as not to hurt her, even if it's not what I want. I simply have no confidence or belief in myself, so I spend my life trying to make other people happy so that they'll approve of me.

The truth of this blinds me, and I sit on the bank in a daze. It's all so apparent now. From childhood, I've erected an outer façade of a strong, rugged, tough guy to hide my own inner weakness. And whenever the shield was threatened, I martyred myself to make others happy. Now the façade has started to crumble, and there's nothing behind it. I have no belief in myself at all. In fact, I'm not even sure I have a self anymore!

Okay. If that's the diagnosis, how do I go about building inner strength? About recreating a self?

Something is seriously missing in my life and I have to find out what it is. In a desperate attempt to find some answers, I hit the books. One in particular deals with establishing a relationship with yourself and the need to feel good about yourself before you can have a meaningful relationship with someone else. That makes sense. Why has no one pointed this out to me before? I don't love myself; shit, I don't even like myself most of the time. How can I expect to feel secure enough to give of myself to another person if I can't even give of myself to me?

So, if self-love is the answer, how do I develop a loving relationship with myself?

A while later, another book falls into my hands, claiming that we all have an inner child within us, which in many people, has been mistreated. This has served to stunt its growth. To move forward, we must heal the damage our inner child has suffered, and help the inner child go through the growth it has been denied. As I read, alarm bells go off in my head, saying, "Listen to this stuff."

It makes so much sense. I see clearly how my lifelong habit of self-recrimination has damaged my inner child. Each time, it slipped further into the darkness to a safer place to escape the pain and blame. What, I wonder, would it take to get it to come out of hiding? I know I wouldn't come out for anything.

I also read that the inner child is the part of us that can give, enjoy life, and love. I realize that I must undertake a quest for my inner child. I must find this beautiful, vulnerable inner self and repair the damage, or I may never escape from the hollow, dark emptiness I call my life. Okay, I tried a new relationship, and it was wonderful for a while, but now I'm right back to square one. Sure Sasha has her problems, but my real problem is *me!*

So how do I get to this inner child? Many self-help books are little more than etiquette manuals, telling me how to behave, when to smile and how to treat people. By now, I know all the right moves, but I still can't do them because they're learned behavior. Sure I've improved, but I've just replaced one façade with another that's more pleasing to look at. And the energy required to maintain the false protective layer drains me, so that when I'm tired or under pressure, I revert back to my old ways. And the struggle robs my life of any joy. Something is missing and I have to find it.

The book continues with talk of spirituality. Now I've read many books that refer to the need for a spiritual aspect to life, and these are not "New Age" authors *per se*, but respected mainstream people, generally from a background of psychology or counseling. So, I ask myself, what is spirituality all about anyway? I'm skeptical about anything "New Age" and have no belief in God, so accepting spirituality is a challenge. But maybe it's not all "out there crazy stuff." After all, wasn't the relaxation treatment beneficial?

Perhaps meditation would be a good place to start. It's only an advanced form of my relaxation exercises. And I've got to do something, by God, so it's worth a try.

It's January 1996, and I enroll in a local one-day meditation class. Like me, most of the participants are looking to reduce their stress level and find inner peace. Impressed, I buy a few tapes on a form of meditation called Yoga Nidra.

After using the tapes, I feel a need to go further. My appetite has been whetted, and I sense that meditation has some answers for me. In February, I attend a class run by a spiritual group and am impressed by how genuinely happy and full of light and joy the instructor is. This particular type of meditation doesn't really grab me, but I vow to myself to find another group.

1996 rolls by with Sasha and I pretty much in a rut. We care for each other, but still cannot dissolve our insecurities. Although the emotional roller coaster continues to inflict damage, neither of us has an answer, yet neither of us really wants it to end.

September finds us in stagnant calm. I continue to see Michelle, but we're just rehashing the same old stuff. I arrive for another session, unsure of where we're going, and after the small talk, she hits me with, "Alistair, we're wasting each other's time. You're coming here trying to get me to solve your problems for you rather than taking responsibility for yourself."

My jaw drops and I'm speechless. With no reaction from me, she continues, "You know what you have to do. We've been going over this for about a year now and nothing has changed."

I recoil from her verbal onslaught and steely eye contact, and steady myself. "Okay, you're saying that I have to end the relationship. I know, but there are barriers I just don't seem to be able to overcome. Can we go over a few things to help me get things in perspective?"

"Sure," she says, her voice returning to its usual soft, supportive tone.

"After our last session, I realized my big problem is a lack of belief in myself. I just don't have the inner strength to make the hard decisions. But I don't know how to develop inner strength."

"Well, there's no easy way. There's no magic recipe for it. But let's start by going back over your marriage. When you left Belinda, you ran right into another relationship. While you felt comforted by this, it didn't allow you to resolve the problems in your life. So you took those problems into the new relationship. And as soon as the euphoria was over, they started to surface. You didn't give yourself a chance to develop your own identity but instead got caught up in a tug-of-war between two women, both of whom wanted to impose an identity on you."

"Okay, so now it's time to be honest with myself?"

"Yes, I'm afraid so. There's no easy way out. Do you really want me to give it to you straight?"

"Yes."

"The time has come for you to spend some time on your own. You're not going to deal with your inner crisis by finding another lover, and clearly this one isn't working. You need to face your fears of being on your own. You need to spend time looking in at yourself and taking responsibility for your own life."

That said it all. As I get up to leave, Michelle adds, "I don't see any point in continuing these sessions at this stage. You know what you must do. Perhaps when you're on your own, there'll be value in coming back to see me again."

Who Are You?

S HORTLY AFTER THE final meeting with Michelle, my job changes. I've reported to Robert for four years and am ready for a change. He's been extremely good for me, supportive when I needed it, and challenging when I needed help to change, both at work and in my personal life. Our relationship has met a need for both of us. I have a strong need for approval from my superiors, and he has satisfied that admirably. However, over the last few months, I've become increasingly dissatisfied, and now I'm breaking free from the shackles of needing others' approval. The process is far from complete, but at least it's started.

My fear of failure and my perfectionist streak make me a very productive employee, but it also makes me easy to control. I'm now beginning to rebel against the control Robert has over me, and this has shifted the dynamics of our relationship. Therefore, when the opportunity comes up to change jobs, I jump at it.

A few days later, I see an ad for free meditation classes close to where I live, and sign up for a three-evening class. I'm surprised to find that it's an ordinary suburban house on a quiet street. Inner conflict tugs at me, part saying, and "What are you doing here? You're a 38-year-old atheist engineer who doesn't believe in anything without scientific evidence."

"But," another part answers, "Your professional training hasn't done much to quell the feelings of hopelessness gnawing your insides. But promise you'll run at the first mention of God, Holy Spirit or any of that religious mumbo jumbo."

For as long as I can remember, I've rejected Christianity, unable to accept the notion that, if there is a God, then Jesus Christ is his only genuine representative to have ever come to Earth, and the only way to get into heaven. How can billions of people be condemned to hell simply because they're Chinese or Indian, and follow someone other than Jesus? Why would God create Hinduism or Buddhism, then turn a blind eye while their followers burn in hell. It's just not possible that God created only Christians, because if God didn't create Hindus or Buddhists, then who did? And how can a just and compassionate God allow so many atrocities to occur in His name? However, having studiously avoided any contact with Christianity, I'll admit that my understanding of religion is close to zero.

As I enter the house, a woman my age greets me, introduces herself as Kapila, and we talk about what I hope to get out of the course. A petite woman, with shoulder length blonde hair, vibrant blue eyes that seem to dance, and a musical voice, she exudes joy from every pore. Three other people arrive, and it's time to begin. The atmosphere in the room is serene, and I immediately start to feel different. Greg, Kapila's husband, demonstrates three different types of meditation, none of which I find inspiring, but what he says at the end really catches my attention. "Next week, we'll talk about who you really are!"

I'm impressed by how calm and happy Greg is. Why are spiritual people always so positive and happy, I wonder. About five feet ten inches tall, he looks, at first glance, like a typical guy around forty. Yet the softness of his face sets him apart from most men I've met.

The week passes quickly, and I arrive early. Before starting his talk, he tells us he runs a small tiling business, operated from his home, but he considers his real job is to help people to discover who they are. Then he starts, with my inner skeptic ready for a challenge.

"Who are you really?" Greg asks each of us in turn.

"Well," I begin, "I'm Alistair Smith. I'm an engineer, a manager, divorced with two children."

"Okay. But is that who you *really* are? Are you really defined by a name or a marital status, or a job title? If you lose your name, your marriage or your job, will you cease to exist?"

"Hell no!" I protest. Okay, so he has a point. I'm not defined by my external status or achievements. I find myself thinking deeper. Perhaps I am my physical body. Yes, that's it; I am my body and all its components—bones, tissue, organs, brain, and so on. Or maybe, I am my mind. After all, I have to be right all the time or I consider myself to have failed. And I need others to appreciate my intellectual capacity to be of value.

"Okay, I've got it," I announce. "I am my body and my mind."

Greg shakes his head.

"Okay, then, dammit. I really don't have a clue who I am. That's why I'm here! Who do *you* think I am?"

"The way we see it is that we each contain a number of different states to our being, including the body and the mind. Our true self, however, is neither the mind nor the body. Now I want you each to point to yourself."

Without thinking, we all point to the center of our chest. After pointing this out, Greg continues, "That's not a coincidence. In fact, it's an intuitive thing. If you were indeed only your body, you could have pointed to any part of your body with equal conviction. And if you were just your mind, you would probably have pointed to your head. No, we're something much more profound and powerful. The fact that you pointed to the center of your chest is significant. It's in the center of the chest where the spiritual heart lies, and it's within the spiritual heart that your true self resides."

This is getting good, I think, and listen, captivated by his words. Is this the inner child I'm looking for?

Greg continues, "There exists a Supreme Being, or God, as most Westerners would call Him. This Supreme Being exists on a different plane of consciousness to what we're consciously aware of. Each person contains within them a life energy that is connected to, and one with, the Supreme Being or God. This life energy is called the Self, with a capital S, and is what gives us life. Some people use the name 'soul' but we avoid this term because of its pre-existing connotation in Western society. When we die, this life force or Self leaves the body and returns to its source, which is God. The body is merely the house in which the Self lives while it's here on Earth."

Greg pauses and asks, "With me so far?"

"Okay," one of the others interjects. "If this is true, is there any proof?"

"Oh sure, there's tons of tangible evidence for the continuation of the spirit after death, plus a stack of scientific evidence to support this concept."

This is remarkable, I think. I know that this is all true; in a way, I've always known it. I don't buy into everything, but the general thrust of what he's saying seems so right. There's not the slightest doubt in my mind.

I have a good laugh as I drive home. I went into the class a hard-boiled skeptic and came out believing in a higher force. Yet there was no weird stuff, no trances, or anything like that. Just an ordinary everyday guy who runs a small tiling business during the day, sitting in his lounge quietly talking about the truth of who we really are. It's as if someone switched on a light inside of me, and turned a darkened room into a brightly lit one. It feels that dramatic, as if the occupant of this room already knew the truth and has finally been given permission to communicate it to me.

The concepts Greg discussed swirl around in my head every waking moment. At the local swimming pool, I'm thinking furiously as I swim a few laps, and am pleasantly surprised to bump into Kapila—it turns out that we've both been coming to the same pool for over two years—so I take the opportunity to pose a few questions. "This concept of the self, living in the heart; I feel it's true, but a part of me is doubting it. I mean, sure, we all point to our heart but isn't that just conditioning?"

"Some people would say that, but it's not so. We have an instinctive knowledge that our true self resides in our heart region. Inwardly, we already know the truth, but we become lost in our own world, busily trying to meet the needs we have allowed society to impose on us."

The way she speaks in her sing-song voice tells me that she doesn't really care whether I believe her or not, that it's not important for her to convert me to her point of view, but only to try to help. When she speaks of society, there's no blame, but rather an emphasis on the fact that we chose to live our life the way we do.

"Okay, I'll buy that, but what about the relationship between the heart and the mind? That's something else I can't quite get my mind around."

She laughs, "Of course you can't. Your mind cannot understand so easily. But think of when you get the most enjoyment and feel the most alive. For me, this is when I shut my mind down and escape its constant demands. Like when I'm listening to my favorite music and simply drift away on the notes, or when I'm reading a great book and become immersed in the words. At these times, the mind is not operating, and we're living in a higher part of our self."

"That makes sense. So if I accept the concept of an inner self, what does it mean for the way I view God? The word God makes me cringe. I can accept the existence of a higher force in the Universe, even that the higher force can impact my life. But a personal God that the Christians talk about; I can't handle that."

She looks at me as if she's about to laugh, and then gives me a smile that softly weaves its way into my heart and opens up my receptivity. "Alistair, God is many things to many people. Take it easy and let your awareness unfold. I can assure you the way you view God will change considerably if you seriously pursue your inner journey."

She looks like a pixie, and flashes a mischievous grin as she adds, "If you're honest with yourself, you may find the problem you have in accepting the notion of God lies within you. Many educated people in the West are too much into control to accept God. To them, believing in God means surrendering control of a part of their life to some external force, and this goes against all their training. Perhaps you are one of those people."

With this, she gets up and strolls off, smiling happily while I'm left to reflect on her words. What she said is true; I *am* so into controlling everything in my life that I could never believe in anything other than myself. To surrender my will to someone or something else is simply too threatening.

No, I conclude. I still don't believe in God, but I am convinced that a higher force exists at some level and I have to find it. I also feel a strange sense of purpose that I've not experienced before. But it's peaceful rather than frantic. A feeling of serene destiny!

In contrast to my peaceful moments with Greg and Kapila, things are becoming more stressful between Sasha and me, and this is manifesting itself as anxiety, which in turn is causing the old physical stress symptoms. I'm fed up with it, but since I haven't yet acted on Michelle's advice and broken up with Sasha, I've no one to blame but myself.

Sasha is happy I'm going to meditation as she thinks it may help resolve my past difficulties, and that it will allow me to commit to her. But she's not seeing any sign of this happening and finds my talk of higher forces confrontational. She hints at coming with me to meditation, but I don't encourage this since it's my alone time, and a break from the strangling dependency of our relationship.

Still looking for answers to help accelerate my journey, I try hypnotherapy with an Indian doctor who specializes in this area. Dr. Jadhav is a jovial man in his fifties with gray hair and flashing white teeth that he displays regularly through beaming smiles. His English is articulate, but his accent is strongly Indian and I have to listen carefully.

For two sessions, he follows a set routine, in which he talks me into a deeply relaxed state, and then implants reassuring messages aimed at reducing anxiety. However, on the third appointment, he tells me he's going to try something different. After talking me through a relaxation, which I find easy to do by now, and asking me to go down a series of steps to a place where I enjoy being, he leaves me in this state of consciousness without talking. This surprises me because until now, he has talked the whole way through.

I'm on a deserted beach at sunset. It's the same beach I've visualized during meditations, but not somewhere I've been to physically. As darkness descends, two bright red lights far out to sea come quickly ashore and hover above me. I see myself rise up out of my body into the air and start to dance with the lights, which have taken on a human-like form, but not quite solid. I feel a peace and calm I've never known before. After a while, the lights begin to draw away, and I hear myself call out, "Please don't leave me!"

The lights turn back and speak to me. "It's okay. We will always be with you when you need us. You are strong enough to go forward on your own for now."

As they disappear into the distance, I'm left stunned but also wonderfully inspired. Excitedly, I tell the therapist about it, and he smiles but says nothing.

At the next meeting of Greg's meditation group, I stay behind to ask him about the lights I saw. "How are you finding meditation?" he asks.

"Pretty good. Sometimes I experience a sensation of light descending from above and entering my heart. Also, I've become adept at visualizing myself in various country scenes, with the wind blowing in my hair, or with a beam of light coming from above."

"Nice. Yes when you tap into your heart and open up to the higher consciousness, many wonderful experiences can occur. But are you finding it making any changes to your outer life?"

"I guess so. Your focus on inner wealth rather than material wealth is helping me see how false my life has been."

"What do you mean?"

"Up until now, my inner life has been non-existent, just a great, empty, dark cave inside me. My entire focus was on outer achievement but it never made me happy. Now I'm starting to see why. That without acknowledging the existence of an inner aspect to my life, I would've been on a continuous search for outer fulfillment, in an attempt to meet a need that's really coming from within me."

"That's great. If you've realized this, you're well on the way."

"Greg, can I ask you something?"

"Sure."

I relate the hypnotherapy experience. "It was much more vivid than anything I've ever experienced during meditation. What do you think it means?"

"Don't know for sure, but it sounds like you had a visit either from some spirits, or a higher aspect of yourself. Either way, it sounds like a very positive experience."

"You mean, I didn't imagine it?"

"Of course, you didn't. It's not uncommon for people to have psychic experiences, where they meet all sorts of spirit guides, or aspects of their higher self, once they open up to the existence of the higher worlds."

As I reflect on Greg's words, Kapila returns, a tray of cookies in hand. "So, how's your relationship going?" I had told her about the problems Sasha and I were having a few weeks ago.

"It's not really going anywhere. I just feel stuck."

"Is she making any progress herself?"

"No, and I think that's part of the problem. She's so busy blaming me for everything that's wrong in her life that she doesn't seem to be doing anything to help herself. I just feel she's standing still, not prepared to look at herself, and waiting for me to solve her problems. And I've got enough on my plate just dealing with all my stuff."

Greg chips in, "Yeah, we often see problems develop in relationships when one person starts to meditate and the other doesn't.

One partner starts to grow, while the other stays stuck. This causes a growing rift between the two."

"Yes, that's certainly happening to us. Sasha is so materialistic in a way. She desperately wants to own a house and have a family, whereas that's becoming far less important to me. But in truth we were in trouble a long time before I started coming to meditation."

"If she's not prepared to look at herself, perhaps it's not the right relationship for you."

"Oh, I know that. I just have to find the strength to end it."

"Keep meditating," Kapila adds cheerily. "You'll find your inner strength."

Is This What Love's All About?

A s January 1997 opens, I resolve to follow Kapila's advice to
unearth the strength to honor myself. Sasha has just moved
out of the house we shared, and despite knowing that it has
to happen, I'm hurting. When I left Belinda, I was emotionally
dead, but the last two years have opened my heart. And worse, I
also feel the pain of forcing the woman who has shared my life for
the past two years into an uncertain future.

However, we don't end our relationship swiftly and cleanly,
but prolong the agony, like a sadistic, slow execution. A dozen
times a day, I ask myself, *"Why don't you walk away? Why do you
still see her?"*

We talk on the phone every day, often making a date that usually ends up in bed. Why? Poor Sasha is going through hell. She
loves me, or at least she thinks she does. But I know that I don't
love her. I thought I did once, but I didn't know what love was.
And still don't. But every time I decide to make the break, my
heart plunges into an ever-deeper pit, so I call her up again. Neither of us is happy; in fact, we're both miserable.

So, in the twilight of the crushing end to another relationship,
I'm forced to ask myself some hard questions, such as what is
love, anyway? And why can't I find it?

I'm walking along the creek bank near my house, trying to
reconcile things. I and sit against an old willow tree whose long,
drooping branches offer a delightful shade against the hot summer
sun. I watch the insects skimming over the water's surface, which
is quickly turning stagnant green in the summer drought. I tell myself, *"This water is just like my life, muddy and murky. Stop pretending and be honest with yourself, Alistair. Your life is a mess."*

Why are my relationships always so damned painful? When they're good, I worry that they won't last, and when they suck, they're emotional shredders. How can this be so? How can the very things I long for cause me so much pain? *You're such a loser, Alistair.*

Suddenly, in a rare moment of clarity, that last remark hits me, and I see the problem. How can I experience love for, or from, another person, if I can't love myself? And I obviously don't love myself. Despite all my outer posturing, all my confident airs, I have zero self-esteem. In fact, I really don't like myself, and at times, I detest myself. So who would want to love me, or accept love from me?

I lie down on the grass and let the pain of my realization sear through my cells. I see myself as half a circle looking for another half-circle to make me whole, to be all of those things I'm not. No wonder I end up in co-dependency. No wonder I can't let Sasha go, because I'm afraid I'll lose part of myself.

I walk home in a daze, consumed by confusion. Mind whirling, I absently glance at the morning paper to see what's on television. My God, look at this junk. It's all about love, or perhaps what love is not. Love must be the most talked about, written about, acted about, and sung about theme on Earth. And the least understood. All these TV shows about people falling in love, and falling out. And what do we see. Healthy, fulfilling relationships? No! Drama, dependency, and murder committed in love's name. We're all being taught to be semi-circles. No wonder I don't know how to love myself. I can't stand to watch any of this crap. I'll be glad when Sasha takes her television away tomorrow. I won't miss it at all.

What about some music? Every track rams a lament about dependant relationships down my throat. One of my favorite tracks wails, *"I can't live if living is without you."* Yuck. Does he really mean that? No, I can't listen to that one. I turn to Elton John, and sit back relaxing, finally escaping the constant torment of my failed love life, but not for long. *"I Guess That's Why They Call it the Blues."* Damn, I used to love this song and would sing along to it with feeling, but today it grates, the words striking me as ridiculous. *"I love you more than I love life itself."* Sorry, Elton, I can't take any more of this.

In desperation, I put on an old favorite, Jackson Browne's *Hold Out* album. Being someone who listens to the lyrics in songs more than the music, I find Jackson Browne inspiring. I let myself float in the deepness of his words until I'm jerked out of my fragile peace.

'Give up your heart and you lose your way,
trusting another to feel that way.
Give up your heart and you find yourself,
living for something in somebody else.'

That's it! That's exactly what I've been doing—living for something in somebody else. Not living for me, but looking to someone else for my happiness. And it's not working. It's never going to work. It's suddenly so obvious. I can't go back to Sasha. I have to find myself, love myself even, on my own, before I can love anyone else.

Armed with my new insight, I visit Sasha, determined to make her see the folly of continuing our relationship. Her face is dark and downcast, her eyes red and puffy, as if she's slept too little or cried too much, or both. My resolve wilts in the face of such sadness, and the white knight in me comes forward to protect the damsel, to assume responsibility for making her feel better.

"Look, Sasha, I just need some time on my own to sort myself out." I know I'm lying, intimating that there's hope for reconciliation after some solitude.

Sasha recoils from her slumped posture and launches an assault. "I don't understand how you could hurt me so much. I gave you everything, and all I ever wanted in return was for you to love me."

"I tried, Sasha. I really tried."

"I just can't believe you want to end it. We're made to be together. We're so well suited. If only you could stop being afraid of making a commitment, everything would be all right. I'll make you so happy."

Oh no. Now, I'm being attacked. I simply can't stand the guilt of my actions harming someone else. But I can't stay here, trapped like a caged bird. *Sure she'll give you everything you need, only don't expect to fly free in the sky of your own exploration. She might as well have said, "Stay in my warm envelope where nothing can hurt you and all your needs are met, and you'll never have to know what it's like out there."*

"I wish I'd never left my husband. At least he loved me. He would have given me children. And now that I've given you two years of my life, where am I? Thirty-one and now I have to start all over again because you're too afraid to see that we're meant to be together. I must've done something terribly wrong in the past to deserve this life."

The anguish in her words shatters my resolve, and I forget why I'm here. Overpowered by emotion, Sasha, tears streaming down her face, falls in my arms. My male instinct to protect a vulnerable woman takes over, and I kiss her. Aroused by the heat of her body pressed tightly against me, I change from deserter to comforter. I lead her to the bedroom where we ravenously devour each other in what can no longer be called making love.

I agree to keep seeing Sasha, even though I know I'm living a lie. I know my oscillating back and forth hurts her, but worse, I know I'm prostituting myself, dishonoring the growing need I have to be free.

Four months has passed since my last session with Michelle, and it's time for another. She's pleased that I'm living alone, but perturbed at my still seeing Sasha, and hits me with one of her typical questions.

"So, Alistair, what's your view of love now?"

"Why do you always ask such easy questions?" My sarcasm belies the relief I feel at having someone I trust with whom I can discuss my feelings. "I realize now that I don't know what love is. I can see that before I can love someone else, I have to learn to love myself. What I've been seeing as love isn't love at all, but rather the fulfillment of my needs."

"Yes," she agrees. "What you've experienced is the sensation of having your needs met by someone else. So many people who come to me make this mistake. They confuse having their needs met with love because when they meet someone who's prepared to meet their needs, they feel whole. And while it lasts, it feels good. Like the feeling of lust and euphoria that accompanies a new relationship. But it's easy for reality to become clouded."

"That's exactly what happened to me. I felt like one semi-circle looking for another to make me feel whole."

"Yes, being with Sasha was making you feel whole, just as by meeting her needs, you were making her feel whole. But the feeling of wholeness that this type of relationship generates can't last. Being responsible for someone else's happiness eventually wears you down.

When this happens, you withdraw your energy from each other, but when you do this, Sasha felt a loss, a feeling of incompleteness. And you felt the same when she withdrew her energy from you."

"Which is why we ended up on a roller-coaster ride, right?"

"Exactly. As soon as one of you started to withdraw your energy, you entered into an energy struggle. Each of you tried, in every way you knew how, to obtain the energy you needed from the other. Did you ever find that when you were feeling up, Sasha was down, and vice versa?"

"Yeah, all the time. I could never figure out why that happened."

"Well, when you were winning the struggle, you were taking her energy. You felt whole and loved, but this feeling was at the expense of her energy. So while you felt good, she felt a loss and resented the fact that you felt good. She then conspired, subconsciously, to recapture her energy, and some of yours as well. When this happened, the pendulum swung the other way, and she felt good. But you then felt a loss, and so the tug-of-war continued, with neither of you understanding."

"Why didn't you tell me this before? It seems so clear now."

"I tried to, several times in fact, but you weren't ready to hear it. My job isn't to tell clients what to do, because that doesn't lead to permanent changes. I tried to help you move down a path where you could see the truth for yourself and integrate it into your thinking."

"Boy, I must be pretty slow. It's taken me nearly two years to work it out."

"Hey, don't beat yourself up. Some people never get it. You've done well to understand as much as you have. It's rare that I meet someone who's prepared to be so honest with themselves."

"So when I left Belinda, I simply ran to another haven of dependency?"

"Yes. From what you've told me over the past 15 months, I can see the subtle games both you and Sasha were using to control each other's energy."

"You know, I can see the truth in everything you say, but I still can't find it in me to really end our relationship."

"I know you pretty well by now, Alistair, and it seems to me there are several reasons for this. If I can be blunt, you still lack the inner strength necessary. You're still afraid of losing the last remaining thread of love, even though you know it's not love, and you're still afraid of being on your own. On top of this, you're still carrying guilt over the way you left Belinda, you're still taking responsibility for her, and you're trying to do it right this time. But perhaps you're overcompensating and causing Sasha more hurt in the process."

Wow, is she ever right, and my guilt, bubbling under the surface, is about to erupt like an enraged volcano. There's nothing I can say. Michelle takes my silence as agreement, and continues, "There's another way. It doesn't have to be like this. But you're not going to find it unless you move on, unless you let go of your need for security. And unless you can find this love within yourself."

Michelle stops, searching for her next words, and I sense that she's grappling with an inner demon of her own. I step in to fill the silence. "So what do I do next?"

She looks me straight in the eye, and I see a flicker of fear. For a brief moment, a scared, lonely little girl looks out through Michelle's eyes. She gathers herself once more, and in a controlled and deliberate voice, she says, "You go searching for your fears. You go right on inside yourself and look them straight in the eye and you don't turn back. You don't ever turn back."

Then she looks away, but not before I notice her bottom lip quivering with suppressed emotion.

A Change in Meditation

S OMETHING IS MISSING. While meditation has brought me a greater awareness of myself, and a wonderful group of people, it isn't stimulating my inner journey, and I'm beginning to feel that it's not the right path for me. In early February, I see an advertisement for meditation classes to be given by the same group I went to a year earlier. It didn't grab me then, but now I decide to go, and invite Sasha, feeling that meditation will help her let me go, and this will make it easier for us both. We arrive early, and find a young man in his mid-twenties meditating in the room. "Would you mind returning in half an hour," he asks, so we go for a drive. Sasha says, "Wow, did you see how peaceful that guy was? He had an extraordinary feeling about him."

The usually bubbly Sasha is oddly serene this evening. I've never seen her like this before, and all because of the brief contact with the young man. When we return to the hall, he introduces himself as Robin and begins the class.

The class inspires me, and I start practicing every day. The results are immediate and dramatic. Two days after the class, I have a meeting with a union committee to discuss the future of the Transport Workshop, which is under threat of closure. Expecting a battle, I meditate for ten minutes before the meeting. In the meeting, there's no sign of the old confrontational, got-to-win-at-all-costs Alistair. Of course, some employees become emotional and blame me for the closure, but I don't react. Rather, I listen carefully, empathize with them, and acknowledge their point of view. I remain calm and peaceful throughout the meeting, while still achieving the required result.

After meditating for a week, calmness and self-control become routine for me, and I find myself interacting easily and naturally, without being constantly on guard.

The change is so dramatic that I feel a pull to this new group, and the next Monday, I attend a follow-up class, being held at the group's Meditation Center rather than at a local community hall. The temperature reached 104 degrees during the day, and it's still hot and steamy as Sasha and I arrive for the class. The packed room is like a furnace, but on entering, I'm overwhelmed by a feeling of family, as if I've finally come home.

There are four follow-up classes, one per week, but Sasha takes a dislike to the group leader and decides not to attend future classes. Despite some interesting sensations, I remain skeptical about how successful meditation will be for me in the long run. After being in control for 39 years, my mind has built up a tremendous capacity to doubt. And despite a belief in the existence of a higher force, I still feel no connection with "God." But for now, I'll continue with the journey.

In the next class, Daphnie, the Center leader, asks us to focus on a particular object and try to shut out any thoughts. I sit cross-legged on the floor concentrating on a photo of the group's spiritual teacher. Suddenly, I get the odd feeling that I'm connected to something within me, and notice that my thoughts are barely registering. Then, wham. A beam of light shoots between my heart and the photo. My eyes open wide, I watch two luminous golden hands emerge from the photo and move slowly towards me. I can't believe this; part of me wants to get up and run, but somehow I sit and watch calmly. The golden hands go right into my chest, remove my heart from my body, and return to the photo. Light pours out of me from where my heart was.

I'm stunned. There's no way I imagined this, yet logic says it could never happen. I hover, suspended in the moment, between the serenity and joy flooding my being, and my analytical mind. After a while, I feel my heart being returned, although there are no images this time.

After the meditation, I approach Robin, still the person I relate to in this group, to tell him about the experience, but before I can speak, he says, "Wow, man, you should have seen your face during meditation. There was so much light pouring out of it."

I go home feeling wonderful. My mind has no idea what happened, but it can't deny the evidence of my own eyes either. For the first time in my life, I have really experienced the power and beauty of my inner self-existing within my heart, connected to the higher energy that Greg described several months earlier.

It's a cool summer night and I wake up about four o'clock to soft warmth caressing the very cells of my body and soothing my emotions. I also sense a presence in the room, a faint glow, and out of nowhere, a tidal wave of joy washes over me. I bask in this delicious feeling until sleep reclaims me. The following morning, I recall the experience and wonder whether God, or whatever is controlling the game, is telling me that I'm on the right path, that I'm where I'm supposed to be.

I arrive for the fourth class knowing that I must decide whether I want to become a member of the Center. By now the original 40 class members have dwindled to 7 diehards, and as the evening draws to a close, Daphnie talks about what it means to join the Center and become a student of their spiritual teacher. The rules she lays down are pretty intense, such as lifestyle changes intended to increase sincerity and purity. We must become vegetarian and abstain from alcohol and drugs. But the biggie is that you join as either a couple or a single, and stay that way while a member. Single people must remain celibate, which means no new sexual relationships.

Now wait a minute. Slow down! I'm not ready for this. My heart sinks as my decision to continue with the group unravels. Coming to class has touched me profoundly, but there's no way I'm ready for celibacy. For me, sex has always been a link to love, and I'm not ready to give up on something so important. And while Sasha has moved out of the house, we're still seeing each other and hopping in the sack occasionally.

Daphnie continues, "Now you don't have to sign anything, but if you're serious about your inner journey, then it's important to be truthful to yourself."

This makes sense. I've been touched deeply and if I'm to head down a spiritual path, I must be truthful to myself, otherwise I'll be wasting my time. So that's it. To stay with this group, I have to comply with their rules. I leave the Center, wrapped in confusion. I ponder my dilemma all the next day, and in the evening, I call Daphnie. After a lengthy discussion, I decide to defer making the commitment. However, I immediately feel terrible. I'm back in turmoil, and agonize over the profound sense of loss I feel.

On Saturday morning, Sasha visits, and says, "You know, I had a really strong feeling this morning that you have to join the Center."

"Where did the feeling come from?"

"I don't know. Just woman's intuition, I guess. But I feel strongly you have to join up, and do it now."

This confirms the knowing permeating me since I decided not to join. "Yes, I feel it too," I admit. "I know it's something I've got to do."

Oh, the relief. I'm overjoyed at the confirmation. Something bubbles up from deep within and spirals through me like a gently exploding star on a moonless night. I literally dance and sing all over the house, knowing it's the right thing to do. Sasha's also happy and I wonder why, when it almost certainly signals the end of our relationship, at least on a sexual level. That night, we go to dinner, and out of the blue, she asks, "Are you going to join the Center as a married person?"

"I can't. I'm not married." Warning bells go off, and I'm immediately on guard. What's going on here?

"No, but you could get married. I'm sure they'd give you some time. Now I understand why she's so happy, and I'm saddened that she can cling to such a tenuous thread of hope, using even the most transparent pretext to hold on to me, especially when the futility of our relationship is so glaringly obvious.

"Look, I'm going to join as a single person, and that means, at least for the time being, no sexual relationship."

The sparkle in her eyes evaporates. "So you are saying we're over?"

"Sasha, I care about you, and I want to remain friends, but I'm not going to miss the chance to discover who I really am."

Like a jack-in-the-box, she jumps up from her chair, knocking the table, spilling a glass of wine, and storms out of the restaurant, screaming, "You can go to hell, Alistair Smith! I have no interest in a friendship with you."

In the past, I'd have gone after her to pacify her rage and take responsibility for her pain, but not tonight. It's finally over. It's time to honor myself and let her go.

The next Monday evening, I join the Center and become a student of its spiritual teacher. I rationalize my doubts about celibacy with the thought that if the right person comes along, I can simply leave the Center. My relationships to date haven't been fulfilling, and I admit that I must change how I relate on an intimate level. The long-term benefits of a period of abstinence will outweigh any short-term loss, so let's give it six months and see how it feels.

The months roll by while I throw myself into meditation and feel the enrichment in my life. An Indian spiritual teacher founded the Center, and I immerse myself in trying to understand his teachings. Starting with a negligible understanding of religion, I find the subject fascinating, like the opening up of a new world, much vaster than the limited world I've lived in until now. The secrets of my inner life captivate me as they unfold, and I soon discover the benefits of not having a Christian upbringing. With nothing to unlearn, I quickly grasp the new concepts and integrate them easily into my life.

The Center teaches what is known as "heart meditation," which the spiritual teacher suggests is the quickest way to approach God. Until now, God has been an abstract notion for me, and while I can accept the concept of a "higher force," the experience of it has remained elusive. But the teacher's books talk about God, or the 'Supreme,' in both a personal context and as universal consciousness or infinite vastness.

The teacher's approach is to nurture your inner qualities and thereby achieve closeness to God. He says, "Love is the most direct way to approach God, and that love expresses the deepest bond between man and God." But, surely this is not the love *I've* known?

The Center also emphasizes the oneness of humanity in that we're all trying to reach the same God, only through different paths. This prospect excites and enthralls me.

Although Robin is only 24 and I'm 39, we develop a close relationship, as if we're brothers. He is full of light and joy, and his humor helps me lighten up, yet at the same time, he's intense about his spiritual practice. Our endless discussions of spirituality help me greatly in my struggle to come to terms with the changes in my life.

Our teacher writes that there are five levels to our existence: the body, the vital, the mind, the heart, and the soul. I begin to understand what the levels mean, but am still grappling with some of the concepts, so one evening, I ask Robin, "I understand the body is the physical body, but surely these five components relate to each other in some way."

"Hey, man, I'm no expert," he laughs. "This is one far out subject that'll take me a lifetime to work out. Sure, separating the five levels is a gross simplification, but it helps at the start. I look at the body as being like the house in which my soul lives. That makes it really important to look after your body."

"So, what about the vital? Is this just the emotions?"

"No, not really. The vital is that part of us through which we express our emotions."

"So are you saying that we should avoid becoming emotional? That if we enter into our heart, we can go beyond emotions?"

"No way, man, no way. The vital operates in two states—a lower state and a higher state. In its lower state, it's restless energy or aggression. In its higher state, it's dynamic energy that can be focussed and powerful. We need the vital and its passion. It's the dynamic energy of the vital that enables us to make things happen in the world."

"But we need to operate in the higher vital rather than the lower, right?"

"You got it."

"Okay. I'm with you so far, but what about the mind? I can see how my mind can be negative, but is it all that bad."

"No. None of us is bad. We need all parts of our consciousness. It's just the way we use our mind. The mind—that part of us that controls our thoughts—likes to complicate things. Left on its own, it will analyze and separate, which leads to judgment and criticism. Like me, you're ruled by your mind, so it's in charge of you. Me, too. What we need to do is to place our heart and soul above our mind, and use the mind's capacity to carry out the instructions of our inner self—our soul—rather than being ruled by it."

"I'm not sure I really grasp the mind yet. I hear what you're saying, but are we talking about the conscious mind, the subconscious, the superconscious or what?"

Robin looks at me with a boyish grin. "Hey, come on, brother. Who do you think I am? A psychiatrist? I just know what I need to know to help me make progress. I don't need to understand all the complications. That's just your ego needing to be in control and analyzing everything."

"Okay, I get the message. Now the heart is not the physical heart but some space in our chest where the soul resides?"

"You're really pushing the limits of my knowledge now. I see the heart as much more than a physical location. To me, it's a state of energy, a state of consciousness, if you like, that we can choose to live our life in. The Eastern philosophies believe the heart chakra, or energy center, is located in the center of your chest. But what's important to me is to live life through my heart's consciousness. This is a state of creativity and spontaneous joy. A state of love and peace. When I live through the eyes of my heart, I see everything in a positive light, but when I move to focus through my mind, I start to judge and criticize and look at things in a negative way."

"So it's easy then," I retort. "I just have to live my life in my heart. It's that simple."

"Ha, if only it was that easy," he says lightly.

Now I'm really getting warmed up. "So, the soul is who we really are, right? That part of us that's truly spiritual and comes from the Source, from God?"

"Yes, and when we go into the consciousness of our heart and stop all the constant chatter of our mind, we're able to receive messages from our soul. This is when you really know what is the right thing to do."

"Hey, you're giving me a headache," I protest. "Let's stop for this evening, okay?"

Robin and I continue to develop our friendship and as we go along the path together, I feel a growing love for my spiritual brother. Our conversations soon become two-way, and I find myself thirsting for a source of knowledge that I can spar with to challenge my growing spiritual understanding. But there's no one at the Center who can do this, so I slake my thirst for wisdom through my meditation and reading.

My meditation technique improves steadily. I sit still, back straight, and focus on an object. This calms my mind and suspends distracting thoughts. Ha, easier said than done, and I find myself playing games to stop the constant flood of thoughts that insist on invading my silent space. Then, concentrating on my heart, I enter into it.

Our teacher also talks about different forms of love. Human love, based in the vital and mind, causes us to form attachments and dependencies, and usually ends up in frustration. I can relate to that. However, there's another type of love that he calls *divine love*, grounded in the heart and the soul. This love has, as its foundation, a love of God, and is far higher than human love. Not limited by dependencies or attachment, it is liberating. Indeed, it places no expectations or conditions on the one being loved. I am struck by the thought that I have no idea how to love God, but wonder if this is what I must achieve to experience real love.

As I continue down the spiritual path, I find myself less and less threatened by the word *God*. I still can't relate to God in any personal way, but at least I'm opening up to the *concept* of a God.

I really notice other changes in my life, however. For example, I give up alcohol overnight. While I wasn't a heavy drinker, I used to drink regularly. But I stop completely, without even having to try.

Things at work are also changing. I'm working on a huge project, which is highly stressful for everyone involved. What other people thought of me used to govern me but now I rarely let that influence my actions. My new boss, Karen, keeps me on my toes. The same age as me, this highly successful dynamic performer rose through the ranks in a male-dominated industry. She has a reputation of being pushy and domineering, but we click immediately, and rather than intimidate me, she encourages me to express myself freely and pushes me to test the boundaries of my capacity. What a difference from the controlling limitations I experienced with Robert.

I also notice that my relations with other senior managers have shifted significantly. They used to be able to push just the right buttons to make me react in certain ways. But now, I don't react as much and feel free to say what I think should be said. Consequently, I'm enjoying my interaction with other executives rather than being constantly on my guard.

At last, the major project we're working on comes to an end and I can relax. I hadn't realized how much pressure we've all been under, and with the release of pressure, my management style changes almost overnight. Once a highly structured, results-oriented manager, I was rigid and inflexible. Suddenly, that's all changed, and now I have difficulty in focusing on process and structure. Fortunately, the payoff is a dramatic increase in creativity. However, the speed of the turnaround troubles my staff, some of whom can't readily adjust to my new *modus operandi*.

It's late June, and I haven't seen Michelle since January, but she's been on my mind for some reason. I feel no need to see her, but part of me wants to, so I make an appointment to bring her up to speed with where my life is going.

She's more relaxed than I've ever seen her, and the session feels more like lunch with an old friend than counseling. Finally, though, she switches gears with one of her innocent-sounding challenges, "So, Alistair, tell me what you think about your progress in life."

"Do I have an hour to prepare?"

She laughs, "I wasn't sure what we'd discuss today, so I spent a few minutes going over my notes from your previous visits. Looking back, it's easy to highlight some of your big challenges. I'm interested in how you see them now, but first, I'd like your opinion on where you're at."

I think about this for a moment and the words flow from my lips, "Well, I guess it's about three years since I genuinely started my journey. For the first two and a half years, it was exhausting, like hacking through the jungle with a machete. And I was always on guard in case a big snake was lurking to jump out at me. But now, I'm making rapid progress. It's as if the jungle has cleared and now I'm walking along a beautiful grassy path next to a crystal clear stream. Not only is the going a lot easier, but also the scenery's improved dramatically. In fact, since I've been meditating, I've made more progress in a few months than I made in the previous three years."

"You should give yourself more credit than that, Alistair. You were ready to take some big steps whether you took up meditation or not." I'm puzzled by what she's getting at, and wonder if I haven't touched a sore spot with her. She continues, "Okay, as I said, I've gone through my old notes and want to share them with you. Here's how I would describe you when you first came to me."

I settle back in the chair, eager to hear what's to come. "First off, you were a perfectionist. You couldn't stand the thought of making a mistake, which meant you didn't try new things. In addition, you needed the approval of others to make you feel of value. This was caused by a low sense of self-worth. The combination of these two traits generated a strong need to control your environment so that you could meet the needs of everyone. I suspect that you were more driven by your expectation of their needs and, in fact, probably strived to exceed their needs."

She's spot on, and I smile at how hearing her say these things doesn't hurt. In fact, I've already accepted what she's saying and am dealing with it.

"With these complex factors at work," she continues, "it's little wonder you suffered from insecurity and anxiety, again being driven by a lack of self-worth. This manifested itself in you not trusting yourself, meaning you worried excessively about the future. It also led to a fear of commitment, as evident in your relationship with Sasha. How am I doing so far?" she smiled.

"Who is this creep? I don't want to meet him," I joke, and we both laugh. "Seriously though, when you say it like that, I was in a terrible mess, wasn't I? No wonder I was unhappy! No wonder I felt nothing but darkness inside! No wonder I couldn't talk about my real feelings to anyone! No wonder I couldn't love! No wonder I was too afraid to face the truth of what my life was really like."

"So where do you think you've got to now?"

"Gee, I still have a long way to go, but I've started to dismantle the barriers I erected around me to shield me from the truth. I'm rebuilding myself from the inside out, and at times, I can see the sun rising in my heart, and can feel a trace of love emanating from my soul."

"So, you've become a poet, too. What do you put this change down to?"

"That's easy. I've simply moved my focus from my mind to my heart."

Instantly, the mood in the room changes. She says nothing, but the smile disappears from her face, and you can cut the tension with a knife. What's going on with her, I wonder, continuing, "Before I took up meditation, I was ruled by my mind. I wanted to judge and criticize everything. I was never happy with what I had, because I was always comparing myself to others and wanted to be the best of everything and have the best of everything. This led to a life of fear and doubt."

"That's a simplistic way of viewing the mind and its capacity," she says defensively.

"Look, you're a psychologist and I'm not going to get into a discussion about the theory of the mind with you. You asked me a question and all I can do is tell you what I believe is happening to me. But I know that by meditating, the focus shifted from my mind to my heart. Consequently, life has taken on a completely different perspective. I'm now able to look at things from a positive perspective and am no longer afraid to face my fears."

"It seems to me, Alistair, that you haven't changed as much as you think. You're still as intense as ever. You've just transferred your focus from your work to your meditation. After all, a leopard can't change its spots, you know."

Suddenly, I feel as though I've become the counselor, and see no point in continuing the discussion, so I look at my watch to signal that I think we're through. As I get up, we're both relieved to end the session. At the door, I turn to her. "Michelle, you may say that a leopard can't change its spots, that people can't change that much. But let me tell you, you may think I'm a leopard, but in my heart, I'm a deer. We can all change this much simply by moving from our mind to our heart. Just think about it."

With that, I turn and walk out of her office for the last time. And as I leave behind someone who has become more a friend than a counselor. I recall her words of a few months earlier: "Counselors can only take you as far as they have gone themselves."

So maybe Michelle has taken me as far as she can. I'm now at a point that's pushing her out of her own comfort zone, a point where she's being confronted by her own fears.

Yes, I think to myself, I'm well and truly on a journey now, and there's no turning back.

Part 3: Wisdom Grows

The Wise Man Appears

AS MY AWARENESS of what's going on inside me increases, I find myself observing an inner struggle as my mind is confronted by the increasing influence of my heart. Like a battle between the different states of my consciousness, my heart is positive, sincere and trusting, while my mind tries to cast doubt and suspicion on everything. Whenever I recognize that the struggle is playing out, I direct energy to the heart, giving it extra strength.

I can't claim that I fully understand what's going on inside me during these little (and sometimes not so little) struggles, but at least I'm aware of them. One of these little battles is raging inside me as I arrive at the local swimming pool. Kapila is just leaving, and she greets me with her usual warm smile. After a little small talk, I tell her about my inner battles.

Laughing in her infectious tone, she says. "Well, what do you expect, Alistair? Your mind has been in total control of you for the best part of your life. It's not going to surrender without a fight."

"So how do I win the fight for my heart."

"Ask God for help on that one, not me. Your mind knows your insecurities and anxieties perfectly and it knows exactly where your vulnerable spots are." As she leaves, she adds over her shoulder, "Enjoy the contest. It will teach you a lot."

Meditation has become a very important part of my life, and I look forward to each session and the wonderful sensations that often come, the occasional flashes of light within me, and the glorious colors that appear in front of my eyes. Also, the photograph of my spiritual teacher regularly moves around in its frame. I can't explain these experiences so, for now, I decide to simply enjoy them.

My rich spiritual life, however, remains separate from my outer life. In fact, I don't view myself as a "spiritual person." I remain skeptical, and while I now believe in the existence of a Supreme Being, or higher source, I still have no direct experience of such a being. Having been a non-believer for so long, my mind has great difficulty accepting what's occurring. I'm also a little concerned that I may be deluding myself. Perhaps my ego is playing an elaborate game to make me feel superior. My heart knows that what I feel reflects the truth, but my mind continues to doubt.

Deep in meditation beside the creek after my morning run, I feel a presence beside me. Looking up, I see an elderly man standing just to my left.

"May I sit with you?" he asks politely.

I've seen him occasionally walking around the creek. A thick crop of white hair tops his lined face, and peering out from over a long, white, bushy beard are the most penetrating green eyes I've ever seen. They emanate a steely strength tempered by infinite compassion—an enchanting contrast.

He sits down and, as I start to speak, a movement of his right hand commands me to silence. "Please do not let me interfere with your inner work."

"I was almost through," I say, aware that his presence would present too much of a distraction to get back into meditation.

His next words take me by surprise. "You are much younger than I thought."

"What do you mean by that? Who are you?"

He laughs apologetically and pats me gently on the left knee with his right hand, much as a grandfather would. "Oh, I'm sorry. Sometimes I forget that we don't know each other in the outer world."

"What are you talking about?" Part of me is uncomfortable about this level of intimacy with a complete stranger. But I also sense that he means me no harm.

"Let me explain. My name is Ashoka. It's an Indian name, given to me by my spiritual master. You could say I am a servant of God. About a month ago, I had a vivid dream that I was to meet a young man who needed my help, a young man I had known well in a previous life."

Now he's piqued my interest. My own teacher talks a lot about reincarnation. It certainly makes sense but I haven't given it any focus.

He goes on. "A few days later, during meditation, I had a vision where I was guided to walk around the creek, and shown I would meet my friend on the bank. Since then, I have been walking every day looking for one whose energy is aligned with mine."

"Yes. I've seen you on several occasions."

"For a few weeks, I have thought you were the one, but I was confused. The message said a young man."

"Thanks," I interject. "I'm not all that old."

"No, compared to me you are a babe, but I had a picture of someone in his early twenties. It is easy to misinterpret the messages of our visions. The spirits must have meant you were young in terms of your current spiritual journey."

My head is spinning with what this encounter might mean. An old man appears out of the blue saying he knows me from a previous life and has been sent by the spirits to help me. My head is cautiously curious about what the old man has to say, but my heart is wide open to him. I know he senses my turmoil, and say, "Look, you'll have to excuse me if I don't embrace you as a long lost friend, but this is all a bit too much. I've only been meditating for a few months and to be honest, I'm still not convinced that it's real. As for these psychic experiences, I just find it difficult to accept."

"I understand. It was the same for me at the start.'

"And when was that?"

"Oh, a long time ago," he says, glancing off to the trees on the other bank, as if reflecting on the duration of his journey. The rays of the morning sun filtering through the leaves creates a serenity that takes me deeper into my heart, so I stop my futile attempts to understand what's happening and surrender to the moment. A sensation bubbles up from within my heart like raindrops of tranquility, and Ashoka seems to sense the shift in my consciousness. "You are on a journey to the truth, but there will be many challenges on the way. What do you do for a living?"

"I'm a senior executive at a large energy company. I'm in charge of a group looking at mergers and acquisitions."

His white bushy eyebrows register surprise. After a moment, he continues, "That explains why I have been asked to help you. Your job requires a very active mind?"

"Yes, absolutely."

"And to go on the spiritual journey you have chosen, you must place your mind to one side and follow your heart. That must be hard for you."

"Well, I guess it is. It's as if I'm living in two worlds. I enjoy meditation tremendously. It's given me back my life, but I still see it as something separate from me, almost as if it's not real, as if it's all a trick of my ego, and that one day, I'll wake up back where I was."

"Tell me about your journey. Did you spend much time trying to find answers before you took up meditation?"

I relate my story, the struggles, the unsuccessful relationships, the sessions with my counselor and my last meeting with her. Throughout, he nods his head and smiles, as if reliving his own life.

"Let me tell you a story," he says as I finish, a smile playing around his mouth and the corners of his eyes.

"There is a man who lives in a dark cave. At first he thinks life in this cave is good, but something inside him does not accept that this is all there is. He senses there must be something outside so he roams around his cave looking for a way out. Eventually, he sees a beam of light shining through an unseen aperture high in the roof of his cave. He doesn't know where the light comes from, but it fills him with hope of a world infinitely brighter than his home. He is filled with a deep urge to reach the light so he starts to dig at the cave wall."

I am spellbound. His words weave a spell around me like spider webs, and I can see myself in the cave. I know that this is not a story at all, but a parable reflecting my own life, which the wise old man can somehow see. I dare not interrupt the flow of his words.

"At first, the man does not know how to escape, but he intuitively knows he has to start digging. In fact, there is no wall, but the man does not know this. The cave is an illusion, the walls representing the man's own fears and ignorance. He is not really entombed, and the only thing stopping him from reaching the freedom of the light are his own fears. But in his life, these are very real."

My whole body vibrates at the clarity the story brings to my life. It describes so perfectly what I've been living for so many years. I want to blurt this out to the old man but dare not disturb the flow.

"When the man realizes that it is his own fears that entomb him, he directs some energy away from fighting the world and into delving into his own problems. The more he does this, the brighter the light becomes, which encourages him to continue. Digging with his hands, he thinks he can break through the wall on his own, and he will be out in no time. But he is mistaken. After much hard work and energy, he has made only a tiny opening in the wall, at the cost of sore and bloody fingers.

"At this stage, he realizes he needs help. So he approaches a wise counselor, who gives the man a shovel and he continues digging every day for the next year, expending an enormous amount of energy, yet something is not right. He thinks he has broken through the cave wall. He can see the light filtering into his home and illuminating it, but he can't get out and if anything blocks the opening he is plunged into darkness."

I can contain myself no longer. This is just too close to the truth and I blurt out, "This is amazing. You're describing my life. It's impossible, but somehow, you're explaining exactly what has happened to me. How can you know so much? How can you come up with such an analogy when we only met half an hour ago?"

He looks at me quizzically, as if he doesn't understand what I'm so excited about.

"It's not so hard. First you told me all these things a short while ago. And while you think I am describing your journey, do you think you're the only one to ever go through it?"

His quashing of the arrogance of the new seeker stops me dead in my tracks. Humbled, I say, "No, I guess not, but somehow I feel that way."

"We all have to go through the same things. I myself went through it all many years ago. We all have our own path to God's love but the steps we take are the same. We all have to go on a journey through our own fears and limitations. It is very easy for me to add a few words to make you think it is only your story, but the plight of the man in the cave applies to all of us. You do not own this journey."

The forceful tone of his words deepens my feelings of being so foolish as to have read too much into the intimacy of the story. "Okay, so it's not just my story, but it really helps me to understand what has happened. I felt exactly like the man in the cave. I knew what to do, I had read all the books, but I still couldn't find happiness."

"Yes, it is here that the limitation of our modern philosophy is exposed. It deals with the mind, and unfortunately cannot answer the big questions in life. Once you start asking, 'What am I doing here? What is the purpose of my life? Is this really all there is? Who am I?' the mind cannot help you. You need to look inside to your spirit. You need to go to a higher source."

"Yes, I feel like my mind lived in the prison, and it just couldn't get out on its own. It was only when I started to meditate that changes began to happen without any real effort."

"You are right. When you move your focus in life from the mind to the consciousness of the heart, miraculous changes occur in the way you view life. It happens almost overnight. You see, the power of the heart consciousness is vastly superior to the mental state of consciousness."

"Yes, I feel this. But do you know why?"

"It is quite simple, my young friend. When you operate in the mind, you try to do everything yourself. When you move to the heart, a power far greater than you descends and offers assistance. In the cave analogy, the mind, with all its professional assistance, has the capacity of a shovel. By expending a lot of energy, you can use it to dig through the wall but you come to an invisible force field that you are powerless to penetrate. In this state, you can see the light but you cannot reach it. But the heart, with the assistance of a higher power, is like a laser beam. With the grace of God, it is able to break down the force field and allow you to escape into the light beyond. Once outside, the heart can help the mind to become illumined and move into the light as well."

Elation wells up in me and washes away all the doubts that have nagged at my mind. A burst of gratitude flows through me for the wisdom of the man beside me who I have only just met, yet have known forever. Spontaneously I reach over to embrace him, but he smiles softly and raises a hand in a gesture that suggests he's not yet finished.

"There is more you need to know. It is not as simple as you think. It is not a simple matter of escaping the confines of the cave and living a life of bliss. It is not all light outside, and you must be careful to travel down the correct path. There is a path in front of you and it is made of light, but on either side of the path is a swamp. A dark smelly fog rises out of it and blocks the sun. The swamp is no different than the cave you have been in. There is plenty of food, and the people living there believe it is the only place to be. But every now and again, the fog clears enough to allow those who are searching to look up and see the light. If they look up with enough focus, they will glimpse a majestic mountain towering above them. They are captivated by the beauty of the mountain and frantically search for a way out of the swamp. The answer they will find is similar to the one you found.

"The mountain represents the path of self-discovery and the swamp represents the sea of ignorance and frustration, and is ruled by fear, while the mountain bathes in love. There is a path through the swamp, which leads to the base of the mountain. And here is the warning. You have just started to walk along this path. As you proceed, you will see many faces looking up at you through the fog. You will see the fear in their eyes, the desperate pleas for help. And a part of you will want to reach down with your hand and help those people out. But you are not yet strong enough, and if you reach out with your hand, you will be pulled into the swamp.

"You must keep your eyes straight ahead, focused on the mountain of light. Once you have safely navigated the path, and climbed part way up the mountain, you will be strong enough to come down and help people out. Resist the voice of your ego telling you to help before you are ready."

Message delivered, the old man sits back and gazes across the creek. I'm not sure that I fully understand what he means. I got the warning, but I'm not about to go out and try to save the world.

Abruptly, Ashoka rises to his feet. I jump up, millions of questions racing and tumbling through my head. "Where can I find you? When will I see you again?"

"God will guide us together when it is appropriate. You have to trust that. It is not right for us to meet too often for you will come to rely on me and that would be to your detriment. You must go on your own journey. When we are meant to meet again, we will be guided to do so. Goodbye, my young one, you give me much joy with your struggle."

With this, he turns and walks away, leaving me to my thoughts. God will guide us together when it is appropriate. Used to controlling my life, I struggle with trusting some God to tell me when I can and can't talk to someone. But then surely it was the same God that guided Ashoka to me. Right?

A few days later, I'm at a friend's house. Walking into his garage, I see a small bird that obviously became trapped inside when the door was closed. In its desperate attempts to escape, the poor bird flings itself blindly against the window. Through the glass, it can see the freedom of the open sky, but cannot reach it.

I am struck by the capacity of nature to present the lessons of our life so clearly, and the similarities between the bird's plight and that of the man in the cave. My friend assumes the role of the higher force in the little bird's life, and goes to the window. As he does, the bird recoils in fear, unable to recognize the help being offered. But once the window is open, the bird escapes to the freedom of the light beyond its cave.

I Meet My Inner Self

A S THE COLD winds of winter sweep in from the southern ocean, I start to see visions during meditation. Whether my eyes are open or closed, the visions occur as pictures or scenes inside my heart, like a movie playing inside me, with me the only member of the audience. They only happen in deep meditation, where I can move beyond the constant chatter of my mind (although my mind tries to comment on the inner experiences).

I am also now hearing voices or messages, sometimes in conjunction with a vision, but other times on their own. The words subtly form in my mind as they come from another part of my consciousness, and gently come to rest in a place where I can receive them. It feels like the very core of my being is communicating to me in its own language, converting the messages to words so I can understand and interpret them.

The mystery unfolds in an intriguing way as I visit a cave during meditation. A vision forms in my heart and I observe myself flying across the countryside to a mountain. The mountain is snow-capped, and at the peak, I find a cave, with a deep, powerful light shining from within it. When I enter the space, a huge room flooded with light unfolds, with a series of doors facing the center of the inner sanctuary. I'm aware of the doors, but don't enter them, rather being restricted to the main inner room, feeling the peace and light permeating my presence.

Over the next two weeks, I visit the mountain on several occasions. Each time, the scene is similar, but the vegetation changes, ranging from barren and rocky to lush tropical forest. One particular morning, the vision takes me aloft to the cave, and I find myself perched on a ledge at the opening. To my surprise, a frenzy of activity is taking place in the valley below, which I intuit represents my family, work and other aspects of my life.

This vision fuels a growing feeling that the rooms within the mountain represent a part of my inner being, a place from where I can observe what's going on in my outer life. Perhaps the doors open up to pathways to different aspects of my being. This day, one of the doors opens and I'm guided down a corridor. Coming to another room of light, I discover a pool of liquid resembling a spa bath. Entering this pool, immersing myself in the fluid, I'm flooded with peace, as if the pool contains a magic essence bringing serenity to my entire being. This is a part of me I've never accessed before.

The concept of an inner self continues to puzzle me, and a few days later, during meditation, a pool of water appears, resembling a shallow puddle in the middle of a huge, horizontal mirror. To my surprise, the "me" in the vision jumps into the pool, and gently descends. The pool seems bottomless, but after a while, the floor of the pool rises to meet our descent, and I discover breathing to be easy under the mystical liquid.

A young man sits with his back to me. He turns slowly at my arrival, and says, "It's good to see you. I've been waiting a long time."

I'm amazed to realize that he's a younger version of myself. This must be my inner self, or at least a representation of my inner self.

I visit the pool on several more occasions, and each time, my inner self speaks gentle words of encouragement and guidance to me. On one visit, he speaks slowly and deliberately, "You are doing well, but you still punish yourself over your mistakes. You do not need to do that. I must admit, there are times when you slip back to your old ways and I cringe at the memory of how you used to act. At other times, I smile at your clumsy efforts, but hey, you're doing great."

I take that as a clear message to stop judging and punishing myself when I'm not perfect, and to accept that I'm still learning. And for the first time, I have a glimmer of understanding about what Ashoka meant by seeking my own guidance.

The next time I find myself at the bottom of the pool, my inner self is not there. Instead, to my surprise, my spiritual teacher reveals himself. Having never met him, I struggle to understand the role he plays in the changes occurring in my life. In recent weeks, I have felt a growing connection with him, and meeting him at the bottom of the pool strengthens the emerging bond. But what exactly is his role? Is he a guide, a teacher or a catalyst for my journey of discovery of myself, or perhaps my journey to find God? Or is he all of these?

These visions reinforce my belief in God, and as my faith grows, so too does my receptivity to the messages. Someone or something is communicating with me, and whether it's God or a higher aspect of myself, it is real. And so I become aware of a growing relationship between my inner self, my soul, and the higher power, this God. I feel an ancient mystery being revealed through my life, but I'm still unable to relate to God in any personal sense, in the way I see others around me relating to Him.

In my naïve exuberance over these visions, I spout forth the wonders of my experiences to my new friends at the Center, but they don't seem to share my enthusiasm. Puzzled, I discuss this with Robin. "I really thought people would want to share their experiences, but instead they seem to be defensive."

"It's probably best not to talk about it. People like to keep their inner experiences to themselves."

"You don't," I retort.

"Yes, but I feel comfortable with you. Not everyone's so open."

"I don't get it. How are we supposed to move forward in understanding what's happening to us if we can't talk about it?"

"Look, Alistair, not everyone has the sort of experiences you're getting, and you've only been at the Center for three months. I don't get anything like you describe, and I find it mind-blowing. It can be pretty discouraging for someone who's been meditating for years without a significant experience and someone who's just started talks about all this amazing stuff as if it's quite normal."

"Oh, I thought it *was* normal." It never even occurred to me that the other people at the Center weren't having similar experiences, but even Robin isn't. Oh boy, what does *this* mean?

Robin picks up the conversation again. "It's not normal in my experience, but then I receive messages in a different way, as do many other people. But I don't really know that much because we don't talk about it."

"I still have a problem with that. Aren't we supposed to share in each other's experiences as if they're our own, and transcend our egos and insecurities?"

"Sure, we're *supposed* to, but we're not there just yet."

Perhaps I've put the people at the Center on a pedestal, assuming that because they've been meditating longer than I have, they're somehow more "spiritual" and have overcome the normal human insecurities of fear and jealousy. Apparently not.

The realization that my experiences aren't normal for anyone who meditates throws me into a spin. I was reasonably comfortable with what was happening, because I assumed others had been there before me and could explain it all to me. Now, however, I'm in turmoil at discovering that I'm having "abnormal" psychic experiences, something I've always dismissed as overactive imagination on the part of people who are either mentally unstable or trying to cash in on a gullible market.

One evening in late June, in a hotel room in Sydney, the turbulence rises to a crescendo and my confusion reaches breaking point. Desperate for answers to help ease my torment, I call Robin, the only person I know who can possibly understand.

"Hey, how are you?" he asks, his voice as chirpy as usual.

"Not too good. I'm just really rebelling against the whole concept of a spiritual life. I simply cannot accept all the things that are happening to me."

"That's just your mind playing control games again. Let it go."

"It's all right for you to say that, but my mind is a part of me too, and I happen to like it. Besides, even you said my experiences were unusual. Why is it happening to me?"

"Just accept it as God's grace. Listen, I gotta go."

The conversation has brought me no closer to any understanding. It's after 10 o'clock, and an urge to meditate tugs at me, but I'm feeling rebellious, so instead I grab the remote control and surf the in-house movies. When I reach the adult programming, I'm hit by a surge of sexual desire. *What are you doing being celibate anyway?*

I press the pay key and sit back to watch nubile young women bounce across the screen, but it provides no satisfaction. *What am*

I doing? This does nothing for me. What the hell's going on inside my head?

After enduring five boring minutes of crass, uninspiring scenes of flesh rubbing against flesh, and no apparent plot, I turn the TV off, disgusted in myself for even thinking it could help lessen my inner conflict. Agitated, I pace around the room, but the pull to meditate persists. In fact, it's now stronger.

I yield and, after a quick shower, sit down to see if I can find any solace in the silent reaches within. I'm not hopeful, as I'm too agitated, but to my surprise, an unexpected energy wave washes through me, and I slip easily into a relaxed state. A vision soon forms in which a young man in white robes takes on the familiar appearance of myself. A group of us are seated, looking intently at an older man, who appears very distinguished and learned. I recognize him as my spiritual teacher, much younger, but indisputably him.

We're sitting by a well in a village square, and I intuit that it's in India, several hundred years ago. Our teacher is talking to us, every student glued to him, totally engrossed in the wisdom being delivered.

The scene changes, and we're in the mountains. Screams, people running, the pounding of horses' hooves. Suddenly, I see the younger me running through a tunnel, apparently to escape pursuing soldiers. My teacher appears in front of me, standing at a fork in the tunnel, pointing the way, and urging us to move faster. A soldier appears and lunges towards our teacher with a long spear. Instinctively, I hurl myself forward to protect my beloved teacher, and as I do, the spear enters my heart. The vision ends abruptly.

I sit in silence, dumbstruck, a tingling sensation pulsing through my body, heart racing despite my deeply relaxed state. As my pulse rate returns to normal, a powerful voice calls to me. "You have been with me before, and now that you have found me again, I am not going to let you go. It is time to continue your journey."

No wonder the pull to meditate was so strong. But I sit on the floor of the hotel room, even more confused. The vision has pushed my mind to a point beyond where it wants to go. It raises so many questions, yet it clarifies everything, if only I will believe.

In addition to conducting spiritual training, the Center also actively promotes peace, which includes staging a bi-annual run in which relay teams carry a torch much like the Olympic torch, and visit schools and councils along the route to talk about peace. This year the run is to cover 5500km, from Townsville in the north to Adelaide in the south. I'm disappointed that I can't participate due to work commitments, but the day before the team leaves Adelaide, a major planning conference is suddenly (and mysteriously) postponed and I'm able to take a week's vacation.

Pairing up with other runners, we cover more ground than I thought possible. On some days, we cover over 50 km between us, with me running over 20 km in two 10-km stages. Carrying the heavy torch and waving it to passing cars is agony, as every muscle in my arms and legs screams in pain, but an overwhelming inspiration spurs me to keep running.

With our leg of the run finished, Robin and I head off for the 8-hour drive home, both feeling exhausted but exuberant.

"So, what did you think of your first peace run?" he asks.

"Fantastic. I don't think I've ever enjoyed anything so much. And I learned so much, as well."

"Oh yeah, like what?"

"Well, the first thing I discovered is just how much I limit myself. I mean if you'd said I'd run over twenty kilometers two days in a row, I'd have labeled you crazy. But I've just done it. And enjoyed it."

"Yes, that's what happens when you access the energy available through your heart. It's only your mental state of consciousness that limits you."

"I can see what you're talking about. All the time my mind and body was screaming at me to stop, but I got such inspiration from the school children that I exceeded what was possibly imaginable."

"It just goes to show what limitations we place on ourselves through our own belief systems. We don't think we can do something because that's what we've always been led to believe. But it isn't true."

"Just think what this means. If we can apply this latent energy to everything we do, we would truly realize all our dreams."

We fall silent as we let that thought infiltrate our mind's resistance.

I continue. "I also rediscovered my sense of adventure. For years, I've been travelling for work and staying in four- or five-star hotels.

While the environment is pleasant, it's also very false. Someone pampers to your every need which, of course, is the purpose, but it's not the real world for most people and it's too easy to forget that."

"Hey, brother, I'm really happy to hear you say that. I wondered how a big executive dude like you would cope with sharing a room with a bunch of young guys."

" I have to admit the first night was a challenge but after that, it was great. I feel ten years younger. I'd never have done it a year ago. I have to be honest though, sleeping with four other guys in a room is okay, but Fred waking up at four in the morning and singing songs is a bit tough. And I could do without the cold shower."

We both laugh, differences in generation and lifestyle peeled away by the shared experience of giving and commitment. We settle into a relaxed state of togetherness, which can only be shared by people who have developed a bond that transcends their natural differences. After half an hour of gentle silence, Robin speaks in a tone of someone drifting in the freedom of a timeless night. "So tell me, brother, did you feel any differently about God on the run?"

The question takes me by surprise and I'm forced to reflect. "You know, I really felt a presence with me for perhaps the first time. When I was running my first stretch on Thursday afternoon, I swear I could see a divine face in the sky. I just wanted to keep running for ever."

"Yeah, it's wonderful, isn't it? I felt He was watching over us the whole way to make sure we could finish."

As the endless miles of the long, straight road disappear under the car, I feel a growing acceptance of God. Even though He is still remote and I can't relate to Him on a personal level, I cannot deny feeling His presence.

As we continue the drive in the silence, the sun long since set behind the western horizon, I think about God and the visions I've experienced recently. I haven't told anyone of the vision where I saw my spiritual teacher in the caves in India.

"Robin," I start hesitantly. "You know these visions I told you about?"

"Yeah"

"Do you think there's any way I could be imagining them?"

"Hey, brother, I told you, you're one cool, connected guy, and there's no way you're making them up. So what's happening to make you think like that?"

I tell him of being with our teacher in a past life, and add, "It's just too much for me to accept. I get scared about what it means, scared of all this psychic power that seems to be flowing into me. And I'm afraid it's all just an elaborate plot by my ego to make me feel superior."

Robin reaches out his hand and places it on my arm. "I believe in you, Alistair, and you should, too."

It's a lovely gesture but does nothing to reassure me. I feel Robin has put me on a pedestal and his faith is unable to overturn my own doubt.

I arrive home shortly after 11 pm and a surprise awaits me. It's a letter from Catherine, a flight attendant I met a month ago on a flight to Sydney. I was waiting to use the restroom and we got talking about our respective spiritual journeys. We swapped addresses and phone numbers, and the titles of books. In her letter, she tells me about a Buddhist meditation class she attended the previous weekend and an experience she had.

I saw a white/golden light and you (although you had no face, I knew it was you) walked out of it. As you walked closer, I could see a hole right through you where your heart was and the light behind shone through you and came out like a beam. I asked/thought, "What's that?" and you go, "Oh that's where I was run through with a spear!" (You were kind of humorous about it.)

I don't know if that means anything to you or not, but I thought I'd tell you about it as it was a pretty mind-blowing experience for me.

It sure does mean something to me. I try to make sense of what I've just read and the connection with the vision I had in the hotel room. Catherine couldn't possibly have known about that. This is too much. Scared, I call Robin at almost midnight, and blurt out what's happened, ending with, "I can't believe it!"

"Hey, calm down, calm down. Stop playing victim and look at what's going on. Why are you denying the grace you are receiving?"

"I don't know. It's scary."

"I think it's great. Look, someone's trying to send you a very powerful message and I suggest you listen. You were given the answer through your meditation, but you're scared that it's just your mind playing tricks on you. So He's dealt a blow to your doubt that even skeptical old you can't deny."

"Yeah, I guess you're right. It's time to stop doubting myself."

"Well, one step at a time. It'll probably take a lifetime to really stop our doubt, but it's certainly time to take notice of your inner messages. As I said earlier today, your messages are real. Believe them."

"Okay. So God's telling me to listen to him?"

"Yes, and I'd say you are in for one mighty fast journey, my friend."

Who *Is* God, Anyway?

AWAKE ON SUNDAY morning to the sound of the south wind howling in the telephone wires. I crawl back under the blankets, but a strange restlessness creeps into me, a message telling me to go running. Begrudgingly, I roll out of bed and prepare to face nature's fury. Dark, threatening clouds billow overhead, and the gusting wind tries to rip off my clothes, but at least the rain looks as though it will hold off for a while.

Once I'm in my stride, I think about the letter from Catherine and its implications. I can't hide from what's happening, as too much is going on out of my control to dismiss it as a trick of the mind. I've become a player in a bigger game, even though I don't know the rules of the game, or even what the game is.

Running along the creek bank, I come to my regular spot, and my heart leaps. Ashoka said he would appear again, and here he is, on this stormy morning, seemingly waiting for me. It must be important.

As I approach, he looks at me, unfathomable depth behind his penetrating eyes. "I thought I would find you here this morning."

Aware that I'm here much later than normal, I ask, "How long have you been here?"

"Time is of no consequence. What is important is that you have come. My dreams told me it was time for us to meet again."

I squat down to his left, and he asks, "Tell me, how is your journey going?"

"Way too fast." I relate the story of my meetings with my inner self, the vision of my teacher, and Catherine's confirmation.

As I talk, his face takes on a strange luminosity, and he says, "That's great," his voice tinged with an excitement absent during our previous meeting. "Doesn't it demonstrate why you are so receptive? You have done all this stuff before in another life."

"Well, I don't know. I'm still struggling with it all. If someone had told me a year ago they were having visions, I'd have thought they were crazy."

Ashoka chuckles to himself. "Corporate executive turns spooky spiritual nut, eh!"

"It's not so funny," I protest at his casual dismissal.

Suddenly, he becomes serious again. "No, it is not funny. What you are embarking on is very serious indeed; it is the journey of life. There can be nothing more significant. Please forgive my frivolity. You see, when I received the message to come and find you today, I was concerned you may have lost your footing on the path of light and slipped into the swamp. I am relieved to find the opposite is the case."

"Well, tell me, how do I explain the visions."

"Who do you think I am? God?" He tosses his head back and looks to the skies. "Look, you have to understand something. Every person's spiritual journey is unique." He pauses, perhaps asking a higher power for guidance. "I am concerned that, if I give you my answers to your questions, you will simply adopt those answers as your own. This would be fatal, for if you did, I would be guiding you down my spiritual path and my path is not necessarily your path. I will not carry that responsibility. You have to grapple with these matters on your own and reach your own awareness. Do you understand?"

Of course I understand, but I don't want to. I want answers. My mind cannot be sated without a logical answer to what's happening to me. Yet the truth of what he says is clear. Already I've run into conflict in the Center's rules and being forced to comply with behavior that doesn't feel right for me. "I guess it's like the lessons I had to learn on love. No one else could tell me, I had to learn them myself."

Ashoka doesn't respond. He appears to be meditating, but I'm too preoccupied to try and join him. Finally he turns and fixes me with a gaze so penetrating that I want to break eye contact. It feels as if he's looking right into me, searching the depth of my inner being for clues of how to continue.

After what seems like hours, he says, "All right. I will share my understanding of these matters with you, on one condition. You must promise not to adopt what I say as gospel, but use it as a guide to help you on your own quest for the truth as it relates to your life. And you must promise, that wherever your life takes you, you will never tell another seeker of God anything other than this: That each has their own unique path to the truth."

I nod my assent to his condition and whisper, "Yes."

His face is filled with compassion and I'm sure he's aware of the thoughts flowing through my mind. He closes his eyes and speaks from a deep level in his being.

"In my experience, it is rare for someone to have visions as you do, with such clarity, particularly so early. But it is not unheard of and, indeed, I have had similar experiences myself. When we connect with our higher self, our soul, we gain direct access to God. God and our higher self know exactly how to communicate in a way that will allow us to receive the messages. For everyone it is different. Some people receive messages through feelings, others through intuitions, while others hear voices and have lucid, revealing dreams. In your case, you see visions and hear voices. Understand, this does not make you any better than anyone else. It is possible God knows the strength of your doubting mind and is aware you would not believe in your dreams, or your feelings, and so He is giving you visions to provide you with a means of communication you cannot ignore."

He pauses to let the information sink in. This gives me a chance to unscramble my brain long enough to respond. "You talk about God and my higher self in the same way. But I have to say that I'm confused. I thought of God in the way I perceive Christians do, as some remote judgmental being sitting on high. But this doesn't fit with what I'm experiencing. It doesn't fit with the love I'm feeling."

"God is all love and compassion, even in His deliverance of judgment. Unfortunately the true essence of God has been lost in the centuries of control imposed by the religious leaders and the structures established to maintain this control."

"Okay, so if God is all love, then what's the difference between God and my higher self? I've met my inner self, and he doesn't appear to be like a God, but you keep talking about them as if they were the same."

He leans back on his elbows and sighs, "Yes and no."

After another pause in which he grapples with the answer to the unanswerable, he continues, "What a question. I doubt any of us will truly understand the answer in this lifetime, but let me tell you how I rationalize it to myself. I perceive my higher self as the true me, the essence of who I am. I could also call this my spirit or my soul, when it takes residence within me. I exist in a continuum of consciousness, at one end of which is "my human," my body, my emotions, and my thoughts. My soul has taken on my human to enable it to manifest its truth on Earth, and to experience what it needs to. At the other end of the spectrum is "universal consciousness," or what I call God.

"My soul came from pure universal consciousness, and will, at some unimaginable point in the future, merge back with it. In the meantime, my soul, or higher self, is caught in a struggle between my human—who sees himself through the ego as a separate being from others, and who therefore seeks to control and possess others to make himself feel safe and worthwhile—and universal consciousness, which is total harmony and oneness. My soul has, and will continue to, manifest many "humans" in order to explore the fullness of the human condition and grow towards the perfection of universal consciousness."

The oracle falls silent and, in awe, I try to wrap my limited comprehension around the enormity of the message. Ashoka, eyes closed, offers no further elaboration.

"Wow, that's powerful. But it's so difficult for me to assimilate."

After another lengthy silence, he continues, "Let me use an analogy to make it clearer. Imagine taking a cup to the ocean and filling it with water. The water in the cup seems separate from the ocean and insignificant compared to the vast power and majesty of the ocean itself. Yet pour the water back into the ocean and what happens? It becomes one again with the ocean, and we can no longer distinguish between the water that had been in the cup and the rest of the ocean.

"If the cup is analogous to my human, the water it temporarily contains is my soul and the ocean is universal consciousness. The challenge in life is to realize, and to remember, that we are not these few isolated drops of water within the cup. That the cup is really only an illusion we bind ourselves with, and that just because part of the ocean is contained in our human, it never stops being "ocean-stuff" and therefore always has access to the majestic power of the ocean."

After a few minutes of silence to let me assimilate that, Ashoka rises to leave. He senses my desire to continue the teachings, and says, "Remember your promise. I have already told you more than is safe. Remember you must go on your own journey and discover the truth of your spiritual identity for yourself, for only then will it be truly liberating. Do not seek me out to answer your questions. Trust we will be guided together again when the time is right."

As he turns to walk away in the chilling wind, a wind I forgot entirely during our conversation, I know there's no point begging this mysterious man of wisdom to stay. I sit back, stunned, transfixed by the clarity of the message. I have received a pearl of wisdom so profound that it must reside above all other thoughts in my conscious awareness: My true purpose in life revealed as being the realization that I am not a separate cupful of water, but part of a vast ocean of love. And while I heard the words, I am aware that I don't really understand what they truly mean.

Robin moves into my house. He has been sharing a house with three other young guys from the Center and, when their lease expires, they decide to go their own ways. He has been unhappy living there for a while, but I don't know why. He tells me about it, but I feel he is concealing part of the story. It's good to have him stay, however, and we enjoy many long conversations on spirituality.

In late August, I visit my family in Perth. It's the first time since starting to meditate that I've been home. I once dreaded these visits and their painful memories but this time I feel different. On the Saturday morning, I run past all my old spots haunted by the ghosts of past painful feelings. This morning, however, it's different. Beauty and joy abound everywhere, and I frequently interrupt my run to admire the scenery. A new sense of freedom releases the painful memories that always clouded previous visits, as if the negative feelings have been sucked from my body and replaced with joy and love.

The relationship with my family is also different, and we enjoy a warmth and intimacy not present on previous trips. Despite the feelings of peace, I'm still glad to return to Adelaide, however, because spirituality is now such a large part of my life that I have a hard time communicating with those not like-minded.

Two days after returning, I receive an inner message to write to Belinda about an emotional situation she's involved in. I heard about it in Perth, but didn't learn the details. The words of a letter just appear in my mind as clear as a crystal pool, like a computer program being downloaded into my brain. Immediately after meditating, I write Belinda a letter, thinking, this is crazy. Belinda and I are civil, but hardly close enough to write a letter like this. Yet I mail it before I have a chance to talk myself out of it.

A few days later, she replies, thanking me for my courage in writing to her. She writes,

> *Your letter arrived at exactly the right time and was just what I needed to hear. I consider myself to have a strong faith in God, but His power through you is awesome. I am stunned by His infinite care.*

With this confirmation that the barriers of my past are being systematically cleared out, I feel ready to move forward with the next stage of my journey. It seems God is devoting considerable energy to convince me of His presence. I'm now past the point of no return on the journey into myself.

Part 4 • Love Evolves

Is This Really Love?

EVERAL DAYS EACH week, I work in Sydney and the evenings in the hotel give me time to continue working or to meditate. One day, a poster in a downtown bookstore window catches my eye. It announces a forthcoming comparative religion class, to be held on three consecutive Tuesday evenings. I have become captivated by the notions of the oneness of all people and a common message within all religions, yet I know nothing of the teachings of the major religions and the great masters who founded them. Excited, I enroll on the spot.

The class involves pairing up for exercises, and I team up with Sabrina, a woman in her late thirties, with medium length, brown hair and striking green eyes, which enchant me. Soft yet strong, those eyes seem to invite me in to explore further.

After class, I catch a cab back to the hotel, feeling a new sense of aliveness that I can only attribute to Sabrina. Lying in bed, I'm excited at the prospect of seeing her next week. What is this feeling? Where is the excitement coming from? Is it just a natural reaction to six months of celibacy, or is it something more.

The week drags, and the next Tuesday night rolls around too slowly for me. When I arrive, Sabrina is already there, and beckons me to the empty seat next to her. It seems that she, too, wants to continue our interaction.

At the break, we share backgrounds. She's a lawyer in a large Sydney practice, married with three children, ages ranging from nine to 14. She seems happy with her family life, and a wave of disappointment surges through me but I quickly rein in my feelings, hoping they didn't show. After all, I'm not interested in a romantic relationship. Meditation is transforming my life and there's no way I'm stopping now for a relationship. And yet?

She talks about her interest in meditation and other spiritual dimensions to life, and admits to a conflict that also bothers me. She says, "I find it increasingly difficult to rationalize the behavior I witness in the workplace with the spiritual beliefs growing within me."

"I can relate to that."

"The problem is compounded," she tells me, "by my husband not believing in spirituality, and I receive no sympathy for my internal struggles from him."

Despite what she says about how happy she is, I sense her inner emptiness, and a deep desire to be with people who understand her spiritual side.

On the final evening of the class, she once again saves me a seat. The class passes quickly and finishes around 9.30 pm. The material has been interesting and has strengthened my belief in the commonality of the message shared by the world's religions, yet Sabrina and I both regret that the class is over. We linger in the room, making small talk and finding excuses not to leave. Clearly, neither of us wants our time together to end so abruptly. After about five minutes, she asks, "Would you like to come and have coffee with me? I know a place nearby."

Once we've settled in and ordered, the conversation turns to our individual spiritual journeys, and our struggles to integrate spiritual awareness with the corporate value systems in which we're both immersed. Her environment is less supportive than mine, and once again, I think how lucky I am having Karen as a boss.

Being with Sabrina feels so right, as if we're old friends. I talk about my feelings and beliefs, with a comfort belied by our short acquaintance. The words flow straight from our hearts, without the need to filter them for safety.

Suddenly, she looks up with a start, "My God, it's eleven-thirty. I was expected home long ago."

We both rise and spontaneously embrace. I hold her close, and her body responds. Something moves between us, some magical essence flowing from my heart into hers, some deep power beyond the mind's understanding, but nonetheless still very real. I walk her to the cabstand, and as she gets in, she hands me her business card, "Please call me when you're next in town."

My heart misses a beat at her words, and as I watch the cab drive off, a peace descends, but back in the hotel room, the peace evaporates, to be replaced by doubt and uncertainty. What's going on here? I've just met this woman, yet feel I've known her all my life. She's married and committed to family life, and I'm on a spiritual path and committed, at least for the time being, to a life of celibacy. Still, her image won't leave my thoughts.

I reflect on how my previous relationships were founded in emotional need. Admittedly, I've come a long way since Sasha, but I know I'm not yet ready to plunge into the mysterious realm of intimacy. Yet I'm enchanted by this woman, whose vibration resonates within me, as if my soul has felt her radiance and is ascending in response. I drift into a fitful sleep, and she awaits me in my dreams.

Back in Sydney the following week, I call her on the first afternoon. After what seems like an eternity, she comes to the phone, sounding harried, distant and reserved. "I'm busy. I'll call you back in half an hour."

The next half an hour drags interminably, filling me with doubt. This is crazy! Why am I feeling like this? And why was she so distant? Alarm bells go off as I recognize the old pattern, and it's not a comfortable memory.

The phone rings and shocks me back to the present. Her voice is totally different, the words dancing like a symphony over the telephone line. Being prepared for the voice I'd just heard, I'm thrown for a loop. "Sorry," she explains, "other people were in my office and I had to put on my 'business' voice. Do you want to get together for lunch tomorrow? How about that same café?"

The next day comes quickly and I clear my afternoon. The conversation over lunch assumes a life of its own, and after an hour, Sabrina says, "It's such a beautiful sunny day. Why don't we go and sit in the park?"

I agree and she adds, "I've freed myself of meetings this afternoon, so I'm all yours."

"What more can I ask for?" I joke, wanting desperately to take her hand as we walk down to Sydney Harbor, around the waterfront, and by the majestic Opera House. We settle on a grassy spot hidden from public view in Macquarie Park, overlooking the harbor.

In our little piece of heaven, our conversation returns to our respective spiritual paths, and our love for God. We each approach our inner life from a different perspective, and yet the similarities are striking. I feel free and complete being with her, and when I look into her eyes, I can see all the way into her heart, as if I'm looking at her very soul. Every word spoken is understood, an exchange between two hearts without the confusion of minds.

Somehow, we stray into the relationship between Christianity and the paths we're on. "I have a strong Catholic background, and although I explore many alternatives, my beliefs are deeply rooted in the Christian tradition," she explains.

"But you believe in the oneness of all people, don't you?" I ask, already knowing the answer from our discussions during the classes.

"Yes, there's room in Christianity to accept that the beliefs of others are valid. But I'm still trying to rationalize this with what it says in the Bible."

"What do you mean?"

"Well, for example, the Bible says that God gave His only son. So if Jesus is the only Son of God, this must place him above the founders of the other religions, and this seems to conflict with the concept of oneness."

"Perhaps it's the way the Bible is interpreted," I venture. It seems obvious to me, despite my limited understanding.

"What do you mean?" she asks.

"Well, when Jesus was on the cross, didn't he say, 'Father, why hath thou forsaken me?' and at the same time, 'Father, forgive them for they know not what they do'?"

"Yes, you're pretty close."

"See, even Jesus, despite his high state of evolution, was still struggling with an identity crisis. The first statement is coming from the human Jesus, and the second statement is coming from the divine or spirit of Jesus."

"Okay," she says cautiously, not knowing where I'm taking this. "I'm not saying I agree, but let's just say I am following you, sort of. Go on."

Ashoka's analogy of the water in the cup trying to return to the ocean inspires me, as I allow my inner voice to guide me into uncharted territory. "Well, I'm just a baby on the spiritual journey, but it seems we're all caught in the same struggle that Jesus' words highlight, trying to understand the relationship between our human self and our spiritual self."

"I'm not sure I'm going to agree with you, but go on anyway."

"Well, if we each embody both the human and spiritual aspects, and if we are each caught in a personal struggle to reconcile these aspects, can we not be seeing the same struggle taking place on a society-wide basis?"

"Yes, if your theory on the struggle of the individual is correct, the extrapolation makes sense. But where are you leading?"

"Okay, it seems to me that, given this duality of human and spirit, there are also two ways to interpret the words of Jesus in the Bible, but that one of these ways has been completely ignored. Christianity, from what I can tell, interprets the words from a purely human perspective, whereas perhaps the answer lies in looking at it from the perception of us as spiritual beings."

"What you say makes total sense, but I can already feel me becoming defensive, because I know it's taking me out of my beliefs."

I touch her cheek gently with one hand, and say reassuringly, "Everything about today is outside of our beliefs. Just stay with me a bit longer. I really need your understanding of Christianity to provide a test for my beliefs."

Responding to my touch, her eyes soften, the mounting resistance swept away. "It sounds so logical as you tell it to me. I'll just have to remember not to react to my own belief structure."

"So back to your original question about the Father giving His only son. If we look at this from the human angle, then we say, 'See, Jesus is the only Son of God.' But what happens if we look at it from a spiritual perspective, what did God give up?"

Excitement rises in her voice. "I see where you are heading. God didn't give up the spiritual aspect of Jesus. We all know that our beloved Jesus still lives and looks over us."

"Yes, exactly!" Caught up in her excitement, I hear my words flow, not quite sure of the source of my newfound wisdom. "From the human perspective, Jesus probably was the only direct incarnation of the Father, on Earth, in a human form, at that time. From a spiritual perspective, he didn't surrender His son at all, and even if we consider He did, then perhaps it still makes no difference."

"I don't follow you there."

"Well, at a spiritual level, if all the great masters have attained a full realization of God, then they are one with the ocean of Universal consciousness, and there is only one son."

"Now you've completely lost me."

I explain Ashoka's analogy of the ocean and the cup of water, and add, "If Krishna, Buddha and Jesus, for example, have all realized the falsity of the cup, and have all fully merged with the ocean, then how can we separate them? How can we say that they are different? It's only the fact that we see ourselves from the human perspective, contained within the walls of our cup, that we think of them as different."

"This is fascinating. I'd like to test another one. The Bible suggests that following Jesus is the only way to salvation. What do you make of that one?"

"Again, if we take the human view, then we think this means Jesus the man is the only one to follow, right."

"Yes, that's how I've always seen it."

"But if we take the spiritual perspective, then perhaps what the Bible is saying is that what Jesus represents is the only way. Now, if Jesus represents the awareness that we are not, in fact, the isolated water in the cup, but a part of a great ocean, could it not be that our road to salvation lies in understanding this, and committing our lives to pursuing that realization?"

"Okay, so it's not Jesus the human but Jesus the spirit we must follow, and we have already established that, at a spiritual level, at the level of the ocean, there is no difference between Jesus, Buddha and Krishna."

"Good girl, spot on. I mean we can play around with this, but it seems to me that the important thing is to try to look at the teachings for their spiritual significance, and not the limited human perspective of separation."

"Oh boy, you've given me something to think about. You certainly learned something in that class."

"Yeah, I guess so." So often finding myself in the role of student, I enjoy playing teacher. "But for me, the most important part of the course was meeting you."

Those words hang briefly in mid-air between us. The feelings we both know are building are exposed for a brief moment, and then we push them back to a place of relative safety.

We're lying on our backs, looking at the cloudless azure sky, when Sabrina props herself on one elbow and looks straight into my eyes. "I'm not sure what I'm doing here with you, but it seems so right."

Her words capture my feelings perfectly. I feel so elated, so alive, and yet there are no sexual thoughts, no thoughts of physical contact whatsoever. It simply isn't necessary. The conversation turns to her family situation, an inevitable extension of the intimacy enmeshing our beings, and the need to restrain it.

"So where does your husband stand on these sort of issues?" I ask.

"He's strictly Catholic. He doesn't like the sort of things I dabble with."

"Hmm. That must cause a few problems?"

"Well yes, it does. Like when I first started meditating about five years ago, we had some real problems. But we've worked through those, and now things are really good."

Her voice sounds far from convincing so I probe further. "Do you find the two of you are growing in separate directions?"

"Yes and no. Marriage is sacred to me, and the notion of us splitting up is inconceivable, so I just have to work at it." The odd combination of pain and resolve in her words is not lost on me.

"I understand. I've been through a divorce. Funny though, I always thought I viewed marriage as sacred too, 'til I just ran away. But I know the pain it causes children, and I'd never want to be the cause of anyone else going through that pain."

Our eyes meet, sharing a deep understanding and mutual respect, both knowing that the conversation, while appearing removed from the intimacy of our togetherness, is really defining the boundaries within which that intimacy must stay.

As a harbor front clock announces four o'clock, we gather ourselves for the walk back to respective offices. Our parting embrace exudes warmth I can't remember feeling previously, and she whispers in my ear, "You know this can't come to anything, don't you."

No answer is needed, or possible.

Once more, I'm in the familiar state of turmoil, unable to get her out of my head. I feel sick at the loss of not having her beside me, and yet have no physical desire. The feeling of want comes from a deeper place, as if our meeting has revived dormant soul memories. I awaken early the next morning, oddly lucid and reflect on the previous afternoon's conversation. The ease with which we encroached on such intimate topics testifies to the strength of the bond we feel with each other.

The next day, I return to Adelaide, my feelings for Sabrina unchanged, suspecting I should just forget all about her and get on with my life, but I can't evict the love that's decided to occupy my heart. As the plane levels off at 30,000 feet, I write her a letter expounding my feelings, careful not to apply pressure or suggest anything should come of these feelings, but still needing to express the wonder of all that is unfolding within me.

The following day, I arrive at the Center still reflecting on my turmoil over Sabrina, and I ask for divine help to understand what it means. Not long after meditation starts, I feel a deep inner cry in my heart. The cry is mournful and agonizing, as if a long buried hurt is being emitted. A vision forms inside me of a barren room, a child in the corner, cowering in fear. He is skinny, without clothes, tears of desperation cascading from his eyes. I watch, knowing this child is part of me. My spiritual teacher appears, represented as a glowing divine being, and approaches the child reassuringly, gently stroking his hair. When he cradles the child in loving arms, I feel a deluge of love inundating me. He gently speaks to my child, "It is okay to acknowledge you have longed for love, that you have desperately missed having real love in your life."

Suddenly, a form materializes in front of me, not in my vision but actually in the room, right before my eyes. It is Sabrina's soul, appearing as a luminous being, the epitome of heavenly beauty descended from her celestial vantage point. The form enters into my heart, and our souls embrace each other in what can only be called ecstasy. Peaceful and composed, she beckons me to join her. Then, as suddenly as she appeared, she fades into the depth of my heart and disappears.

With no context for handling this experience, I want to believe it's coming from my soul, that this is what divine love is like, that I'm experiencing love on a deep spiritual level. But the spiritual or divine love that my spiritual teacher writes about is a love without attachment or expectation, a love that liberates. But with Sabrina permeating my every thought, I feel anything but liberated. I descend into an unpleasant space, powerless to halt the slide. Being trapped between anxiety borne from an expectation of something and an expectation of nothing is a feeling I remember from the past and it's far from healthy. In one fell swoop, my emotions take my heart prisoner, and plunge me into the dark swamp of self-indulgence. Just as Ashoka described, I have fallen from the path of light leading to the mountain, and have disappeared beneath the surface of the swamp.

On the Friday, I return to my Adelaide office and learn that Sabrina has called. I immediately return her call, but when she answers, she quietly asks me to call back in half an hour. I watch the clock tick off each of the next 30 agonizing minutes. I cannot believe how nervous I am. Oh, God, sending that letter was a horrible mistake, I tell myself for the hundredth time.

She answers in a warmer tone but her first words throw me. "Alistair, what are you trying to do to me?"

My heart sinks. Time stands still. "I ... er ... I'm sorry," I splutter.

"There's no need to be sorry. I wrote you a letter as well, but I ripped it up before I sent it."

We talk for an hour, during which I'm transported from my office to a mountain stream gently caressing its grassy banks in the summer sun, as colorful butterflies play carelessly among banks of flowers. I forget where I am and once more feel the caress of her soul. Every feeling I wrote about she shares, and she says, "I was totally surprised at the strength of my feelings. When we talked in the park, I could see right into your heart. And I know you could see inside mine. And all I could see was love, a very pure love."

The conversation flows easily between us until the topic of her marriage comes up. "There have been some difficult times, and it's not a perfect marriage, but we've worked very hard to get the relationship to where it is now."

"I'd never do anything to harm your family," I reassure her. Continuing, I add." Even if you wanted to, I wouldn't let you. I feel what you and I have is so pure and special that it wouldn't tolerate an act that could taint it with the destruction of a family unit."

There's nothing else to say. We both understand how the other feels, and the depth and purity of the emotions. But what do we do with a relationship that has nowhere to go in the traditional sense?

Should I tell her about how her soul visited me? Coming from a Christian background, and despite the exploration of our thoughts at our last meeting, she'd probably react negatively. And besides, I don't want to put her under that sort of pressure. So I say nothing. I wonder if perhaps we shouldn't end it right here, but neither of us wants this, so we agree to stay in contact and try to be friends on a spiritual level.

"My project in Sydney has come to an end and my trips there will be far less frequent, so I don't know when I'll see you again."

"That's probably a good thing."

I feel a deep sense of peace. Sabrina has validated the love that flows so freely through our hearts, without any opportunity of a physical manifestation of the relationship. Comforted, I convince myself that this is a divine relationship, that our souls have been invoked during our meetings, creating a merging of our beings at a deep spiritual level, which transcends the need for physical contact.

But as the next few days pass by, I wonder, in moments of honesty, if this is completely true? Am I simply kidding myself in the euphoria of a new romance? Does how I feel about Sabrina, even though it's only by letter and telephone, meet a deep emotional need which is not being satisfied by my current spiritual life? And in the process, am I really creating an attachment that will have to be undone in the future?

Several times, I've seen Ashoka walking on the other side of the river, and have resisted the urge to chase after him, remembering his words that we will be guided when it is time. This morning, I see him coming towards me. In excited anticipation, I slow down to a walk. To my surprise, he shows no signs of stopping. Instead, he looks through me with those penetrating eyes, flashes a smile across his aging face, and walks on, beads in hand as he silently chants a mantra.

What a strange little man, I think. I wonder when I'll talk with him again.

Whose Game *Is* This?

As winter turns to spring, ushering in October, Sabrina and I continue our long-distance friendship. Several beautiful, lengthy phone calls sprinkle the symphony that my life has become with a sweetness surpassing the most exotic spice. Despite her words to the contrary, a growing sense that we are destined to be together takes hold in my heart as I convince myself of the future possibilities.

My involvement in the Center grows, as I take an increasingly active role in its management. Students openly approach me to discuss their concerns, and part of me feels drawn to help them in whatever way I am guided. They're like brothers and sisters to me and their energy and enthusiasm towards the selfless service they offer the community, through meditation classes and other activities, is inspiring. Another part of me, however, wants to hold back and enjoy the anonymity that comes from being the newest member of the Center.

My relationship with Sabrina is also a source of inner tension. To pursue the relationship beyond platonic would, of course, require me to leave the Center, and yet my spirit feels so alive when I'm with her. Even though this is only a remote possibility, I'm still confused as to why I couldn't combine the two, and I know I'll need to confront this at some point.

One evening the opportunity arises to discuss this conflict with Robin, and after relating the story, I conclude with, "Our love is so different from anything I've known before that I'm sure it's a spiritual love."

"Be careful, that's all I say," Robin counsels, a worried frown etched on his face.

"Robin, the vision I had was real, her soul was calling to me. You're the one who keeps on telling me to believe in my visions and feelings."

"Yes, I know. I want to believe your feelings, but I just don't have any frame of reference to fall back on."

"That doesn't make it wrong," I argue.

"Well, no," he hedges, clearly uncomfortable with the conversation.

I'm not going to let him of the hook, so I pursue him with my burning question. "Why can't I stay on the path if I have a relationship with Sabrina. It seems that every time I talk to her, my spirit comes to the fore and I open up further to God."

"You may be different. You may be able to handle it, but for most people, the dangers of attachment are too great. I'm not saying you would, but in the main, when people get involved romantically, it makes it harder to pursue God with the same intensity."

"Well, surely they can be flexible?"

"At one time, our teacher used to allow marriages, but it got out of hand. You have to remember, there are a lot of young people at the centers, and it would be very easy for the centers to become romantic hot beds. That wouldn't be fair to the people who wanted to make real progress."

I can see his point. The young women at the Center are beautiful, and emanate a purity that heightens their appeal. "But I'm not becoming emotionally attached," I answer a little too firmly.

"I hope so, my dear friend, but just remember, the appeal of a woman is a powerful force, and you need to be very careful not to fall in a trap."

It's clear Robin doesn't share my enthusiasm for the magic of my love with Sabrina, so there seems little point in further discussion.

At work, the few people I mention Sabrina to are equally convinced that it's simply a case of the euphoria of a new love, not understanding the magic of the merging of two souls. Still I remain convinced I'm being shown a love that transcends the limitation of a normal relationship, one that has moved into the realm of the spiritual, and I yearn for someone to share my discoveries.

A few days after the conversation with Robin, Karen arrives in Adelaide for a series of meetings, which require an overnight stop. Our relationship has flourished and we decide to catch up over dinner. The first hour of the conversation centers on work and we're well into the main course when an opportunity arises to relate my love for Sabrina. I've freely shared many of my spiritual experiences with Karen, and while she doesn't fully comprehend, she's always receptive, with a depth of understanding that belies her lack of exposure to the spiritual path. As I finish the story of Sabrina, I add, "It's such an amazing feeling when I communicate with her. It's hard to believe that we've only seen each other a few times."

"It doesn't surprise me at all, Alistair. You're probably unaware of just how open you've become. When you talk of spirituality, there's a fire within you that's enchanting. And you're so incredibly open about your feelings, it's hardly surprising that, if you meet someone who's the same, a fire would ignite between you."

"So you don't think I'm imagining these feelings?" I'm relieved to find someone who seems to understand.

"No, not at all. But tell me, what does it mean for your spiritual path?"

"What do you mean?"

"Well, I know you're on a path that requires celibacy, and to have a relationship with Sabrina would require you to leave, wouldn't it?"

"Yes, I guess so, but there's no way I'm going to have a relationship with Sabrina in the physical sense. What we have goes beyond that."

"Yes, I understand what you're both saying, but I'm not sure you can keep it that way. If she has the same feelings for you as you have for her, then how long will it be before one or both of you want to make more out of it?"

I'm silent for a moment. She's touching on a critical point. "It has to stay at a spiritual level, Karen, at least for now, because I know I'm not ready for another intimate physical relationship. I've already felt the pull of emotional dependency with Sabrina, and I'm not going back there."

"It would be a real shame if you ended up having another ordinary relationship. But I sense you have a real challenge on your hands."

As I say goodnight to Karen with a warm hug, I think about how fortunate I am with the people who come into my life just when I need them. Robert helped me so much, and just when that relationship was turning sour, along came Karen, who provides exactly what I need right now. And then, of course, there's old Ashoka, who just appeared out of the blue. It seems I'm being blessed with the teachers I need at exactly the time I need them.

Our Center is organizing an ultra-marathon championship, which provides me an opportunity to get more involved in the organization. The event is intended to demonstrate what we're capable of if we can cast aside preconceived limitations. The race is set up for a world record attempt by Greek champion Yiannis Kouros to become the first man to run 300 km in a day. This amazing man succeeds, running 303.5km in a relentless display of courage that just eats up the distance.

Yiannis stays in my house for a few days, giving me the wonderful opportunity to get to know him and form a friendship. The night after the run, he's lying on the floor with Robin massaging his swollen feet, and I ask, "How do you do it?"

"It's a gift from God," he replies, with a humility I've rarely seen in a sporting champion.

"You make it look so effortless, though."

He looks at me, a pained grimace on his face. "You can't train for an ultra-marathon. You must run it purely on the strength of your will. After seventy kilometers, my knees were in agony, but you have to go on. I have to focus my mind to overcome the pain rather than give in to its protests and accept its limitations."

"Yiannis, I've always thought that humility and intensity didn't go together. I mean I've always been proud of the intensity with which I live life, and I'm afraid that if I become humble, I'll lose that intensity."

He looks straight into my eyes, and I'm engulfed by his love and understanding. He nods to encourage me to continue. "I've always craved humility, and desperately want it. You seem to have both."

Yiannis winces in pain as Robin touches a sensitive spot on his left foot. "Your fears are without basis. Humility is a blessing that does nothing to reduce your intensity. In fact, it can enhance it."

"What do you mean?"

"Well, to be genuinely humble, you need to accept yourself as you are, and consider what you have as a gift to be shared with your brothers and sisters, no matter how small or insignificant the gift may seem."

"But how does that increase your intensity?"

"When we achieve this level of self-acceptance, we can go beyond the ego. I have no need to devote any energy to worrying about what others think. I am totally focused on my performance."

Yiannis lies back, closes his eyes, and drifts off, enjoying Robin's gentle fingers on his aching feet. I sit back and reflect on how much energy I still devote to feeding my ego, and worrying about what others think of me.

After his massage, the exhausted Yiannis goes to bed, leaving Robin and I to resume our earlier conversation. "On the one hand, I feel a real pull to become more involved with the Center, but part of me still wants to hold back from total commitment."

"Well, I think you have to choose," he says, much more forcefully than usual.

"Let's see what happens when I get back from New York."

"Delaying the decision for another month isn't going to help. If you get the message to do it now, you should do it now, and not make excuses to put it off," Robin persists.

"Perhaps, but I'm not ready. Listen, I'm tired, too. I think I'll turn in."

The next morning, however, the inner pressure to become more involved at the Center is overwhelming. A sense of duty rises up like a cobra responding to the snake-charmer's command, so later that day, I discuss it with Daphnie. We agree that I should run a strategic planning session to help plan priorities and resources for the coming year.

Since I have the necessary skills, I start by interviewing the other students to identify the vision people hold for the Center, and the problems they see blocking the realization of the vision. Some people feel challenged by being made to look beyond the status quo, but for me, the process brings to the fore my old nemesis, the corporate, power-driven side of me, accompanied by a new demon—self-importance. As the inner struggle intensifies, during meditation, I ask my spiritual teacher for guidance on whether I'm doing the right thing.

In the following morning's meditation, a powerful force rises up from deep within me, like an invading army charging into an unprotected valley. As it leaves my body, this unidentified energy crystallizes into the shape of a speeding railroad train pulled by large, powerful locomotive. As quickly as it appears, the vision of the train changes into an intense beam of light emanating from my heart.

As a detached observer, I enjoy the sensation of light flowing out from my being, and drift into a state of blissful oblivion. After a few moments, however, the vision changes, jolting me from my peaceful state of detachment. Objects begin to appear in the light, and I watch them solidify and increase in density. Horrified at the stream of emotional garbage gushing out of my heart, I want to escape but am locked into the experience, mesmerized like a rabbit startled by car headlights. Scenes of anger, screams, the faces of people who have caused me pain, flashbacks to sexual experiences, and excruciating inner torment inundate me as the painful experiences of my life pass before me. Fortunately, this horrendous outpouring lasts only a few minutes, but it feels like hours.

Suddenly, the stream of painful memories is replaced by a cascade of pale blue light that streams into my heart, filling every crevice of my inner existence, enveloping me with tender warmth. As the soothing light caresses my soul, I'm overwhelmed with a feeling of profound love for all things known to man, and especially my spiritual teacher. I leave the meditation exhausted and wrung out, knowing that I've just experienced the first stage of an internal cleansing process.

Two days later, I'm meditating at the Center and suddenly my heart fills with a purple light interspersed with flashes of white that slowly changes to a glistening gold. Then my heart expands and the gold light explodes to fill the Center. The ever-expanding ocean of gold transforms into a vastness, seemingly without boundaries. From out of the light, a being emerges, spiraling mystically outwards from somewhere deep within me. It is a young, beautiful angelic being that clearly looks like me, but is composed of light. His beauty carries me aloft to higher dimensions, like an eagle riding a thermal current.

Continuing his spiraling journey, the light being drifts unhurriedly into the ocean of gold, joyfully dancing and diving like a playful dolphin. Soon, he's joined by others like him, also frolicking in the ocean of gold. Are they souls? Are they the inner selves of the other people in the room? I let these questions float through me unanswered lest they disrupt the majesty of the moment.

Eventually the images fade, leaving a peaceful lightness exuding from my heart. There's little time to indulge in the flood of love sweeping through me, however, as the great cavern within my heart once more expands so rapidly that I'm barely able to follow it. First, it encompasses Adelaide, then the whole of Australia and, finally, the entire world. I watch in awed wonder as it expands to encompass the entire Universe.

A sun emerges vividly from the golden light, with giant solar flares reaching up, like fiery orange claws trying to engulf a comet that careens by just beyond their reach. The image fades and then returns, and over the next two minutes, comes and goes, until my celestial experience ends.

I sit engrossed by the incomprehensible scenes that have just played out both before my eyes and within my body. But as soon as my heart returns to its normal state, it expands again, this time to envelop my whole body. My mind gives up, stretched beyond its limits, as my heart expands beyond my physical form, yet oddly, the vision is completely contained within me. Somehow, I am both within myself and beyond myself.

The light that fills me moves gracefully outwards, embracing Robin who is sitting next to me. As if it's alive, it seeks out and envelopes everyone in the room, until the entire Center nestles within my heart. Suddenly, a great shaft of light appears before me, a luminous pathway through the dimensions. Now my heart, with all the Center members securely within it, is drawn inexorably along this luminous pathway. Like a space ship accelerating to light speed, it moves ever faster along the beam of light as time and space become meaningless. An immense image of my spiritual teacher appears and my heart, the space ship, comes to a halt. His heart opens up like a gigantic astral aircraft hangar, allowing our dwarfed craft to enter. As we do, the loving confines of his heart close around me, the scene fades, leaving only an unforgettable memory.

That evening, as we drive home, Robin comments, "You look like you're not here, like you're in another dimension."

"Oh, I'm sorry." I was unaware how silent I had been, still in a vacuum of timelessness following the experience. "I'm just trying to come to terms with what happened tonight." After I explain the vision to him, all he can say is, "Wow, what a blast."

"Yes, it was. As if the entire Universe was within me, and yet I was part of it."

"Yeah, well, you know what our teacher says in his books—that we're a finite human and an infinite spiritual being at one and the same time."

"Yes, I read that, but couldn't really grasp what it meant. It's all very well to read these grand statements about the Universe being within, but until you experience it, it's only theory. Robin, remember I told you about what old Ashoka said about the water in the cup, and the ocean. How our journey is all about remembering that we're not the isolated water in the cup, but are really a part of the infinite ocean."

"Yeah sure, it's a really great analogy."

"Well, can't you see? What I experienced tonight is confirmation of this. The finite human in me thinks that I'm totally contained within a body that I can observe with my senses, that my body is the cup. But this evening, for a few minutes, I became the infinite ocean. As if my cup of water was poured into the ocean and I became aware of being the whole ocean."

"Yes, yes, of course," he stammers excitedly. "The cup is the body, and the water in the cup is the spirit. So what your vision tells us is that, from the spirit's perspective, the ocean represents the Universe, that we embody the entire Universe within us, and that we can experience it if we can let go of the illusion of our finite body."

Immersed in our own thoughts, we fall silent until we arrive home. Neither of us can comprehend what I experienced, the glimpse of the infinite that lies within us all, but which the limited capacity of our minds simply can't grasp. All I can do is accept that it exists and dream of a time when I may see it again.

Three nights later, during meditation at the Center, the messages resume. A sensation of freedom permeates me, and the now familiar luminous representation of myself appears, arms outstretched, flying effortlessly yet purposefully. Slowly, I become aware of the terrain below me, and the landscape is a barren, scorched wasteland, as if ravaged by a ferocious fire. Suddenly, a massive rock jutting into the sky fills the horizon and interrupts my flight.

As I approach the huge rock, I see my teacher, sitting cross-legged on a ledge, and surrounded by a circle of about a dozen other beings. The luminous being of light, an inner aspect of myself, lands on the rock and takes up a position in the circle behind the teacher.

Our teacher elevates his eyes to the sky and following his gaze, we meditate in unison. The sky is filled with ominous clouds that threaten a storm, and as I watch, a bright light spears down through the clouds. It's a divine light descending to bless us, I think. Well, think again. The light transforms into a whirlpool of darkness like a vicious tornado that tries to pluck us from our tenuous perch. It attacks with the ferocity of an enraged demon, and I struggle to hold on to the rock. As the wind batters savagely at my body, I fight desperately to resist the forces of negativity that pour from it. I feel an opening within my light body, and something floods through me and emanates outwards, glistening energy. It exudes from each of us and covers the surface of the rock, creating a strong bond between our souls.

Linked by the wonderful substance, we combine our efforts and render the storm powerless. Knowing it has lost the battle, the tornado withdraws, spiraling away into the distance. Suddenly, a flash of light pierces the clouds and they disappear, revealing a pristine blue sky.

Bathed in the love of my spiritual brothers and sisters, I want to savor love's victory over the forces of fear. However, we warriors of light are afforded no such luxury. On some inner command, we leave our roost and ascend once more into the sky. As my luminous inner self flies back in the direction from which he arrived, I notice the ground beneath has totally transformed. No longer the seared devastation by an inferno, but now a lush, verdant paradise. From one horizon to the other, flowing rivers and streams criss-cross vast tracts of green pasture, and I'm captivated by the panoply of nature's abundance as it unfolds beneath me.

Alone at home, I puzzle over the symbology of the vision. Is it that if we combine our inner capacity, if we unite in our love for God, then we can withstand any negative force and transform barren wasteland into an oasis? Or is it more personal? Does the wasteland represent my life prior to taking up meditation, and the lush vegetation the possibilities if I continue with my spiritual journey? Is this a variation of Ashoka's swamp of darkness and mountain of light?

Whatever the case, I'm pleased with how my relationship with my spiritual teacher is maturing. Never having met him in the flesh, initially I struggled to relate to him, but as his presence in my visions increases, I feel his guidance. And I'm excited at the prospect of attending a spiritual event he's hosting next week in New York.

As for my dilemma over my role in the Center, I take my latest vision as a sign not to lead in the same way I do in the corporate world. Was I not shown the importance of combining the capacities of everyone to overcome problems?

I'm still deep in thought as Robin arrives home. As is our custom, we talk into the night about our unfolding spiritual journey. As I relate this evening's experience, he listens intently, a smile slowly growing into a radiant glow. Suddenly, he leaps out of his chair and throws his arms around my neck, saying, "Hey, what a guy. You're simply awesome, man. This is great."

I don't share his enthusiasm, but he continues anyway. "Wow! Can you see what this is saying. You're being asked to play a leadership role at the Center."

"Yes, I know. But I'm not sure I want to."

"Hey, why not, if that's what God wants you to do?"

"But is it? Is it what God wants me to do, or is it my ego trying make me seem important?"

"Oh, come on, Alistair. Something like you just experienced isn't coming from your ego. There's no doubt it's coming from your soul. You could never make up something like that."

Part of me knows he's right, but I'm still scared. All my life, I've sought to take control, to fuel my need for achievement, and I can't shake the fear that I'm doing this again. Even so, I take Robin's words with a grain of salt, because I don't think he really understands what I'm concerned about.

Lying in bed, struggling to sleep, Michelle's words at our last meeting come back to haunt me. "It seems to me, Alistair, that you haven't changed as much as you think. You're still as intense as ever. You've just transferred your focus from your work to your meditation. After all, a leopard can't change its spots, you know."

It's a crisp spring morning as I run. When I see Ashoka on the opposite side of the creek, my heart jumps. "Oh, how I long to talk to him. Surely it's time? Surely he'll talk to me about my fears?"

I turn around, and run back to cross the creek and intercept him. I'm relieved when he greets me with a genial smile and a warm embrace.

"Hello, wise one. I'm in need of some gentle guidance."

"Why certainly, young one, it is time we met again." Taking my arm, he says, "I know a wonderful place where the energy is just right at this time of day."

Following this mysterious old man along the creek bank, I wonder about his life. He's told me nothing of himself and my probing has been gently deflected. But he seems more open this morning and I decide to try again.

"Ashoka, do you have a family?"

He answers distantly, as if from another world, "Yes, I had a family once, a long time ago. It seems like another lifetime. We were young and restless, and in search of wealth. She left me for a richer man, and I left her for God. I am not quite sure which came first."

I sense a man caught between two worlds and think of the similarity to my own position. "Did you have any children?"

"Yes, we had two boys," he answers, sadness in his voice at the question that has to be asked.

"Do you still see them?"

"No. They rejected their father as a crazy fool who tried to force them to share a dream they did not believe in. They got caught up in pursuit of their own dreams, in ways I could not support."

I sense the hurt fomenting in him as he continues, seemingly oblivious to my presence, "I drove them way from me. I cannot take responsibility for others, but I tried to control their lives. I could see where they were going with their lives and I wanted to change the direction."

Pain sears the old man's eyes as he grapples with a flood of emotions raging inside of this usually peaceful man of wisdom. Tears start to fall down his cheeks as he continues. "You see, my boy, I thought I knew what was right for my sons. I thought I had to tell them the right way to live their life. But what did I know? How could I possibly know what God's plan was for them? So when they needed a gentle ear, when they needed a father to trust them to go on their own journey and to be there when they needed me, I couldn't do it. I had to tell them the way I thought it should be done. And in the end they left their father behind."

We arrive in a grove of trees nestled against the bank of the river, where a meander forms a secluded lagoon, well off the path. Ashoka stops and we stand together, sharing space, the aging teacher, overcome with grief and the younger student, wondering what to say. The silence is overpowering and it seems unthinkable to disturb it, but after several minutes, I ask the question I know I must.

"Where are they now?"

Ashoka pulls himself together and turns to me. "Please, can we sit, I find this spot so soothing." After we sit, he continues, "My older boy, who is 43, is a corporate executive with a large merchant bank in Sydney. He gets his picture in the paper every now and then, and people say he is doing well, but I see the loneliness in his eyes. By God, I see the emptiness, even in a newspaper photograph. He is a lost soul, and I let him down when I could have helped him!"

His voice rises as the pain of a helpless father spills through the inadequate layers of protection. Just when I think he's going to collapse in my arms, he breathes deeply, gathers himself and continues. "My youngest boy, oh, he was so sensitive. He could have been a great writer, or perhaps a painter, such creativity he had. But he lost his way and looked for his dream ..." He stops, tears once more interrupting the flow of words, grief wracking every cell of his aging body.

With all the strength he can muster, he straightens his hunched body and looks me fully in the eyes. My heart plunges at the heartache in my old friend's eyes and I wish I'd never raised the question. When he speaks, there's no other sound in the Universe, just the intimacy that springs from the sharing of one's deepest secrets with a fellow traveler. "My younger boy thought he would find his dreams in a syringe. He died of a heroin overdose ten years ago. Today would have been his thirty-ninth birthday."

My God, he'd be the same age as me. There's nothing I can say, so I just embrace him as a lost son would an aging father. For the first time, I realize our relationship is not all one-way.

We sit in silence for well over ten minutes. Finally Ashoka speaks. "So what is it that brings you in search of me this morning?"

In the wake of his revelations, it's almost unthinkable to burden him with my dilemma, so I reply gently, "It doesn't matter any more."

"Listen, my son, you came to me today for a reason. Had you not found me, I would have sought you out. Please forgive an old man his painful reminiscence. The fact is that God has blessed me many times over with a love most men never feel in their lives, but there are still some fears I have not faced. Perhaps that is why you have come into my life. But do not belittle me by thinking I am not ready to hear your story."

We sit together listening to the water gurgling among the rocks on its journey downstream, and I tell him about the visions, about the leadership role I'm being asked to play in the Center and about my fears concerning my ego's need for control and self-importance.

"I feel a real turmoil over my role in the Center. I just can't seem to throw off the fear that I'll become controlled by my ego once more."

"Yes, it is a real fear, one you should not underestimate." He pauses and I'm relieved that he agrees that my concern is justified.

"You see, we live in a world where there are two games being played. There is our own little game in which we try to control everything, in which we try to define the rules and contrive the outcome. Then there is the big game, the game of the universal consciousness, in which we are but a player, one of many players. Let me use the analogy of a football team. If I am a player in a football team, then the universal consciousness is the coach. My job is to align myself with the other members of the team so that we do what the coach wants us to do, albeit colored by each player's own flair and creativity. If I take it upon myself to define the game plan, then all is lost."

"Yes, that makes sense."

"But most of us do not understand this. We do not see our brothers and sisters as fellow teammates. We see them as opponents in the game of 'looking after number one.' So we try to play our own game, unaware of the bigger plan. But this is impossible. Think about it. Every person is trying to plan his own game, making up his own rules, expecting others to comply with these rules. But the others also have their own game plan and they are playing by different rules. What else can happen? We end up in conflict, in frustration and in constant anxiety and insecurity. Even the richest of people suffer from this, because no one can control the game."

"But surely there's another way?"

"Yes, of course. We can forego our own plan, the plan of our ego, and surrender to the big game plan. We can let go of our need to control, to understand every move the coach makes, and take our part as a willing member of the team. Only then can we get satisfaction, and only then will everything happen for us in the way it is meant to."

"I can see so clearly what you mean. I'm caught in my own plan. But how do I get out of my ego?"

"Ah, that is for you alone to work through, my young friend, but let me tell you something. It is this battle between the two games that is the source of your inner turmoil. Do not worry. The very fact that you *are* in turmoil means you are becoming aware of your ego's games and are ready to tackle it. Give yourself time."

"So should I take responsibility for making changes at the Center?"

"Oh, that word responsibility—what a curse it is to the human species. Many people will tell you to take charge of your own life, to create your own reality. To me this has connotations of the ego, of the human taking on the obligations of the bigger picture. This really means we are trying to control things, to get what we think is the right outcome. Yes, the onus for your life is yours, but that means listening to what the higher power wants you to do, listening to the coach."

"So the visions I'm getting are messages from the higher self, instructing me in what to do?"

"It seems that way to me. Your inner self is intimately connected to the universal consciousness, to God, and receives messages from the source, which it passes on to you for implementation."

"So I *am* to play a leadership role."

"Perhaps, but what is the definition of leadership. Not the one your ego would select, but the one your inner self would choose. This, it seems, is the question you are being asked to work out. And I cannot give you the answer."

"You know, you're right. I hadn't looked at it in that way, but all the visions have something in common, and that's a feeling of love. This is why I've been so confused, because I've always seen leadership associated with power and control, which are in conflict with love."

"You are in for an interesting journey, young man. It is time for me to go. Thank you for helping me release some pain today."

As he leans over and embraces me, I feel a security that could surely only come from contact with a trusted elder.

Inner Cleansing

S THE END of October approaches, I prepare for the long trip to the USA. Around midnight the night before leaving, I sit down to meditate. During the short time I spend inside myself, a strong feeling of love for God emerges. An inner cry echoes within me of a lost child desperately seeking its parents. As the cry inside me fills the voids of my heart with its deep vibrations and then slowly wanes, an inner voice says, "I'm coming home, Father. I love you, Father. Thank you, Father."

As I bask in an overpowering sense of being loved, I reflect on the fact that I called Him Father. For perhaps the first time, I feel I'm calling to God in a personal sense. My feelings toward Him have changed, almost without me being aware of it and I think the trip to New York will be a homecoming for my soul. I have no doubt my spiritual teacher has a very close connection with the Universal consciousness, and going to see him is taking me closer to the source.

I go into the lounge to join Robin who's something of a night owl. "Hey, brother, you look really spaced out and peaceful."

Coming from him, this is a compliment. "You know I just felt a really intense inner cry. Sometimes it's so powerful, yet I've no idea where it comes from. I can't bring it forth myself."

"Yeah, it's all a matter of faith."

"You're right. The more I believe in God, the more receptive I become and the more guidance I get in my life."

"So your mind is finally accepting God?" he beams.

"Well, I guess so, but it's not that simple. I thought it was just a matter of deciding to believe, but it doesn't seem to work that way. Tonight, I think I finally realized that faith has to be earned, it has to be developed like a muscle. I feel it has to come from deep within me and every time I deal with one of my fears, each time I break through one of my protective barriers, I'm blessed with an increase in faith."

"I guess if it was as simple as just believing, then thousands of people, perhaps millions of people, would just decide to believe in order to gain the wonderful gifts of God. No, it must be much harder than that."

I know I still have many barriers to overcome but for one fleeting moment, I felt God's love flood through me, and the feeling is so divine, so beautiful, so intoxicating, that I know I have to pursue it with all the intensity I can muster. So with this feeling of love in my heart, I board the plane for New York.

The flight is uneventful until about half way to Los Angeles. Courtesy of my boss, Karen, I have some meetings set up on the trip, so I'm lucky enough to fly business class. Since I have plenty of legroom, I can meditate, and out of the blue, my inner voice says to me, "You have to write a book."

"What? I reply. "I've never written a book. Never even considered it."

My inner voice speaks again, "You have to write a book about your personal change. Write it and have it published."

A deep excitement boils within me. I grab a writing pad and immediately start scribbling a structure for the book as the words simply flow from somewhere beyond my knowledge. I write for two hours, then the voice speaks again, "It's me again! Listen, you're to actually write a series of four books. The second one will be about teaching people how to pursue their dreams, and the fourth one will be about a new way of looking at love."

In the excitement, I fail to see the irony of a 39-year-old successful corporate executive who's been meditating for about a year being told to write a series of books, and embracing the concept with unbridled joy.

My first night in New York is one of intense emotions, few of which I can identify. Lying on an air mattress on the floor of a room shared with two other people makes sleeping difficult, so I put some music on my Walkman. Lying in my makeshift bed, I become aware of a wracking sobbing within me. Spontaneously, tears roll down my face, as I'm consumed by an overwhelming need to be released from my raging emotions.

Some energy inside me thrashes about until it consolidates into the forms of individual energy beings that work diligently to reconstruct my anatomy at the cellular level. As this is happening, a glow appears in mid-air, and a loving presence descends to my rescue, taking my heart in His arms and gently nurturing me. A powerful feeling of well-being pervades me as this presence tenderly caresses the very core of my existence, reassuring me that I am secure.

Then a voice resounds in my ears, powerful yet soothing, "It is safe here. You are here to be cleansed. It is safe to let out your emotions, your pain, your fear and your guilt."

During the night, I awaken several times with hot flushes in my head, too intense to be ascribed to the head cold I picked up on the flight. Conspiring with jetlag from the 15-hour time difference, the cleansing makes sure I get little sleep. At 3 am, I resort to another tape and as I drift off with the soothing music, I enter an unfamiliar space, suspended between sleep and alertness. Almost in a dream state, yet conscious of everything happening, I am observing my dreams from a wakened state.

Unlike the visions I've been seeing, this is taking place out of my body. I'm walking on a path of light, which leads upwards to some unseen world. I walk slowly and deliberately, the path shimmering with translucent light beneath my feet, reflecting from my white clothes. The path is lined on each side with beings of light, also dressed in white, who are cheering me.

As my ascension continues, the path dissolves into cloud-like, misty whiteness. I sense I've arrived at the top of the Universe, but my upward journey continues until I emerge into a vast peaceful expanse in which everything is made of light. The entire area revolves around a figure standing a short distance away. As I approach this figure, I'm engulfed in a gentle wave of love lapping over me, like the morning tide against a sandy beach on a windless day. As the initial feeling subsides, I feel many additional qualities emanating from Him. Compassion, wisdom and strength radiate from the Source. Somehow I know there's much more, that what I'm seeing is only a representation of God Himself, and that it is my capacity to understand that limits what I can perceive.

I gaze in wonder at this being, whose body consists of different shades of light held together into a solid form by an invisible force. Faint but powerful rays of light emanate from Him and spread across the panoramic view before me. Rendered immobile by the sheer enormity of the realization that this is God, I stand in awe as He walks forward and embraces me. I am swamped with the essences of heaven and overcome with serenity, joy and love. I see my teacher, off to one side, observing the scene with a smile of satisfaction on his face.

Awakening before the sun, the memory of the experience is fresh in my mind. How do I comprehend the significance of what occurred? Robin kept telling me amazing things would happen here, but how could I be prepared for this? Seeing God in such a personal way is overwhelming. My teacher seemed to be playing a passive role in the dream state adventure, almost as if he is guiding me to look past him, not to focus just on him, but to keep my focus on God. Whatever it means, I know I'm on my way home to the source of my existence and that my teacher is showing me the way.

After two days in New York, I'm confused. Yes, I'm having some powerful inner revelations, but at the same time, feel I simply don't belong here. The inner connection with my teacher has intensified, and my love for God grows, but I'm disgusted at how the other students shower our teacher with their adulation. I try to stand back and accept it, recognizing that my ego may be obstructing my judgment. After all, I'm not used to surrendering control to another being, no matter how divine he may be. Even so, I'm uncomfortable with their adoration, much of it appearing false, almost insincere, as if it's expected rather than occurring spontaneously.

On the third morning, in meditation, I pray for an answer, pleading to know what's going on. I try to invoke light in my heart but no light comes, only a cold, chilly wind. Vibrations echo within me, and in a vision, I see myself flying through a windy night, emerging into light at the top of a mountain. As I watch the small, lonely figure in my heart, sitting on the mountain, bathed in light, an overwhelming feeling of loneliness descends on me.

Suddenly, the mountain opens up to reveal an internal cavern flooded with light. I float down into the light and slowly descend into the heart of the mountain where another being waits. I'm looking at an image of myself. Made of light, he glows, as did God two days earlier.

After a moment's silence, my inner self says, "Do not stress yourself over your confusion. Accept that everyone has a different role to play for God, and not everyone is meant to be comfortable in this environment. You have to find your own place and your own role. But in doing so, do not ever think you can do it all on your own. You will need constant guidance."

With this he disappears and leaves me to ponder the message. I continue to struggle through my confusion, which is not helped by a conversation with another Australian living in New York. He says, "I'm really surprised that someone of your age would join the spiritual path and seem so right for it. Usually people your age are too fixed in their ways to accept the path of a spiritual master."

Perhaps he's right. I certainly come from a different background than everyone else here. And perhaps I am just too fixed in my ways, too independent of thought. But is that necessarily a bad thing? Surely people of my age who have spent half their life punishing themselves in the pursuit of a false dream of materialistic pleasure are as much in need of salvation as anyone. I feel there's a message in the conversation for me.

The next morning, the cleansing continues and I wake at 5.30 flooded with anxiety. As I meditate, my deepest anxieties pour in torrents through my awareness, my thoughts, and feelings. This startles me until I recall Robin's advice about accepting whatever comes up and offering it to the higher forces for transformation. This is not easy as the black, ugly creatures parade inside my heart, and jump out and attack me, attempting to destroy my tenuous hold on the security of my faith. Many doors lead out from my inner sanctuary, and as each door opens, yet another monster of darkness leaps at me.

To avoid coming out of meditation, I call on the strength of my beliefs. I manage to hold my inner state and stay with the ugly scenes until I suddenly realize that the creatures are not actually capable of harming me. Anyway, retreating to the false safety of ignorance is pointless since whatever I'm observing represents my own fears, and I must face them. No external enemy has come to ravage my inner garden. Instead, I'm faced with my own anxieties, which does little to lessen the ordeal, as even my neck and shoulders ache from the painful memories of my past sweeping through me like a raging river.

Along with the flow of human agony streaming from my body, a huge magnet extracts the negativity out of me, like a vacuum cleaner sucking at the darkness. As the tidal waves of anxiety wane, I return to the surroundings of my room feeling drained of energy and wondering just how much self-inflicted pain is still inside me.

The cleansing experience continues the following day, once again junk pouring out of my heart, but this time I don't recognize it. My God, this is gruesome. Surely this doesn't belong to me? Liquid filth, akin to the putrescence in a festering boil, pours out across my inner movie screen, obviously depicting my polluted emotional state. Now my inner workings are being depicted like a great waterway, the protective barriers I erected throughout my life portrayed as a great dam across a mighty river, holding back a reservoir of filthy, polluted water waiting for a chance to escape and flood downstream. The floodgates open to allow a lifetime's stagnant pollution to spew forth. The release of decades of self-persecution continues for some time, but eventually the evacuation of a tormented life is complete, and the putrid flow stops, replaced by a crystal clear stream.

In stark contrast to the dark, polluted sewage, the beautiful stream originates in the upper regions of my being and gently cascades into my heart, flowing down to a crystal-clear mountain lake, situated at the bottom of my inner cavern, which takes on the atmosphere of a temple. The scene of beauty captivates me like a child to an enchanting fairy tale, and a voice says, "What you have seen symbolizes the transformation possible in your life."

I go back over the "dream" and the emphasis on the word "possible" dashes my fleeting hope that it's as simple as just letting go of the past through internal experiences. As I ponder a return to sleep, a new vision shows a laser beam mounted on a swiveling base searching the extremity of my inner recess. My heart once again resembles a vast cavern, and the laser beam shines its light over the roof and walls, as if patrolling for intruders. As it pokes and prods in the ceiling of my heart cavern, little trap doors open and more garbage tumbles from unseen rooms.

Suddenly, I feel a sharp pain in my right shoulder that shoots up the right side of my neck into the back of my head, as though someone or something is pulling stuff out of my body. However, the negativity being extracted by the unseen forces of divinity seems well-anchored in my brain. As the pressure being applied to my screaming body increases, I feel the darkness move, and visualize a long serpent working its way out of my brain, down my left arm, and out through my hand. I watch in fascination as the snake slithers slowly from my body, taking unwanted emotions and pains with it. I feel a tremendous release as a shaft of light moves into my arm and fills my brain, illumining it. Slowly, the pain subsides.

I have no idea what's happening. I know I'm being worked over relentlessly, but can't interpret the visions. Am I actually letting go of past hurt? Is it symbolic of the journey I have to go on, or somewhere in between? Whatever the snake and the river of filth represent in my life, I don't want them to remain in me. I wish I could talk to someone here about the visions, but this is obviously something I have to work through on my own, at least until I can talk to Ashoka.

I recall the words spoken during the experience—"What you have seen symbolizes the transformation possible in your life"— and am sure that what I've just seen is an omen of the journey ahead.

Sunday is New York Marathon day, with over 30,000 runners, and I'm working in the aid station at the halfway mark. Before the main runners start, the disabled athletes from the Achilles Club run. In particular, I notice two young runners. One young girl with a plastic leg runs by and doesn't even stop for a drink. Later, a young man, one leg removed above the knee, passes on crutches. I am astounded at the determination behind running over 42km with crutches under his armpits. The inspirational performances of these two courageous young people reinforces just how much I limit myself because I don't believe in my own capacity, and don't have the courage to pursue my dreams. I'm inspired to think that if they can run a marathon, then who do I think I am making excuses and pretending, at the age of 40, that I'm too old for such madness. On the spot, I make a promise to myself that I will run a marathon before the end of 1998. If I start training after Christmas, I'll be ready for the Australian winter.

The struggle over the role of my spiritual teacher escalates. While I feel a strong bond on an inner level and credit him with retrieving my life from my own darkness, I simply don't relate to him in the outside world. I can't accept the fact that he allows his students to shower him with their adulation. My perception that some of his followers are putting on an insincere performance because it's expected is now really bugging me.

Also the strict segregation of male and female seems to foster antagonism towards the opposite sex. People just won't talk about it, however, instead pretending that they've overcome their physical desire, but I sense they're simply suppressing it, and as a defense mechanism, belittling the opposite sex.

Am I just being overly judgmental? Are my own insecurities in this area simply being invoked? After all, I'm totally confused over Sabrina and the celibacy issue. No, it's not that. Something really isn't right here. Divine love, that precious jewel, is supposed to liberate us, to be inclusive, not divisive. I refuse to end up like the people I see here, and my rejection of certain aspects of the spiritual path becomes more deeply ingrained.

It's my last day in New York, and my confusion and insecurity intensify. Waiting for our teacher to arrive, I start to meditate on the sky, and as the rays of the midday sun dance through the leaves of the overhanging trees and warm my face, a beam of light comes from the sky and enters me. I feel as if God Himself is shining down on me and I bask in the beauty and peace that descends.

My serenity is interrupted by a voice coming from within me, "Release yourself from bondage. You are free to make whatever choices you need to make in your life. I know you are a believer in Me, and will be a good instrument of Mine. You do not have to follow everything you see other people doing, so stop torturing yourself, My child. Stop feeling pressure to comply with what you see everyone else doing. You are on the right path but you should, you *must*, follow your heart, because your inner self knows what is right for you and now you are listening, it will guide you."

The words reverberate through me, unleashing a great torrent of release. My heart is flooded and bursts open with a silvery, luminous light so vast that it stretches forever. As I am shown the freedom that can exist in my life, my inner being knows no boundaries.

Leaving New York for Washington DC, I know without a shadow of doubt that my connection with God is strengthening as He plays with my life. And despite my uncertainty about whether my destiny lies with my teacher's path or in another direction, I still feel a deep gratitude towards him.

My Life's Mission Unfolds

IN WASHINGTON DC, I continue the work component of my trip, and after spending three days at a conference, the weekend is free before I fly to San Francisco for the final leg of the journey. As I meditate on the Saturday morning, a pain grips my heart just as a tunnel materializes that leads deep within me. Something in the tunnel beckons me, and I follow the inner call to enter. I find myself flying through light and emerge in a large room bathed in even brighter light. I find my inner self waiting for me, and he says, "I am very happy with you. I used to cringe at some of the things you did but now you are listening to me a lot more. Your mind is gradually accepting what is happening to you. It doesn't understand because what is happening is beyond the mind's capacity to understand, but it is starting to accept it all."

With that, he explodes in a dazzling array of silvery blue light, emanating in all directions to the outer reaches of my inner void. As I watch the magical beauty of the light show, a sensation of self-confidence streams into me. Aware of my inability to cope with the sudden overwhelming influx of positive energy, he glides gently back to its source. Everything stops momentarily, goes backwards and then retraces its movements, only this time more gently so that my cellular structure can absorb the gift of self-confidence.

All morning, I'm flooded with inspiration and I head off into the November rain to jog around the national monuments, a run of some 5 km. Even a cold, wet, East Coast morning can't dampen my inspiration on this day.

At the far end of the park is the Jefferson Memorial, an enormous, circular, domed building with Roman columns. As I enter it, I feel a powerful presence. About 50 people are milling around inside the memorial's dome, but as I sit down against one of the walls to gaze at the statue of this imposing man, the entire place empties. Remarkably, I have the entire building to myself for five minutes, and sit in silence captivated by the words the great man had composed. One of the verses in particular impresses me with its contemporary relevance:

> *I am not an advocate for frequent changes in laws and constitutions, but laws and institutions must go hand in hand with the progress of the human mind. As that becomes more developed, more enlightened, as new discoveries are made, new truths discovered and manners and opinions change, with the change in circumstances, institutions must advance also to keep pace with the times.*

If we replace the word "mind" with "consciousness," these prophetic words offer a clear message to the traditional religions of the world today that as people awaken to the need to establish a personal connection with God, the traditional view of God, as something contained within the structure of a religion, has to change. That if God is presented as a being of judgment and wrath, people will continue to look outside the established structures for the truth.

Just as I rise to leave the majestic dome, visitors start filing back in, and I'm thankful for the blessing of a rare moment of solitude in this awesome temple of wisdom.

On Sunday, my last day in Washington, I meditate as usual first thing in the morning, but it proves to be a struggle. However, just as I'm about to stop, a light appears, glimmering like a candle flame in the mistiness of my heart. As the mist clears, a priestly figure holding the candle comes into view and beckons me to follow him. We come to a place where the entire Universe spreads out before me, as though I'm on the flight deck of an intergalactic spacecraft. As I take in the breathtaking scene, the priest at my side says, "I am here to reveal something about your mission on Earth."

"How do I know I can trust you?" I ask.

"Look out at the sky."

As I do, the smiling face of my teacher materializes among the stars, and I am aware of his message, "It is all right, I have sent him to you."

The priest continues, "You are to be a bridge between spirituality and the materialistic, intellectual world you come from. The path you are on will give you strength and act as a base to fill you with light and energy. To fulfill your role however, you must read and understand other views."

My first reaction is to reject this as a trick of my mind, but as I come out of the meditation, I know it's not. I have a hundred questions. What's he talking about? My mission here on Earth? Who does he think he is? For that matter, who do I think I am? And what implications could this have on my life?

Running always clears my head, so I head for Rock Creek, the banks of which are lined with lovely trees. I don't want to think about what just happened, so I focus on the trees, and see them in a splendor and clarity I never have previously. So taken am I by the wonders of nature resonating in the trees that I don't even notice the heavy traffic roaring alongside the creek. I see the beauty in everything, as individual leaves stand out and the trees glow with an energy of their own.

In San Francisco, I meditate in the hotel room early in the morning, and an uneasy feeling swarms around my lower abdomen, like a caged creature searching for freedom. As I slide deeper, my focus is drawn to feelings of over-responsibility. I know I need to work on this trait, and this morning it lurks like a hungry leopard stalking its prey.

Suddenly, I find myself in the deepest quadrant of my heart, standing in the center of my being as my heart expands, taking the shape of a great cavern. Doorways lead off from the cave walls, and out of one, a black monster scrambles. The pitiful hunchbacked creature has long matted hair and little stumps for arms. Its face is an ugly collection of pieces mashed together. It hesitates for a moment, unsure of its bearings in the lighted environment of my heart, and then throws a smoke bomb that explodes, sending a dense cloud of smoke billowing upwards, blotting out the light.

From somewhere beyond my awareness, I understand that the creature represents my need to take responsibility for everyone and everything. When I let my responsibility monster out of its cage, my light is clouded in darkness, and in this state, I cannot enjoy the freedom, peace and joy that is blossoming within me.

Clearly this issue has been simmering away and this morning is ready to erupt, which is why it plagued my earlier thoughts. With graphic clarity, the trait is exposed in relation to my feelings towards my teacher. I know my confusion over my relationship with him is manifesting itself in bursts of insincerity and anxiety, but why am I taking responsibility for our union, for the way I react to the things I observe? Surely my only obligation is to be sincere to myself, to be honest about my feelings, and to act accordingly, not to try to manage all my interactions with others, or their relationship with him.

I now see clearly just how much I do this. I have always played martyr to my need to respond to the expectations of others, or at least what I perceive their expectations to be. I've convinced myself this problem is overcome, but as I sit in meditation, I know it's not. I know I need to acknowledge my true feelings and act on them, but since I've never done this, I don't know where to start.

I slump into desperation, fatigued by the long journey that has barely begun, and with all my intent, cry inwardly to God to rescue me. I cry to understand, to be shown how to release myself from this inner monster.

Whenever a genuine inner cry has sprung forth from the bubbling rebirth of my spirit, it's always been answered, and this morning, I'm shown a vision of a young child crying for its mother, helpless without the loving embrace it so desperately seeks. A light appears in the ceiling of my heart, which once more expands until the ceiling is transformed to a vast horizon of blue. As the light streams down from the sky to illuminate the cloudy darkness of my cavern, an angel appears, a young man, beautifully featured, dressed in white and glowing like a luminous beacon.

"I have come to chase away your feelings of responsibility," he says, softly and tenderly. "But for me to rid you of these creatures, you have to help me. You must create a tunnel in your heart, from the back of your inner cave right out of your heart, otherwise as I chase them from their hiding places, they will simply hide elsewhere. This tunnel has to be strong enough so that they cannot break through its walls. The only thing that is strong enough is love, your spirit's love. You must build the tunnel out of love."

How do I do this? How do I invoke the love he talks about, this divine love that comes only from my spirit, or from God? Faced with the task of invoking it, I suddenly realize that I have no idea what it is. As if reading my thoughts, he says, "Do not worry. Do not take responsibility for it. You will know what to do. It will be done for you. Just trust in that."

Okay, I think, let's try to invoke a tunnel, and at the same time not take responsibility for it, to trust it will indeed be done for me. This paradox graphically highlights my confusion over what I can do and what God does for me. As I try to let go and build a tunnel at the same time, I realize the conflict between trying myself and simply allowing a higher force to manifest through me. Eventually, a structure starts to form in my heart, and as I invoke a yearning for love, the tunnel grows stronger and takes form.

Suddenly, I burst into tears. Not just an inner cry, but hot, burning physical tears that spring from nowhere like a hot geyser venting steam. I'm crying to God, asking Him to forgive me for doubting His love and compassion. I cry in joy to Him, for releasing me, and yet the tears do not feel like tears of joy but a great release of years of suppressed anger and frustration, of carrying burdens for others, of self-imposed martyrdom.

I call out aloud to God, the words squeezed out between wracking sobs. "Father, please forgive me for my feelings of insincerity, for my doubt over my spiritual teacher."

As these words come out from somewhere inside me, I realize just how much of an issue this has become for me, just how much conflict I feel, and how much I want to carry the burden of the success of my relationship with him. And as the tears pour down my face, the response echoes through my heart, tinged with a trace of laughter. "My child, that is not a problem. Your angel guide will explain it all."

Inspired by the reassurance in the voice, I try to build the tunnel again, but each time I do, my crying just intensifies. Now I'm sobbing uncontrollably, my body convulsing with each wracking sob. Totally out of control, I just surrender to whatever is happening. As I relinquish control, I feel a great love flowering within me, and I'm overcome by a tremendous oneness with the Creator.

Suddenly, the crying stops and I'm left with renewed freshness and energy, as if I'm no longer called upon to commit my own energy. I concentrate all my strength on building the tunnel, on strengthening it with love. The tunnel takes on a solid luminous form, stretching between the depths of my heart and into the photo of my teacher on which I'm meditating.

Just as the tunnel nears completion, another monster runs out and throws a smoke bomb. My angel friend is still here, and suddenly I find myself inside him, aware of his thoughts, but at the same time, he is inside my heart. We enter the room from which the monster launched its assault, and are surprised to find the chamber full of maybe thirty dark, hunched creatures, all racing around in frenzy at the appearance of my angel. "Okay, you guys, it's time for you to leave," he commands.

They laugh and joke to each other, and then almost as one voice retort, "Oh yeah! And whose gonna make us leave?"

My angel produces a trident-like instrument, presses a lever, and bright light shoots from its forks and ricochets off the ceiling of the creatures' hideout. The room fills with light and my angel speaks once more, authority and power in his voice, "Leave now! You know you cannot stay here once I have illumined it. Go!"

The tunnel opening is right in front of the door of the creature's refuge, and as the angel pours more light into the room, the creatures can no longer stand the light, so with shrieks and screams, they hurry through the door, into the tunnel, and out of my body.

The release of having these monsters removed is profound, but is it really this simple, I wonder. Are they really gone, or is this just the start of a process? Or is this God's way of showing me they are gone now if I can only believe it? The same questions I'd raised about the cleansing vision in New York. However, there's no time to ponder as my angel speaks to me again, "Well, now we have some things to discuss about your role."

I'm excited at the prospect of clarity on where my life is heading, but there's something more pressing on my agenda. "Can we talk about love first? What about Sabrina? Where does she fit in?"

"Sure, but I am not the best person to do that. If you don't mind, I will call down your female angel."

While he concentrates, sending a powerful beam of light into the sky, I reflect on his words. A male and female angel? Who are they? Are they external angels, or aspects of myself? But before I can pursue these thoughts, a beautiful woman angel appears and embraces my male angel with a deep sense of intimacy.

"He is ready to learn the truth about love," my male angel says. "I think it is better coming from you."

Flashing me a beautiful, loving smile, she starts to talk. "Everything you have felt so far is true. Our Father, the Creator, wants you to manifest love here on Earth, but this must be true love, in the most beautiful form. The world is not ready yet for a spiritual life, where physical love is no longer required. There is a need for a transition, and you are to help in that transition."

I am enchanted but also apprehensive at how much I must evolve before I can even think of playing such a role. And yet in one sentence, she has confirmed my sense that one day I would have another relationship, and this would cause me to leave the path.

She continues, "To enable this to occur however, you have to be highly evolved and this will take time. What would happen if you went into a relationship with Sabrina, or someone else you love at this time? You would simply throw yourself at that person with your newfound love, and the addiction would start all over again. All would be lost. It would just become another love affair. You have to get to the point where you can look at love in a totally different way, from a spiritual or divine perspective."

My male angel interjects, "Now it is time to talk about your role. You have been worried about your loyalty to your spiritual teacher, concerned about learning different perspectives. Well, tell me, what do you think your mission is here on Earth?"

A few days ago, I couldn't answer this question, but now, recalling the words of the priest in Washington, the response flows easily. "Is it to be a bridge for intellectual, professional people to discover spirituality?"

"That is close enough for now. And how are you going to do this if you do not have a wide understanding of a range of opinions? Our Creator, God, and your teacher are one. At your teacher's level, there is no differentiation, there is only oneness, so how can you be doing anything to hurt your teacher if you are following God's inner guidance."

After a pause to let that sink in, he continues, "Let me tell you something else. Much has been written lately about the new sources of energy that people are tapping into around the world. There is an increasing awareness of this energy by people who are evolving through all types of means. But God has sent the spiritual masters to Earth throughout time to be a direct source of this energy, in a very concentrated form. The energy you have been receiving is very, very powerful. But your transformation will not be an overnight thing; it will take time, dedication and trust. Some people make huge personal progress by being around a spiritual master, while others will have to take this energy out into the world. You are one of the latter, that is your role. Don't you see how it is all connected, how everything is connected? How, for you, God has His own plan, and it requires you to remain in society, but also to keep your connection with the source that your spiritual teacher gives you."

My mind reels at the profundity of his words. Their import is life-transforming yet so sensible. Exultation sweeps through me, an expanding horizon of freedom unfolds before me.

"Now just sit back and enjoy the view in your heart."

I am already deep in my heart, and slip sublimely into the state of observer once more, as the vision in my inner movie theater resumes. A multitude of stars appear in my heart, and I sense the entire Universe unfolding within me. A tremendous ball of fire emerges in the center of the scene, expanding rapidly to form the solar system. From the central orb, balls of fire are hurled off in different directions, sweeping outward like missiles. One of the these solidifies to become planet Earth. As the empty planet spins in an erratic orbit, it is magnified until it occupies the entire focus of my viewing screen. Then a light sweeps over the land, a soft, multicolored light, a mystical beam of radiance dancing, as if alive with the exuberance of a new birth. And I'm aware of watching the creation of life on the planet.

The scene jumps ahead and thick forests emerge. My mind can't cope with the wonder of the revelations and tries to cast doubt, telling me this cannot be real. In response, a massive volcano erupts in my heart, magma blasting straight up, exploding the limitations of my mind, and casting its doubt to a distant oblivion. With my mind silenced, the evolution of the planet continues and I see dinosaurs ruling Earth until their extinction by a great ice age. Next come the prehistoric mammals, and finally mankind emerges.

The panoramic replay of history moves forward to show ancient spiritual beings. Somehow, I know they are the ancient Vedic priests, and I witness how they could consciously cross over to a higher dimension at will, and how they left instructions for mankind before returning to their home. A succession of peoples I do not recognize appear, doing the same thing as the Vedics, leaving this plane to go to another dimension. I'm totally aware of what every scene represents as if knowledge is being implanted in my mind, or perhaps an already present source of information is opening up. I now understand why and how the lost cultures of the past that had advanced architecture and societies simply vanished from the face of the Earth.

Moving forward in time, I see a shift from the beauty of the spiritual man to the ugliness of the egoic man. Scenes of repression and brutality parade before me through the First World War, and the Second World War, ending with atomic bombs exploding over Japan. Oddly, I feel no sense of horror or disgust at these events. Instead, it is obvious to me that these tragic events were necessary to show mankind how dangerous the newfound technological power could be.

Next, I see the emerging consciousness of man. Light emanates from somewhere in North America throughout the world as the overall consciousness increases. I wonder if this represents my teacher, but the answer is not clear. This light reaches up into the sky like a searchlight leading the way for humanity, and I feel the emerging consciousness around me, so powerful, so awesome. And I know that humanity's apparently inevitable rush to self-destruction is not the only outcome, that we stand at the dawn of a new era of conscious evolution.

As this astonishing panoramic experience comes to an end, the whole Universe appears in my heart again, this time with serenity that wasn't present before. I intuitively know that the serenity pulsating gently throughout the Universe is the direct result of mankind's acceptance of its spiritual reality, and its capacity to transform the planet to a haven of peace and spiritual enlightenment.

As the vision slips quietly away, some two hours after I started meditating, I settle back and enjoy the feeling of love and light permeating my heart. I notice my angels are still there and suddenly feel a concern about them going. Sensing my apprehension, the male angel says, "Do not worry. Now that you have made the breakthrough, you can access us whenever you want just by calling out to us."

And as the most profound and enlightening experience of my life ends, the thought occurs to me that the real issue is faith. Once I experience something like this, I know it exists. Believing this opens me up to even greater awareness. But underlying all the beauty and enchantment, I sense that I'm being prepared for responsibility, being given this privilege for a reason.

The long flight back to Australia gives me plenty of time to think. In San Francisco, the question I blurted out to my angel about Sabrina was fueled by a desire to pursue an intimate relationship. The paradox is that I feel drawn to explore love on all levels yet I'm plagued by fears about intimate relationships. While enjoying the freedom that comes with celibacy, I'm aware of festering sores lurking away in the cesspit of my wounded emotions, sores that the avoidance of celibacy will not heal. And my angels told me that I must one day face the challenge of taking the concept of a divine love into a relationship, of transforming my fears and pain into a beautiful manifestation of God's love as a living reality in my relationships.

From my angels, I also learned that my path is not to be with Sabrina, at least not yet. But such love blossoms in my heart when I think of her. Sabrina has shown me a taste of what a divine relationship could aspire to. But I'm not ready for it yet, because mingling with the magic of divine love is a need, an unhealthy emotional thirst. Still, hopefully, a time will come when my feelings for Sabrina can manifest themselves.

As the plane's tires scorch the runway of Sydney airport, I reflect on how the last two weeks of intense and memorable experiences have changed the way I view my self, my spiritual teacher, God and, in fact, my whole world. What happens now that I'm back to the normality of my life? Will my life ever be the same again? Or am I simply deluding myself?

Who's Making These Changes?

A T THE END of a grueling trek, I stagger off the flight from Sydney to Adelaide, and am met by Robin. "Hey, brother," he greets me in his usual way and we embrace. "I can't wait to hear all about it."

Driving home, I tell him all about my experiences, except that is, for the revelations on my mission, which I'm not yet ready to share. "You know, I'm really starting to accept that it's not me doing the work."

"What do you mean? I think you've accepted God's grace for several months?"

"In a way, yes, but I didn't understand. You know we read something and have a certain level of experience that makes us think we understand what's happening. But it seems every time I think I know what's going on, along comes another experience that sheds a whole new light on my understanding, and I discover that I didn't really have any idea after all."

"Yeah, I know what you mean. I suspect that will be the case through our whole lives."

"Robin," I say with a note of urgency that causes him to look across at me. I pause in indecision, unsure whether to continue with my line of thought, but he is a very dear friend and I trust him to be honest with me. "What I'm experiencing is pretty remarkable, isn't it?"

"I've never met anyone on the path who's moved as quickly as you. You're amazing, man. I really admire your intensity."

I can always rely on Robin to boost me up, but that's not why I asked. "Just over a year ago, I was an atheist, a complete skeptic on spiritual matters. Since I joined the path in March, my life has gone crazy. There have been no amazing life transforming incidents, no near-death experiences, just a gentle tap on the shoulder by God and a gradual increase in awareness."

"I wouldn't call it so gradual, but I know what you mean."

"Well, everything just seems so clear, as if I knew all this stuff about God already. It seems so natural. But I can't understand why it's happening to me and not other people who are far more spiritual."

"Just accept it as God's grace."

"That's exactly my problem. I do accept it as God's grace, 'cos it can't be anything else. And if He is investing so much energy into me, if He is blessing me so much, then He must have something important He wants me to do for Him, right?"

"Yeah, I guess so. He probably has something important for all of us, but you're really opening up to it, so what's the problem?"

"No problem, other than being scared witless. It's all happening so quickly and I don't think I'm ready for it. I just want to go back to enjoying being the new kid at the Center, having blissful experiences."

As he turns the car into the driveway, Robin looks at me, a slightly miffed expression on his face. For a moment, I think he's going to push me for a clarification and I realize he can't possibly understand the full reason for my fear as I haven't yet told him about the mission.

During the next week, I feel a change in my life. I sleep less, and have much more energy. I'm also more creative, even at work, but the greatest change comes in how I relate to people. Everywhere I go, people smile at me, as if I'm emanating a totally different vibration. My life is filled with a new joy and peace, and despite the ongoing conflict over my role at the Center, my love for my teacher continues to grow.

On Sunday morning, I go running, and am meditating in my regular spot by the creek, when Ashoka plops himself down beside me, a beaming grin on his face. "Well, young one, tell me all about it. Are you ready to transform the world yet?"

Very funny, I think to myself. Over the next half hour, he is captivated as I relate the story of my trip, all except for the messages about my mission. I'm surprised at the depth of fear over the messages about my future role, strong enough even to prevent me raising it with my wise old friend. "I still can't quite believe that God Himself appeared to me." I say as my story comes to an end.

"Hey now," he retorts, "don't you go reducing God to a grandfather image. God is the Universal consciousness, the Creator, the Source. Our human mind tries to define God, to contain Him to a form we can understand. Impossible!" he says, with emphasis on the final point.

"But I saw Him, He spoke to me."

"Yes, you did see Him, and yes, He spoke to you. I believe you. I have no doubt about it at all. But this is God the all-pervading spirit, revealing one aspect of His vastness to you, appearing to you in a form you can accept. What would you think if God appeared to you as the Infinite? You would not recognize Him."

"I see. Well, no, I'm not sure if I do."

"Look, I talked about the ocean and the cup before, remember?"

"Of course."

"Well, if you go to the Pacific Ocean and sit on the beach in a peaceful little bay, you are looking at the ocean, right?"

"Yes," I say eager to hear another of his analogies.

"But what you see is not *all* that the Pacific Ocean is. The ocean is revealing itself to you as one limited aspect, which you can see from where you are sitting. But you know the ocean is many more things. It is far vaster than what you can see."

"I get it. So the aspect of God I see is like the inlet, just one part of the whole, only a tiny part of creation?"

"That is how it seems to me."

"Ashoka, has God ever appeared to you?" As the words come out I feel slightly ashamed for considering even the possibility that God could have appeared to me and not to my mentor, but he seems unfazed.

"God is in everything if you choose to look at it in that way."

His habit of answering in riddles and avoiding the question frustrates me sometimes. I want to ask him what he means but let it pass. He takes the conversation onto another level, "Oh, but young one, this cleansing you are having, this is wonderful. Never before have I seen someone who was given such a graphic understanding, so quickly, of his or her own fears. This is marvelous."

"I hope you're right. It was intense and I can't say I enjoyed it."

"Your inner self, God—oh, let's call it your higher self for now—knows exactly what issues you have to deal with in your life. It also knows when you are ready to deal with them. Consequently you will be provided with challenges, your fears revealed for you to encounter, exactly when you are ready to face them."

"So I'm just a puppet in a game?"

"In a way, your higher self, through the directions it receives from God, is controlling the game plan. We talked about this before. It is presenting the challenges to you."

"So what do I do? It sounds like I don't have to do anything."

"Don't fool yourself into that trap. God will present you with challenges when you are ready to take them on. But at every step of the way, you are provided with a choice. You can either accept the challenge or ignore it. If you accept it, you move forward. If you ignore it, deny its existence, then you stay where you are, and the fear you refuse to acknowledge will continue to plague your life. We are all provided with choices all the time, but many people do not even recognize them. It seems to me you are very diligent in accepting the challenges."

A pang of guilt flows through me. If this is true, why am I not prepared to share with Ashoka the messages about my purpose in life? But I push the guilt to one side and continue with my questions, "So, what do you think is happening in my visions? With the responsibility monsters and all the anxiety I shed. Is it all gone?"

"Ha, ha, you talk to me as if I have all the answers. I can only relate to you what I understand from my own learning and hope you can apply some of it to your life. I don't know what is going on with your visions, except that it seems there is a major internal cleanse going on."

I have come to see Ashoka as a source of wisdom, and suddenly, I realize that he's just like Michelle in that he can only take me where he's already journeyed himself. Puzzled, I ask, "But surely you have an idea?"

"Yes, but remember, they are your visions so you must discover their truth for yourself. I suspect they are telling you that the inner work has been done. That at the level of your spirit, you have been released from these things."

"So why can't I just let them go?"

"If you totally believe, then you probably can. Now you recognize the fears, which have been exposed, now you accept them as a part of you, they can be transformed. "

"I just don't find it that simple."

"Nor me, either. It sounds easy, but first we have to bring the realization into our outer life and this takes effort. We have been reacting, almost in a pre-programmed way, for so long, and it seems to take a lot of work and experiences to overturn our old habits."

"So I have to go back and work through all my stuff, relive the trauma and rebuild myself?"

"No, that is not what I mean. That view is a creation of our passion for psychology and the workings of the mind. If we are trying to deal with these things in the mind, you probably need to do all that work. But in a spiritual sense, I do not believe this is at all necessary. Once your spirit reveals the true nature of an issue to you, it is telling you that inwardly you understand the falseness of your fear and are ready to let it go. It is a matter of accepting the way you were, letting it go and moving into the light."

"It all sounds so simple."

"Yes, I suppose it does. But life is meant to be simple. We have made it complicated. Doesn't your teacher say this?"

"Yes, but I guess I never really understood what he meant."

"We have trained ourselves to think we have to do all this hard work, that it has to be difficult or we are not making progress. But if we just let go of our fears and embrace life through love, then it really is that simple."

We pause for a moment and I reflect on these words. But while what he says makes sense, my mind can't accept that it's so simple. Surely I have to go through the darkness to get to the light? After a minute or two of inner debate, I decide to take the plunge. "Ashoka, there is something I haven't told you before that I would like to share with you."

He leans forward intently as I relate the story of Sabrina.

Ashoka laughs, "My boy, do not ask me for advice on love. I can talk about God's love, but not on how that relates to the love for a woman? Can you integrate them? What a question. No, young one, I cannot help you with that one, for I have not been there myself. You will have to explore that path on your own."

As an afterthought, he adds, "Oh, and when you find the answer, come and share your wisdom with me."

"I have to be honest, I feel a turmoil between my teacher and my love. His path is one of celibacy and I feel I'm betraying him by thinking that, one day, I will leave his path to pursue a relationship."

"Oh dear, how foolish we humans are. Your teacher is a great man, a great soul. These masters are connected directly to the universal consciousness, they are one with the ocean. He already knows inwardly everything that is happening to you. Look at what came out of you in his presence. But he will not bind you to his path if your mission for God takes you somewhere else. He is not attached to you, only to your soul's manifestation."

"But some of the things I hear that he's said make me feel uncomfortable. I can't accept them."

"He has thousands of students and what he says outwardly is meant for everyone. And often his words will be interpreted by others and communicated to you based on their own journey's experiences. Remember, you all have your own unique path to follow to manifest your soul on Earth, so his words will not mean the same to everyone. It is what he says to you inwardly, what he communicates to you through your inner self, during meditation, that is really important."

Ashoka's answers have raised yet more questions, and as I walk home, I'm drawn to think more deeply about the conflict over my feelings for my spiritual teacher. Thoughts of my own father flicker through my mind, and it occurs to me that there's yet another aspect to this inner turmoil. I had craved for my father to be more active in my life, for him to guide me and help set boundaries. But from the time I was about twelve, he withdrew from this role and took a more passive role. When I was growing up, I desperately needed an older man to act as a role model for me, to show me how to behave, but there was no one who would do that. Instead, they saw my aggression as a threat and put me down, and this made me fight harder than ever to win their approval.

Perhaps I'm still searching for a father figure to show me the way. Is this what I'm looking for in my teacher? But I'm afraid to trust him, because I've been let down by the older men in my life and I'm afraid to give my trust to another man. But God is different. I don't see God as anything like a person.

In an inner sense, it's the same with my teacher, as I view him differently than other men, so can accept him. But I simply can't surrender when I see him standing in front of me, looking like an ordinary man.

Suddenly, I'm hit with a profound thought. Perhaps my father was *meant* to play a passive role in my life, perhaps my soul deliberately chose my father so that I specifically wouldn't get this guidance. And perhaps it was no accident that I never had a mentor in my life to whom I could relate. So, because I never became attached to any form of male role model, my thirst to find my ideal father remains. Perhaps it's this thirst that's now driving me to pursue God with such intensity, to pursue the higher aspect of my Father. As this thought crystallizes, I feel overwhelming love for my father, my earthly father, and the possibility that all the time, he was simply giving to me exactly in the way my soul asked him to for my own development.

Then a lightning bolt of truth hits me. For the first time since I was twelve, I have met, in the form of Ashoka, a man who provides the very sort of wisdom I've always craved for. And I'm sure Ashoka senses this, and it drives him to keep his distance. I know now that I must not become too dependent on him.

A New Attachment

T HE PLANNING PROCESS I initiated at the Center before going to New York has been reactivated, and I'm not prepared for what it unleashes. I like to believe that my friends at the Center are angelic spiritual beings, and not prone the same difficulties as people in other organizations. But, as December arrives, the folly of this naïve notion becomes clear.

Of course, it's certainly different than any other group I've been involved with. People have a genuine love for each other and in many ways, we're a big family. Overlaying this, however, are our human limitations, with each person at a different stage on the journey, dealing with their own issues. So, early in December, I raise the subject with Robin. "I'm not sure if I'm doing the right thing at the Center. While I can see the value in what we're doing, the Center isn't a corporation, and bringing all the skeletons out of the closet into the open isn't necessarily a good thing is it?"

"People feel threatened by change, I agree, but it's time there was a greater level of openness. We've never had someone before with your skills. I think you have to continue."

"Yes, I feel that too, but something's not right. Maybe I'm approaching it too much from the mental direction. I'm not sure my leadership approach fits with how a spiritual group should work."

I go to bed that night grappling with how to implement structured planning process without losing the inspiration and spontaneity of people operating from their hearts. At two o'clock, the phone rings. Being a lighter sleeper than Robin, I get to the phone first and am surprised to hear the voice of the Center leader,

Daphnie. The flatness of her voice takes me aback. "Can I speak to Robin please, Alistair?"

I hand the phone to Robin who's just emerged from his room, and they have a lengthy conversation. I realize that the only reason she's calling in the middle of the night is to do with a call from overseas, and a different time zone. Listening to only his end of the discussion, it's obvious they're talking about another young man in the Center. I know that he's been breaking some of the rules and suspect, although no one has told me, that he's smoking marijuana.

After about twenty minutes, Robin hangs up and says with a long face, "Jeff is going to be asked to leave the Center."

For us, this is a big thing. We're like family, and anyone asked to leave can't attend any of the functions and Center members are supposed to eschew contact with you, something I have a problem with. When in the past, I mentioned this to Robin, he answered, "Yes, I can understand your concern, but remember, most people at the Center are impressionable young people. If one of their friends is out drinking every night and smoking joints, and they're trying to pursue a life of purity and sincerity, it's just not going to work. The rule is designed to help people."

"Well, Jeff had enough warnings, so I guess it had to come," I reply.

"Yeah," adds Robin, "but I have an uneasy feeling that it's not going to end there."

It's nearly three, and we head back to bed. I have a sense that Robin isn't telling me the whole story. He used to share a house with Jeff and some others, and I never really found out why they split up.

I just fall asleep, and am shocked awake for the second time by the phone. What the hell is going on? It's Daphnie again, her tone even more stony than last time. "Can I speak to Robin?"

Judging by Robin's body language, it's bad news. After a very brief discussion, Robin hands me the phone and walks, ashen-faced, to his bedroom. I take the phone and the pain in her voice is evident. "Robin and three of the other guys have also been asked to leave the Center."

I'm stunned and collapse into a chair in absolute disbelief. Robin has been an inspiration to me. I've looked to him as a shining light of spirituality. And in the few months he's stayed with me, he's been a model of aspiration, pursuing higher levels of inner purity, with intensity unparalleled by other members of the Center. Daphnie tries to comfort me, but I am not listening any more and hang up.

I quietly enter Robin's room to offer comfort. He's meditating, a tear rolling down his cheek, and I'm filled with sorrow. Meditation is the focal point of his life, and being asked to leave the Center is like a jail sentence. I kneel down and wrap my arms around him. He nestles into my chest like a baby, looks up at me with eyes full of sorrow, and says, "Thank you, my brother. Can I be alone now?"

There's no way I can sleep, so I sit in a recliner rocker in the lounge, questions tumbling through my mind. "How can they do this to him? How can they kick him out when he's so pure and so devoted? I can't accept this, I won't accept it!"

A storm rages in my heart as the anger grows inside and in my frustration, I contemplate a life without the Center, and I panic. Joining the path of my teacher has saved my life from a downward spiral of self-destruction. If I leave, do I lose all that? Do I slip back into the swamp of darkness? Surely, I can't do that? But what about Robin? I can't just sit back and let this happen to him?

And in my rage, all the teachings of my spiritual life, all the wisdom of Ashoka, are cast aside as my ego rises up, an enraged avenger, ready to assume responsibility for Robin's predicament. Destructive thoughts are consuming me as Robin emerges from his room, looking sad yet peaceful.

"Hey, Alistair, I need to go for a run. Want to come?"

Running is the last thing on my mind, but I'm not about to let him go on his own, so I agree.

It's still dark as we step out into the hot, steamy summer morning. We don't talk as we run, but there's an eerie feeling, as if a presence is running with us. My energy is so charged that I'm running faster than I can ever recall. Robin is an excellent runner, generally slowing his pace so that I can keep up, but this morning we're both flying. As we near the end of our 5-kilometer sprint, he asks, "Do you feel the energy around us?"

"Yes, it's wild. I can't run this fast."

"I know, but you did. I feel our teacher is putting a force on us to help us get through. I feel everything is going to be all right. We just have to trust."

Sunrise hangs in the east as we sit by the creek bank, in the same spot I talk to Ashoka. This is weird, I think. Robin is the one being kicked out and yet he's as peaceful as I've ever seen him, and I'm raging with anger. "How can you be so peaceful?" I ask.

With a serenity and acceptance that stuns me, he says, "Our teacher loves me. I've been to see him many times and I feel total love and trust for him."

"But how can he kick you out when you're so focused on purity? I don't understand. I won't accept this."

"Look, I did something wrong. I dishonored my spirit. In your eyes, it may be a small thing but over the past few months, it's hounded me continually. I haven't been able to forgive myself. Our teacher knows this and he is blessing me. He's giving me a chance to feel I've paid for my dishonor and let it go."

"I just don't get it. I can't see it that way."

In a strange twist of circumstance, it's Robin who comforts me in his calm, gentle voice, "God has two sides; a compassionate side and a judgmental side. He always prefers to use compassion, but sometimes it doesn't work. Sometimes out of His infinite compassion, he has to use His judgment to help us to work through our fears. I'm being blessed by Him bringing His judgment to me now."

"I still don't buy it. I'm not sure I can stay in the Center under the circumstances."

"Now listen to me, brother!" his tone deadly serious. "You are a powerful soul. You are destined for the spiritual life. You must not throw this away because of what happens to someone else."

"And why not?" I say defiantly.

"Stop being so bloody childish and self-indulgent. Do you want me to carry the guilt of having you leave the path? Do you want me to be burdened with that for the rest of my life? Grow up."

The truth of my friend's rebuke snaps me back to reality, and I realize that I'm reacting to Robin's situation out of my own fear of inadequacy, of being unable to transcend my need for control enough to accept the will of God. And my heart is filled with admiration for my young friend as he shows me a faith in the Creator to which I can only aspire.

Robin moves out of my house, to undergo a forced period of solitude in the hopes of being invited back to the Center soon, and I reflect on where my life has taken me. When I joined the Center, I promised myself six months to see how it went. It's now eight months and time to reassess the situation.

My life is careening along, full of activity and transforming experiences. Opening up to the true essence of who I am and acknowledging the spiritual being within provides a sense of well-being and purpose that was totally lacking in my previous existence. Having gotten over my childish tantrum in response to Robin's demise, I simply can't envisage a life without the spiritual aspect, and for now, my spiritual needs are being met by my current path.

Beneath all the wonder and progress, however, I'm aware that there's a disturbing element to my life. In many ways, I've become attached to the Center. The other Center members are now in large part meeting my needs, previously met through work and Sasha. Interaction with them fuels my achievement need, and provides security. Sabrina is meeting the needs not met through the Center, particularly intimate emotional contact, in part, even though I haven't contacted her since my return from the States. The messages I received sounded a clear warning, and I'm giving myself some space, but I still think of her frequently.

I know that I must not allow attachment to take hold again. Combined with the problems I experienced in relating to the other students in New York, it's clear I'm seeing the spiritual path and the students on the path as the same thing, and this is an error. My relationship with God and my teacher is entirely different than that with my fellow Center members. I love them as brothers and sisters, but I'm on the spiritual path to develop my connection with God. I can play an active part in the Center and share my love and oneness with the people there, but must not see them as substitutes for the relationships I once used to hide behind. I must learn to support myself through my connection with God. Equally important is to forge my own relationship with God and lead my life in accordance with my inner guidance, not the expectations of others.

Despite the inner agonizing over my role in the Center, I feel blessed and guided inwardly towards my destiny. So many meditation experiences allude to this destiny and the need to understand my unique connection with God, yet I cannot fully commit to all that's happening. The fear of my ego deceiving me and creating an illusion of spiritual awakening is still a powerful barrier.

This morning, I pray intently for a sign that my understanding is true. A few hours later, my brother calls from Perth, and immediately begins to read a passage from *The Return to Love*, a book by Marianne Williamson:

*Our deepest fear is **not** that we are inadequate.*
Our deepest fear is that we are powerful beyond measure.

It is our light, not our darkness, that most frightens us.
We ask ourselves, who am I to be brilliant, gorgeous, talented and fabulous?

*Actually, who are you **not** to be?*
You are a child of God.

Your playing small does not serve the world.
There is nothing enlightened about shrinking
so that other people won't feel insecure around you.

We are born to make manifest the glory of God that is within us.
It's not just in some of us, it is in everyone.

And as we let our light shine, we unconsciously give other people permission to do the same.
As we are liberated from our own fear, our presence automatically liberates others."

I've long since stopped believing in coincidences and I thank God for once more answering my prayers. One line in particular sums up my inner struggle perfectly:
     It is our light, not our darkness, that most frightens us.

I'm afraid of my own light and in reading this to me, my brother delivers a clear message that it's time to emerge from behind my fears, accept the grace descending my way, and move forward.

Standing back from all the activity allows me to see other imbalances in my life. In particular, I'm neglecting my work. My work habits have changed dramatically, and I no longer take work home. And I no longer blow a fuse if the occasional deadline is missed. Internal customers are beginning to complain, which wouldn't bother me if I knew I was doing my best, but I know I'm not, and suffer uncomfortable twinges of letting myself down.

If my job wasn't satisfying, it could be a sign to move, but I love my job and can't think of a better one. The environment is challenging, stimulating and allows freedom to be creative, innovative and express myself without fear. I have the ideal environment and the perfect boss to help me grow. Karen and I often talk in the evening, and tonight, I'm having a guilt twinge, so at about 10.30, I call her.

"You don't need to say anything in response to this," I begin, "but I'm just calling to apologize for not giving you as much support as I should have over the last few months. I'm now a lot more focused and I'll be giving you a greater effort once more."

The challenge of not being able to respond is too much for Karen. "I wouldn't say you haven't been giving me support. It's very rewarding to see people who work for you go through such major personal growth, and I understand how much energy that takes."

That's her way of saying, "Yes, I know you've been off the boil and it's good of you to acknowledge it, but I understand."

The Danger Of Love

M Y INNER PROGRESS is so rapid that sometimes, I feel it's easy, that in some way I'm invincible. A mood of complacency descends on me that I'm unable to reverse. To be honest, I feel I'm pretty good and my pride is rising, growing menacingly within me. It's evident in the way I talk, and little alarm bells are sounding in my heart, sending messages to my mind, but it isn't taking any notice. I'm powerless to stop the downward slide, as my ego and pride once more ascend to a place of prominence and control in my daily actions.

Feeling threatened by God and my spiritual master, my ego, master of the mind game, launches a vicious assault on my self-confidence. Using its intimate insights into my vulnerabilities, the self-talk turns negative, dredging old doubts from the depths of my past, challenging the very reality of the visions I have and the validity of the messages about the future.

Who do you think you are? What gives you the right to experience the bliss of the inner life? Remember, Smith, you're a corporate executive and you're just going through a midlife crisis. People can't really change this much, you know. Within a few days of receiving the confirming message from my brother, Marianne Williamson's inspiring words are cast to the ground and trampled on.

For the first time in months, I feel defensive and threatened at work. Instead of being outgoing and positive to everyone, a negative and sullen cloud descends over me. The smiling responses I've grown used to disappear, and darkness spreads within my body like a cancer.

On the return flight after a dismal business trip, gloom has control of my heart and I'm forced to reflect on the never-ending nature of the inner battle. Arriving home, a card from Sabrina awaits me. Several times, I've almost acted on the impulse to pick up the phone and call her, but it has felt wrong. This is the first contact for nearly two months. The card ends with the simple words:

> *I'll be home on my own on Friday night if you would like to call me.*

A lot's happened since we last spoke but when I call, it seems as though we've been communicating every day, so free is the conversation. But something is different. An intimacy stretches further than we've previously allowed, which encourages me to tell her how I really feel about her, prompted as I am by a need that creeps stealthily into the unspoken voids between the words. She reaffirms the status of our relationship as one of friendship, and I agree, even though my feelings don't. However, I sense that, behind her brave words, she is also struggling with her feelings.

After the conversation, I feel uplifted. It's been a difficult week and my energy has been low, but talking to Sabrina has made me feel whole again. But it doesn't last; the following morning, I awaken to an uneasy feeling that the phone call with Sabrina was somehow wrong. I replay the call in my mind, and icy fear grips me as I realize I overstepped the bounds with my expression of love. Surely I'm putting pressure on her when I promised not to. I recall the pain and vulnerability in the silence between her words, and rather than honoring her position, I took advantage of her confusion. Oh, my God, when will it end? I don't even have the strength to honor this beautiful being's needs.

I realize that the strength of my emotional need is so great that I'm manipulating my visions, using the messages on divine love to create a dream of a possible future with Sabrina. But this isn't what the inner messages say at all. The angels told me that I'm to have only a divine love relationship, but that I'm not ready yet, and that I must be careful of my feelings for Sabrina.

As the depth of their warning becomes clear, I plunge into an abyss of despair at the realization of just how far I still have to go. The deep emotional need that has ruled my life for so long still lurks within me, ready to prey on any unsuspecting sign of love that enters my life, ready to entwine my energy in the heart of another and bind myself with attachment.

The pain of the previous week, swept away by our telephone call, returns with a venom, magnified by the pain of my betrayal of Sabrina's trust. I want to call her and apologize, to put things right, but am I really only looking for another excuse to talk to her, to swim in the dripping emotions that seep from every pause in our words? So I don't call and the confusion feeds on itself, growing ever stronger.

I start to panic. How could I possibly have lived like this in the past? How I want to talk to Robin, but I cannot. I haven't seen Ashoka for several weeks, and I don't know where he lives. I'm alone and sinking fast. In a moment of revelation, I see my previous existence of emotional need for what it was. It was like living in the slums of a city in an underdeveloped country. If that were all I knew, I wouldn't realize how bad it was. Since taking a spiritual path and finding the light, I have been transported to a lovely home in a plush, upper class suburb. From the comfort of my carpeted lounge, I can look back in horror at where I came from and realize how desperate the situation was.

Right now, however, it's as if someone uprooted me from my lovely home and dumped me back in the roach-infested slum I once called home. My old friends come to the door to greet me. Smiling, they invite me in, and I'm surrounded by insecurity, fear of failure, not meeting others' expectations, guilt and, of course, self-doubt. All my black, ugly, distorted monsters laugh and say, "We knew you'd come back. We knew you couldn't leave us for long."

I'm visualizing them grabbing me and pulling me back into their hovel. In terror, I run into my bedroom, slam the door, scream at the top of my voice, and cry ... for help that doesn't come.

I can't go back there. It's impossible to live in those conditions now I know what it's like on the other side. I can't let myself be dragged into the swamp. I've spent a large part of my life in inner darkness, and I cannot face the prospect of living any more of my life in it, not now that I know the joy of living in the light.

No matter what I do, I can't throw off the negativity. It haunts me all weekend and as I wake on Monday morning, the tentacles of doubt wrap themselves tighter round my heart, strangling the joy out of my life. There's only one way I can sever those tentacles and cast out the doubt—the same way I got to the light in the first place—meditation. My morning meditations over the previous week have been very ordinary, thoughts constantly intruding on the silent spaces of my inner being. This morning, I approach meditation with renewed enthusiasm.

In a desperate search for the light, I cry like a helpless child, my inner tears searing through the shields of darkness defending my ego castle, an inner cry not of my own doing, but a gift from the creator, given through the descending grace of a Father whose child appears before Him and says, "Father, I'm helpless without your love."

From the very depth of my soul comes the cry, with strength beyond both mind and emotion. With the sincerity of an innocent child, my pleas reach beyond to a place so deep within me that my impoverished faith can't reach it. But this morning I go there, as if my soul, swooping from its place of silent observation, is intervening in a previously uneven combat. Watching me patiently from its point of all knowing, examining my forlorn plight, waiting only for an admission of inadequacy, it charges to my defense.

Once I surrender, I'm transported to a place I've visited before, to a large rocky outcrop overlooking a valley stretching into the horizon. I sit near the edge of the outcrop, high above the gently meandering river drifting its way through the valley. The sky resounds to the crash and boom of thunder rolling across my tenuous perch as great clouds of blackness battle for space in the cluttered sky. Lightning streaks from the densest clouds towards the ground, searching for a target for its fury.

Watching this scene, I'm aware of a fear gripping the inner me perched atop the rock. The "me" on the rock tosses his body back and forward, thrashing in turmoil, grappling with an unwelcome intruder who has encroached on the sacred ground of my inner peace. The storm rages fiercely, lightning crashing to the ground nearby with intimidating ferocity. The inner struggle persists for an eternity, but in outside time, no more than five minutes elapses. Suddenly, the body in my vision arches backwards at an improbable angle and streaks of blackness explode from his chest. My body involuntarily responds, and as the darkness gushes into the universe, the sky clears and I slip out of my sacred space. I feel totally exhausted, both physically and emotionally, as if I've been through the struggle myself rather than watching an inner aspect of me in the vision. And then again, perhaps I have. Perhaps the veil between my inner experiences and my outer perception is disappearing.

I feel much better during the day. The apprehension and doubt remain, but the darkness prowling my inner jungle appears to have receded.

The next morning, back on the rocky outcrop once again, thunder crashes and lightning splits open the sky, raging in outer fury, but this time, I sit calmly, unaffected by the protesting tempest. And I know, in my state of serenity, that the storms of ignorance are but irritations, incapable of inflicting serious harm. After a few minutes, the lightning stops abruptly, the thunder ceases its grumbling and the storm clouds clear, to reveal the azure sky.

The experience has shown me just how vulnerable I am when I believe I can do things on my own. God blessed me with a remarkable transformation and my ego took the credit. The resulting fall from grace has been a timely reminder of who is really doing the work and highlights the length of the journey to come. In less than two weeks, the fragile pretence of my own invincibility has been demolished, and my ego has been pounded on the rocky cliffs of its own arrogance. How I long for a break.

During the struggles of December, the wonderful meditation experiences I have grown accustomed to stop. However, the day after my second experience on the rock, the light returns with renewed clarity as I see a vision forming in my heart. Flying along a river, I arrive at an old town. Descending to the only street in the town, I observe a row of rundown buildings. A disheveled structure at the far end of the street catches my attention. Walking through the front door, I'm greeted by an old woman sitting in a rocking chair. In a croaky voice, she says, "Welcome to the house of God."

I turn to leave and hear myself say, "I can't stay here, I'm looking for a lady that I love."

"Wait," she calls out urgently, "You're in the right house, you don't have to run away to find her."

I stop, turn to face the old woman, and see her transform before my eyes. A soft light emanates from her body and the beauty of young innocence radiates from her face. I am gazing upon an angelic representation of womanhood. She speaks again, only this time her voice is soft and musical. In shock, I hear her words as if spoken by Sabrina, "It is the divine in me that you love, not the physical human form. The only way to find me is through God. So do not fear and do not run."

The power of the message echoes throughout the scene as the beautiful young woman of innocence reverts to the crone and beckons me to follow her to a room at the back of the house. In an instant, we are high up, looking down on a beautiful golden city. Reminding me of a space city from *Star Trek*, it is new yet, at the same time, majestically old.

Suddenly, the city disappears and I'm back with the old lady sitting patiently in her rocking chair. She says, "It's okay. We can wait. There's plenty of time."

I drift back and forth a few times but can't regain the vision, or perhaps I don't want to hear what she has to say. As I come back into my bedroom, the message is clear. As with the experience in San Francisco, my inner self is telling me that my emotionally attachment to Sabrina is becoming dangerous, that it's not what I'm supposed to be doing. This relationship is testing me and I have to find the strength to overcome the emotional dependency and pursue a truer love.

I'm having the day from hell at work. Around five, I'm thinking about finishing early when Sabrina calls. "I've been stressing out all week. After our conversation on Friday, I felt all wrong. I couldn't sleep at all that night and at three in the morning, I got up and wrote you a letter. Ever since, I've been worrying that it would hurt you and I couldn't let you get it without talking to you first."

"Now you've really got me worried. What did you say?"

"Oh, I don't want to say over the phone other than that I felt all wrong after our last conversation. But if my letter comes across as being cold, please know that I don't feel coldness to you. It's just that I had to be really strong when I wrote it, and I can't afford to be any other way."

Like the script of a romantic tragedy, pain and heartache accompany each syllable and pause. My God, I wonder, what's in the letter. She mailed it on Monday, so it should be there when I get home tonight. "Don't worry," I reassure her, recalling my own turmoil, "I felt confused and uneasy after that call, as well."

As soon as we say goodbye, I head for home. The letter is waiting, and with a feeling of dread, I tear it open. My heartbeat increases as the truth of what I read echoes through each word:

> *There is so much to say to you and ideally it should be said face-to-face, but I know there's no way that that can happen right now and yet I feel such a coward writing it. I feel that I've done it all wrong between us and now I need to put it all right again, but doing it by letter is getting out of it too easy.*
>
> *Alistair, my dear friend, what I write may hurt and for any ounce of hurt that I cause you I'm sorry from the bottom of my heart and your pain is my pain.*
>
> *Okay, so by now you're really worried so let me begin. I've let things get all wrong between us and I'm sorry. My only excuse, if I'm allowed one, is that I hadn't expected to feel so close to you and I was unprepared for the whole situation. It was good for me when you went to America, and since then, I've been so very busy. With you out of contact, it has given time for the dust to settle and for me to stand back and see things clearly. Speaking to you on the phone today confirmed what I thought.*
>
> *So here is how I see it. I've let our relationship get to a place where it shouldn't be. I know I haven't been unfaithful to my husband, but it feels like it and so the warning bells ring. My family deserves my best and so I need to put things right.*
>
> *I've let you develop a romantic notion of our relationship and have let you say things that should never have been said because of where I am. I fear that you hold some hope that somewhere down the road there will be a time for us and I need you to let go of that because it will never happen and it's wrong to believe otherwise.*
>
> *I know that you respect my situation now, but I need you to know that my situation isn't going to change. So, my friend, it's a funny situation that we find ourselves in, not one that we planned or expected, but one that we need to put right – if we can. I need to know if we can get to a place where we can be good friends, friends that are always there*

for each other, but without any romantic notions that put the relationship in the wrong place. Alistair, I will never be anything more than a friend who cares so very much for you. I can't be and so you're not allowed to think otherwise.

I won't put my marriage in jeopardy for anything – it has to be my top priority, and as much as it would hurt me very deeply, if we can't have a proper friendship, as friends, then I must let you go. OUCH!"

With a huge sigh, I put the letter down. Part of me wants to cry, and yet a deeper part of me feels a great relief, for I know what she says is true, that we're not supposed to have a romantic relationship. However, I can't hide the grief that itself reveals the level of romantic attachment I've developed for her. She's right, I have been hanging onto the hope that one day we'll be together.

It's less than 24 hours since I received Sabrina's letter, and I've agonized over how to respond to it for what seems like an eternity. The temptation to run away is strong, but I've been here before, and haven't I always run in the past? What has running ever achieved, though? I simply admit defeat, admit my emotional attachment is too powerful for me to overcome, and condemn myself to go through this the next time someone captures my heart. How am I supposed to experience a divine love if I run every time things get tough? And clearly Sabrina doesn't want me to run. The pain in her letter is barely disguised, and she is torn by her own emotions. The feelings we share for each other are mutual.

A sense of shame creeps up on me for even thinking of running. Look at the strength she showed in writing the letter, the courage to risk losing all interaction with me, when she feels so much love in her heart. Surely I can show the same strength, and stand up to my insecurities.

The thought of cutting off her friendship completely seems impossible. For the first time in my life, I've met someone who brings my soul to the fore, who unleashes my heart to sing in the freedom of love, without the complications of sexual implications, so how can I turn my back on this? Surely if I'm to experience a truly divine love in the future, then I have to learn from this relationship with Sabrina, but in doing so I must honor her request.

At the Center, the woman chairing the meeting in Daphnie's absence announces a 14-mile run (just over half a marathon, but still more than I've ever run) for the following Sunday as part of a celebration. My inner voice speaks to me with such clarity that I turn to see if anyone is standing next to me. "You're going to run a marathon on Sunday."

"What? Are you serious?"

"Yep, you're going to run a marathon on Sunday."

I expect my poor old mind to challenge this, after all, it's ridiculous to expect me to run a marathon with no training, and at my age. To my surprise, I don't challenge it at all, but just accept it with an excitement that bubbles over with anticipation.

As I drive home, suddenly the Sabrina question clarifies, and I know I must write to her to put her heart at rest. As I write, the words flow from my pen as if divinely guided and appear as much as a message for me as a response to her:

> *You said you let me develop a romantic notion of our relationship and let me say things that should never have been said. It's inappropriate for you to take the sole responsibility for that. It's simply that we're both human and we were both totally unprepared for the power and beauty of what occurred between us. Yes, I did get some romantic notions. I certainly did not plan to. I felt I was strong enough to have overcome that in our situation, but I was not. It wasn't until you raised the issue that I realized how strong and powerful it was and that hurt me a lot. This has always been my biggest area of vulnerability and weakness in many ways. I have always needed someone to lean on and to love me. I really felt that I had overcome that need, but I suspect the enormous changes I'm going through in my life, changes I'm going through on my own, are taking a greater emotional toll, at times, than I admit to myself.*
>
> *I know that you will not put your marriage in jeopardy, and I could never forgive myself if you did as a result of me. So I guess this is where we come to the crunch – can I respond to your beautiful self in a way that enables us to maintain our special friendship without placing you under*

pressure or making you feel as if you're doing the wrong thing. Well as I see it, the situation is like this;

I can have a physical relationship whenever I want to – not a good one necessarily, but they are always around. I don't want one!

I can have a romantic relationship less easily, but they are not uncommon. I've had a few before and if I want to, I'm sure I could have another one. I don't want one!

But what I've felt with you, the free flowing of our spirits, the way we can see inside each other's heart, the peace that I feel when I'm with you, despite the lack of any physical involvement – this is unique. This is not something I've experienced before, it is something that transcends the physical and romantic experience. Neither you nor I can explain what happens to us, why we feel this way, but I have no doubt that it has been an experience gifted to us by God.

My dear friend, we are humans and that means that romantic tendencies are always a danger. And it seems that there are two options that I can take now. The first is to run and hide and try to forget you. This is the easy option. I can admit to myself that it is too hard to overcome my own weaknesses and accept defeat. Or I can wallow in self-pity and self-indulgence. No! That is not the way. I will not do that.

Your friendship deserves much more and I will not surrender it out of fear of facing yet another inner challenge. So no matter how difficult it may be, I will overcome those weaknesses and enable us to achieve the sort of friendship you can feel comfortable with."

As I mail the letter, I wonder about the bravery in my words. Can I really achieve this, or am I just kidding myself so that my involvement with Sabrina can continue? Whatever the case, I have no choice, since giving into my emotional insecurities is simply not an option. But at the same time, I need a rest from the intensity of this situation.

December has already been a difficult month, and just when I thought it was safe to take it easy, this is thrown at me to reveal something that is still to be overcome. Unsure of whether I can go on, I go to bed and pull the covers over my head. As I indulge in bemoaning the intensity of the journey I'm on, I start to cry and find myself talking aloud to God, pleading for mercy, "Father, You're throwing everything at me, and I can barely cope. I'm trying so hard to be what You want of me, to take everything that You give to me, but I need help right now. I need a rest."

Subtle warmth creeps into me and moves through my body, like an unseen lover entering my heart and caressing it, as if God Himself descends and takes me in His loving arms to let me know everything is all right, that I will be looked after. With this sensation flowing through me, I cry buckets of tears of release and drift off to sleep.

On the Sunday morning of the big run, I rise before dawn to prepare. Part of me still can't believe that I'm going to run a marathon, but somehow it feels right, just something I'm going to do. The furthest I've run in my life so far has been 12km., but deep down, I've always wanted to run a marathon. Previously though, because I didn't think it possible, I would make excuses about my knees not being able to take the training.

Experts recommend that before running a marathon, you train for three to four months, and build up to 30km training runs. This must be one of the craziest things I've ever done in my life, since despite the promise I made to myself to run a marathon in 1998, I've made no effort to train.

Since I'm the only one actually running the full 27 miles, while the others run 14 miles, I arrange with the organizers to start early so that I can finish the marathon at the same time as the others

From the minute the run starts, I just know I'm going to do it. A feeling of light enters me and I'm relaxed, as if God Himself is running for me, my only contribution being to make my body available as a vehicle. The run involves 27 laps of a one-mile circuit, and after about an hour, I begin to see light flooding out of me, and I continue the run in a state close to meditation.

Once beyond the 12 km lap, I'm in uncharted territory, but instead of worrying, I wait expectantly for the dreaded wall so many runners talk of, but it never comes. I finish the run in 3 hours 44 minutes, which by all accounts is an excellent time.

Equally amazing is the recovery. I expect to be a wreck afterwards, but that night, I go to the Center's Sunday meeting feeling great, a few sore muscles, but nothing to worry about.

After meditation, I talk to Eugene, a dear friend and one of the older members of the Center. He's a jovial man in his seventies who's seen a lot of life, and I enjoy his insights. "Oh, young fellow, you did very well. We are proud of you."

"You know, Eugene, I don't feel like I did anything. It was such a joy."

As we continue our discussion, I realize how much faith I showed in myself by even doing this run, and how I never doubted it at any stage. "It's funny, Eugene, December has been such a tough month, and at times, I've lain on my bed and cried for the intensity to be eased. And today, I feel I was blessed. Like God came down and borrowed my body for four hours and said, 'Here, My child, let Me do something to show my appreciation.' "

"Oh, I'm so happy to hear you say that. It's amazing for one with such a strong mind to be able to show such faith."

Eugene is always praising my ability to overcome my mind. I don't think he would be so gracious if he could see the view from my side of my eyes, but what he says sparks a thought in me. "Eugene, you just triggered something really important. Despite everything that's happened to me, I still doubt myself. Am I just imagining everything? Am I really receiving messages from my inner voice? Or is it my ego playing tricks on me?"

"Hey, you're way too hard on yourself."

"Well perhaps, I always have been, but whatever the case, I needed some concrete proof, something my mind couldn't dispute. I needed solid, tangible proof of the presence of God in my life. And you know, today I got it. We all have our own ideas of what's possible. To me, running a marathon was only possible with months of hard training. But I just did it, no training, nothing."

"Yes, indeed. The capacity came from God, did it not?"

"There's no other possibility."

A note Yiannis Kouros sends me after the run reinforces my feelings on the grace I received in running this marathon:

> *I'm very happy that you ran the marathon for the first time in such a fantastic time! Congratulations. Many people try for many years to run under 4 hours and they can't. It seems that you have found the key of success in your inner world.*

Yes Yiannis, my dear friend, you're right. The key to success does indeed lie in the inner world!

December 22, the day after the marathon, and the blessings continue, as I'm inundated with bliss all day. My focus and productivity at work is way up, but at the same time, I'm aware of a deep sense of "something" floating through me. It's indescribably magical, as though I'm wafting over my life on a cloud of unreality, suspended in a heavenly paradise, going about my daily work, connected into a world of love and serenity. I feel unusually warm towards the people around me and a oneness with all things that's beyond my comprehension. Sitting in meditation that night, I realize the feeling is love! Real inner love coming from my heart, the sort of feeling I've experienced on one or two occasions when God floods me with love during meditation. But this time it has lasted all day.

Having read about real love in books, I thought I'd grasped it, but not until now, that I'm actually experiencing the feeling, could I possibly have understood. I'm being blessed with a glimpse of what it's like on Ashoka's mountain, so wonderful is the feeling of total freedom that I virtually dance round the house, and it's well past midnight when I call it a day.

Lying in joyful reminiscence of a special day, it all seems so clear. The love I thought that was coming from Sabrina is actually emanating from within myself. In some way, being with her brings my soul, my inner self, to the surface, and I feel the love flowing from within me into my life. Now that I've accepted that we will have no romantic involvement, my own inner love can surface and be recognized for what it truly is.

I remember the vision of a few days ago when I was looking for "a lady that I loved," and God, through the old woman, tried to tell me something but I didn't get it. Now it's clear. I wasn't looking for a woman, but for my inner self. I thought I had to look to a woman to give me love, but God is trying to tell me that I have to find this aspect within myself, that I won't find it anywhere else.

Part 5 • Guides Appear

Christmas, Time of Celebration

CHRISTMAS EVE, AND my children and I fly to Perth to see my family. The wonderful feelings of love have subsided and I'm in a contemplative state, wondering why I can't maintain the bliss of those few days following the marathon. Why do I still feel a need for Sabrina despite everything the visions have shown me? Why am I still in conflict over my role in the Center and my future there?

With these questions simmering in the background, I begin to meditate. I am surrounded by light and mist, out of which emerges the shape of a house. I enter and find an old man smiling at me. As I approach him, the house expands, walls moving silently outwards until I'm dwarfed in a vast area of light, seemingly without boundaries. The old man starts to walk away down a path, beckoning me to follow him. We come to a cellar door.

"Where are we going?" I ask.

"Inside yourself," he replies.

Through the door, we go down a flight of steps and into a brightly lit tunnel. We enter another room, even more brightly lit, and as my eyes adjust to the glare, I see another, much younger man, and I'm struck by how sweet and angelic he looks.

"Who are you?" I ask.

"We are you!" the younger one says. "I am the divinity in you," he continues. "And my friend here represents your wisdom."

"What am I doing here?"

"You want to be here. You want to know the truth," the younger one continues.

"What about the conflict I feel about my spiritual path, and all the things that are going on in the Center. I don't accept all the things I see," I protest, surprising myself at just how much conflict I feel over my spiritual direction.

"That's simply your ego. You will transform it," he continues unperturbed.

"What about my feelings on love, and Sabrina?"

"You *want* love, but you must *do* is to reach for divine love," he says, his voice softening considerably.

"But I don't feel I can let go of my emotional need."

"Yes, but you know you can't experience divine love unless you do."

I have more questions, but one of them says, "You have had enough for today," and the scene fades.

It seems as if my inner being is manifesting itself to me in different forms. Are they all different aspects of me? Or is God using these images to communicate with me?

What of the larger question: the nature of this divine love? Does it mean a life of celibacy, a life without an intimate relationship with a woman? Or is it possible to transcend the limitations we place on the relationship with our sexual partner, and move to a new dimension, where the love for the divine and the love for another person can be merged? It's a fascinating question, one I'm becoming increasingly drawn into.

Later that evening, the men from the Center put on a Christmas play in which I play the role of Jesus. I've no real feelings towards Jesus, but am thrilled inwardly to be given the role. I've never been in a play before, at least not since school, and I thoroughly enjoy it. As with the marathon, I'm not the slightest bit concerned about whether I'm successful or not, and I'm struck by how much enjoyment is possible when I'm not concerned with the result.

Driving home, I feel a complete peace and total oneness with the Universe, as well as a closeness to Jesus that never existed previously.

The next morning, the Center holds a five o'clock meditation to start Christmas Day, before everyone goes about his or her own family commitments. Only six people show up, and the intimate gathering, combined with the stillness of the early morning, heightens my meditation.

Someone I can't focus on is leading me down a path of white light. "Where am I going?" I ask.

"Somewhere you've never been before. But your soul has been there."

In a series of scenes that flash in front of me, which I intuitively know represent scenes from past lives, I first see natives, maybe African bushmen or possibly Malaysian Dyaks. Then I see the Crusades, a political scene in which there is heated debate (I sense it's the early British Parliament), and then a city being gutted by a violent fire, possibly London. Next, I see a war scene, with cannons firing and buildings being blasted, but don't know where or when.

The final scene has the biggest impact on me. I recognize myself in the scene for the first time, and I'm a young boy, standing on a hill overlooking a vast expanse of land. I've seen it before, shortly after returning from the States, and I'm with a man who I assume is my father, clearly an important man, perhaps even a president of the USA. Somehow, I know that in this past life, I could have done something meaningful but didn't have the courage to follow my inner guidance, and I lost the chance, but that in this current lifetime, I'm being given a chance to atone.

At the vision ends, I feel the presence of Jesus around me, and I wonder why he's visiting my inner sanctuary. Did I play Jesus last night only because it's Christmas, or is there some other reason?

Later that day, I head for the airport. This will be the first time since my son was born that our whole family will be together in the one place. The relationship with my children has developed considerably, our love for each other blossoming. They are a source of great joy, and yet I feel I'm still not giving them what they need. The guilt of a father who put the pursuit of freedom ahead of being home with his children every night still gnaws at me.

On the way to the airport, my son, who is nearly six, asks, "Dad, all people who love God are really peaceful, aren't they?"

"Yes, mate."

"You love God, don't you, Dad?"

"Yes, I sure do, mate, and I try to be peaceful, too. Daddy is usually really peaceful after meditation in the morning, but sometimes during the day I lose my peace."

He bursts out laughing. "What's so funny?" I ask.

"You, Dad! Saying that you lose your peace during the day. I think that's really funny."

"Don't you think that Dad loses his peace sometimes?"

"Nah! I think you're always peaceful."

His words reach into my heart and touch me like a soothing balm, and a feeling of love for them swamps me, tears welling up in my eyes. Perhaps I'm doing better than I realize.

Being at my sister's house allows time for quiet reflection. She's a wonderful woman, a few years older than me, and has always been protective towards her little brother. With a gentle frankness, her words are sometimes misconstrued, but always spoken through love. The day after Christmas, the children are busy enjoying her swimming pool and we can finally talk to each other.

"Alistair, you're looking more relaxed than I've seen you for a while."

"Yes, I feel like a completely different person. Like I've discovered a new me."

"Perhaps you're just returning to the person you always were. The Alistair I knew when he was younger was always giving and joyful, if not a little volatile."

"I guess I just got caught up in the fight for life and lost my way. Perhaps I should call it the fight for identity."

"You know, I could never work out why you were so unhappy during the past 20 years. You seemed to have everything going for you, but you were always struggling with something."

"Yeah, I had everything except a sense of self. I never knew who I was, and so I didn't have anything to fall back on inside. I didn't know it back then, but I've spent my whole life searching for a sense of self."

"But you were always so good at everything you did."

"Sure, because I thought if I proved how good I was, then I would feel good, I would be someone. But it didn't work. I convinced myself that I was fighting the world to prove my worthiness, yet all the time, I was really only trying to prove it to myself. And in doing so, I erected more and more barriers around my true self, ensuring I exposed no vulnerabilities for anyone to attack."

"So spirituality is becoming a big part of your life?"

I think about the obvious question for longer than necessary, "Yes, Janette. In fact, you could say that it *is* my life. Spirituality has given me my life back, stopped my downward spiral of self-destruction."

"You always were a bit dramatic."

"You may think I'm being dramatic, but I don't. If I hadn't taken up meditation, God knows where I'd be now. I simply couldn't go on punishing myself any longer and I couldn't get out of the hole on my own."

"So when are you heading off to the Himalayas?"

Her quip catches me off guard, but she has a point. Before I took up meditation, I, too, thought a spiritual person was someone who lived in a hippie commune, or went trekking off to Nepal. Yet here I am, a week short of my fortieth birthday, an executive in a large corporation, and a part-time single parent. It would be easy to use spirituality as an excuse to drop out and immerse myself in the pursuit of God, but that's not what it's all about.

"It's not about renouncing the world, Janette. I haven't given up my job, nor broken off relationships with friends or family. In fact, the opposite is true. I derive more enjoyment from work, my career is blossoming, and my relationships are much better."

"Yes, that's certainly true," she agrees, with a wry grin.

"The spiritual path I'm on is an intense one, which suits me, but it has enhanced the other aspects of my life rather than disrupt them."

"Well, you certainly seem happier."

"Thanks, but it isn't without its moments. I'm constantly being challenged, but I'm learning to see challenges as opportunities to make progress. No matter how difficult the challenge may seem, I know it's just part of the journey, and when I get through it, my life will be flooded with even brighter light."

As Janette goes off to prepare a snack for the children, I find myself looking forward to the next challenge.

The time difference between Adelaide and Perth, further to the west, means that I wake up early, so on the second morning, around five o'clock, I get up to meditate before the house becomes active.

I settle down and see an ocean growing in my inner space, except that it's made of light. As the ocean expands beyond the limits of sight within my heart, I know that it's made of peace, an ocean of pure peace. Suddenly, I'm pulled over the ocean through a tunnel of light, and land on an island about fifty meters across, also made of light, a glowing radiance, both brilliant and yet gentle on my eyes. To my surprise, a luminous form of Sabrina sits gracefully on the shore, and I throw my arms around her in a loving embrace.

The warmth of her body washes me in a familiar feeling of comfort and security, a feeling that, deep down, I know is false. However, I savor the moment, captive to the magic of her embrace. Suddenly, a luminous form "emerges" from the ocean of peace. Emerged doesn't actually do the scene justice, as the form explodes out of the water like a missile launch, making a wave that sends spray cascading out to the horizon, and I feel droplets of peace falling on me. When the form takes sufficient shape, I gape open-mouthed. It's Jesus! Never before has he appeared in one of my visions, yet here he is in luminous splendor, light streaming out from behind his white garments.

Jesus looks at us, and a glimmering, silvery-white light radiates from his heart, shining down on the island, which he towers above. Turning, he walks away over the ocean, beckoning me to join him on a path of light over the ocean. I start to follow, but I don't want to leave Sabrina, or at least what she represents. I don't want to let go of my need for emotional attachment, of the needy sort of relationship I've lived in before. I desperately want to stay with her, despite knowing it's wrong. I try to embrace her again. "You must go!" she says firmly but softly.

Jesus returns. "Yes, you have to go. You must let go of your human attachments."

I know that this is a crucial choice point in my life, and that there's only one choice to make, but still I linger, wavering between clinging to Sabrina and striking out on my path. A crippling fear grips me, like a crooked talon wrapping itself around my ankles, dragging me into the murky depth of the swamp once more. Near panic threatens to extinguish my light, powerful enough for me to even consider turning my back on Jesus.

In this moment, I'm afraid that leaving Sabrina means banishing the possibility of any future relationships. I'm not ready for this sacrifice in the pursuit of God. My heart shakes with the conflict as the inner struggle rages, my mind tormented by confusion.

But, as Jesus waits with unwavering patience, the truth starts to seep into my consciousness, that despite having been celibate for nearly a year, despite the challenges I've endured with Sabrina in the past few months, I still have not dealt with the pain contaminating my emotions as a result of my past relationships. And that while this pain lays dormant within, lying in ambush for the slightest sign of intimacy, I cannot move forward in my quest for love.

I make my decision. I must leave Sabrina on the island. I cannot stay and wallow in the emotional dependency that's tormented my life and caused such self-degradation. If ever an intimate relationship is to again play a part in my life, it must be on an entirely different basis, devoid of dependency. And to achieve that, I must trust in God's guidance and leave my attachments on the island.

Aware of my thoughts, Jesus speaks once more, love and compassion evident in his voice, "You have a big job ahead! You cannot afford to waste energy on an emotional love attachment. My Father has told you to pursue divine love. You must maintain that goal and not bind it with emotional human love. You know that already! With your human love, you cannot fly, you cannot pursue your dreams. With divine love, you can and will do both of these things."

I turn my back on the island and on Sabrina, and walk down the path of light towards Jesus. I follow him along the path for some distance until eventually a bridge of light appears in front of us, spanning a deep ravine. He stops in the middle of the bridge, looks at me, and softly says, "Look below."

I look down and see a huge crowd of people, fighting and squabbling. Jesus says, "They need to be united. We need inspirational leaders to show them that they are one."

Confused over his appearance, I ask, "Why are you here and not my teacher?"

"You don't trust him when it comes to love. You think that he will direct you to a life where you will not be able to experience intimacy again. My Father knows this. He wants you to have a divine relationship, and you must trust that. I am also here to show you that you must forge your own path and understand many aspects."

He's right. I do feel a conflict, and I'm afraid of the path down which my teacher may direct me. I'm also afraid of being restricted by the path, of becoming narrow and judgmental of other paths, as have so many other students.

Once again Jesus interrupts my thoughts, "Your spiritual teacher does not want to place limitations on you. Only some of his students seek to do this."

His message transmitted, Jesus fades, and as he does, I'm flooded with power, light and energy. And as the meditation comes to a close, the significance of the message reverberates through my being, yet I don't know what to do with it.

The Next Challenge

O N NEW YEAR'S Day, a phone call from the leader of the
meditation center in Perth catches me by surprise, "Guess
who I've got in my car!"

My first thought is Robin, and sure enough it's him. He's been
invited back to the Center and has flown to Perth for the New Year's
weekend.

On the surface, I'm very happy for him, but something is
bothering me, a strange sense of disappointment and loss that I
don't understand. That evening, while with some friends on an
8km fun run, the reason for my strange feelings about Robin
becomes obvious. After the run, I drive him back to where he's
staying, and we have a chance to talk in private. Knowing I can
trust him, I open up about my feelings. "You know, I felt really
weird when I heard you were back in the Center."

"Yeah, why was that, brother?"

"Well, at first I simply couldn't understand it, but during the
run, I realized what's bothering me. The way you were kicked out
of the Center gave me an excuse to leave, if I wanted to. It gave me
a justification to distance myself and not to commit. Your return
has taken away my escape hatch."

We both reflect on my words, then I continue, "I never realized
my fear of commitment is so deep."

"Why do you think that is?"

"I don't know. I guess it means I still have an underlying lack
of faith in my ability to make the right decisions in the future."

"But the only person you're committing to is yourself."

"I don't follow you."

"Look, your commitment to spirituality is a commitment to yourself – no one else. It's about your own life and your relationship with God, and you can choose to walk away from it at any stage."

"Yeah, that makes sense. Looks like I'm even afraid of making a commitment to myself."

I meditate with the people from Perth and some others who are visiting for the weekend festivities. We also watch a video documentary on the life of Mother Theresa, showing the early days of her mission work and how God spoke to her and guided her in what she should do. The video affects me deeply, and I watch it trance-like, oblivious to what's going on around me. I'm aware of a presence working within me, implanting a message so deep that my mind can't grasp it. And, as 1997 ends with an unheard, yet deeply felt message about my future life, I feel destiny unfolding within me.

Although I enjoy the time with my family in Perth, part of me wants to be in the company of people who share my spiritual thirst. Caught on the horns of this dilemma, I enter my first meditation for the new year.

The usual tunnel of light is different, well-formed, with solid walls. I emerge into a large room or cavern. Normally, I don't try to invoke anything, but rather hand over control to my higher self to give me what I need, but this time, for some reason, I try to visualize myself being attacked by ignorance.

Almost immediately, a deep voice demands, "Cast off these feelings of being sorry for yourself and playing victim. They do nothing for you. It is time to get on with the job."

I'm back in the tunnel, and arrive at a junction from which two branches head off in different directions, one representing aspiration and the other desire. The tunnel of desire beckons me, parading scantily clad woman and wealth. In the past, it may have been a difficult choice, but today the tunnel of desire has absolutely no appeal. I stop at the entrance to the tunnel of aspiration, presenting itself simply as light, and kneel.

"Am I worthy of entering this tunnel?"

"Of course, you are. All My children are, but most of them would not choose it, they do not even see that it exists. Only those who have made spiritual progress can choose it."

I enter the tunnel and find myself in an area of immense beauty, but my attention falls on the elderly man seated in a secluded peaceful spot, his back resting against a tree of light. I recognize him immediately as my wisdom, there for me once more. I ask, "Am I going the right way?"

"Oh, yes. But as you explore the world, be careful to keep your eye on God, and strive for a better understanding of your true purpose."

Later on New Year's Day, I take the children to the zoo. The following day is my birthday and a few old friends are invited over for a quiet day at my sister's house. When we return to her house, Janette tells me that other people will here for my party and I will have to switch bedrooms. It's no big deal, but I feel oddly angry. I try to suppress my anger, but dammit, it's *my* birthday and I have to change rooms for a bunch of people I've never met!

Janette senses my mood, and when I suggest my children and I should spend the night at my parent's house, she explodes. "You haven't changed at all, have you? All this spirituality stuff hasn't really changed you. You still need to control everything. You still need to get your own bloody way. You still can't cope with having your own little environment disrupted."

Wow, right between the eyes. In the past, I would have had a shouting match with her, but this time, I just sit passively and listen. After she storms out of the room, I go out to the pool and ask my children how they would feel about staying at their grandparent's house for the night. But they love the pool and won't hear of it. They're going to stay with their cousins, no matter what.

I return to my room to stew over the predicament, and to feel sorry for myself. Then I remember the message from this morning's meditation, and I suddenly understand. My reaction over Robin's return, my need for excuses, the words from this morning about not feeling sorry for myself, and now this. God is sending me a message about my next challenge. Janette put it so succinctly, and now, instead of reacting, I am listening. She nailed one of my major problems, something that's plagued me all my life, and now I know it's time to deal with it.

I find Janette in the lounge, looking a bit sheepish for blowing up at me. I give her a big hug, tell her I love her, and thank her for helping me. She's stunned; this isn't the reaction she expected. We sit in silence for a few minutes, two people with a deep affection for each other, both caught in thoughts, yet both enjoying the closeness of the other. Eventually I say, "You know, you've just done me a huge favor."

"I don't know how, but I'll take the compliment anyway."

"You know the other day, I was telling you that the spiritual life was not all joy, that I was constantly being presented with challenges."

"Yes. Go on."

"Well, I'm finding that the challenges are presented to me at exactly the time we're ready to receive them."

"And I've just presented one to you. Is that what you're saying?"

"Exactly. You've stuck it right in my face, where I can't ignore it. This is fantastic, because it means I'm finally ready to tackle it."

"So what is this challenge?"

"You said it with your own words. I need to control everything. I need to control my own space and environment; not just my physical environment but my mental, psychic and emotional environment, as well. Sure, people need their own space, but I seem to carry mine around with me and claim ownership of the emotional, mental and psychic space around me wherever I go. If anyone enters that space uninvited, I react negatively."

"Yes, I've seen you do that, but not all the time. Sometimes, you're very relaxed."

"It's fine for people to enter my space as long as they're safe people. The act of inviting them in means I'm in control of the situation. But when I'm not in control, like today, I get agitated."

"And then you react like you did just now."

"Yes, the fear results in anxiety and triggers defense mechanisms I've learnt over the years."

"I'm sorry, I had no idea it was that bad for you."

"Hey, don't be sorry, sis. How were you to know. I didn't understand it myself until today, thanks to you. But suddenly, it's all so clear. This explains why I experience the wonderful feelings of love, freedom and happiness in my safe environments, but can't carry them out into the wider world with me."

"Well, I'm glad I could be of help."

Once more we embrace in a hug of genuine love and shared understanding, and I leave the room knowing that two big challenges have been presented to me in the past few days. It's time to address my need to control my environment and my fear of commitment. And underlying both is a common characteristic; I'm still not secure enough in myself, still not trusting myself enough. There is still something missing in my life.

It's January 2nd, my birthday and our last full day in Perth. The meditation group has organized a fun day at the beach, following an early morning meditation. I arrive for the meditation, planning to return to my sister's house for my family birthday.

In meditation, a powerful force rises within me, taking the form of a raging flame burning in my heart that engulfs the interior walls I erected there, and I realize it represents the flames of my inner aspiration burning the barriers of fear I've constructed around me, burning the walls restricting my flight to freedom.

Suddenly my heart expands and as I watch the scene playing within, I see myself rise far above the Earth. A sensation of leaving the ground overcomes me and I sense that, not only am I flying in the vision, but in my outer reality as well, although my body remains firmly anchored to the chair.

A sudden explosion of beautiful purple light in the Center of my heart sends streaks of purple pulsating out like a celestial firework display. A form takes shape in my heart Center, and crystallizes into a divine baby of light. I immediately understand that the baby represents me, or at least my soul, in the beyond, the other dimension, preparing to make the journey to Earth in this current life. Then the scene changes to Earth. In pairs and groups, frightened, confused people are fighting and arguing out of frustration. As these scenes of conflict fill my vision, a message drifts into my conscious awareness that I've come to Earth this time to play a role in helping these people, to play a love-based leadership role rather than the traditional leadership role.

The arguing people disappear, and I am on Earth, with a tunnel of light connecting my heart to the other dimension. At the top of this tunnel, groups of souls stand around the edge, pouring love down to Earth. They seem to be rejoicing because it's my birthday and because I'm opening up to the possibilities of my mission on Earth this time.

Filled with love, joy and purple light, I watch a series of scenes depicting events in my life that focus on my intensity and natural leadership. However, they also show how I became lost along the journey, and fell into the control trap. The next scenes show a gradual move towards a more compassionate leadership style at work, culminating in my recent initiative where I took up the fight for some employees who were going to be replaced by contractors.

I'm also shown the role I'm trying to play at the Center, attempting to lead in a totally different way, from the heart, and how my new style of leadership needs to pull together the complementary aspects of the mind and the heart. The messages then focus on the books I'm to write and how the fourth one is about a new way of looking at love.

The next scenes look at my need for love, and show me that love is so important to me and deeply ingrained, but that I had lost my way and failed to remember God's love. I'm shown how I tried to find it in the form of other people and how my desperate need drove me into attachment and dependency. As I watch the scenes playing out, I know that this is not the first lifetime this mistake has caused me to lose my way.

The purple light from earlier returns, and as I bask in its beauty, I hear the others in the room sing "Happy Birthday" to me. The tunnel of light between heaven and my heart reappears, and now all the people in the room appear in the vision as angels standing in a circle round the top of the tunnel, their hands joined as they sing. As their voices harmonize perfectly, they direct love down the tunnel—beautiful purple waves streaked with gold. As I bathe in the ecstasy of the moment, my heart dancing in a sea of purple paradise, a grandfatherly face forms in the center of the heavenly circle, a huge smiling face that I know represents God Himself, and I feel complete. I try to come out of meditation but can't, unable to focus on anything but, overcome with joy, and overwhelmed with the significance of the messages, I simply don't care.

After a brief swim at the beach, I head back to my sister's house for my outer birthday party, knowing they it can't possibly compare to the inner celebration I've just been blessed with.

The next morning is my last in Perth, and I meditate before anyone else is awake. Immediately, the flames of aspiration once again rage in my heart. Drifting deeper, I lose my identity, as my body dissolves into light particles. Some old friends appear before me, people who played a significant role in my life when I was struggling through my teens and early twenties. When I see them, love sweeps through me, penetrating deeply, enveloping my essence like a soft velvet glove. So *this* is divine love!

The purple light appears, exploding all around me in another astral firework display. After a few minutes of enchanting wonder, the scene changes. I am sailing alone in a boat on a beautiful ocean of shimmering light as angels dance gently above the water to the soundless music that softly permeates the air. Somehow the boat finds its way to the base of a pristine waterfall that cascades from high above and down the walls of a cliff face made of beautiful light.

As the boat moves closer, I feel the spray, and am surprised that it isn't wet. My boat actually enters the torrent and comes out on the other side. An elderly man, my wisdom, sits on a ledge, and smiles at me. I disembark and sit next to him on the ledge. After a moment, he says, "You must let your actions and your own personality speak to people for you. Don't tell them all about what you are doing or how much you have changed. Let them see for themselves."

Message delivered, he rises and starts to leave. "Wait! Why are you going?"

"Because I am only to tell you things when it is appropriate. Otherwise, you must work it out for yourself."

"But, you *are* me, so why can't you guide me?"

He laughs and wraps me in an embrace of total love. "Well done! You have realized a great truth."

Then he turns and disappears.

God Becomes Personal

T HE FEELINGS OF love I experience in Perth continue to grow, and during the early part of January, I'm overwhelmed by outpourings of love whenever I meditate. Peace and love sweep through my body, and at times I visualize a tidal wave of ecstasy emanating from my heart and spreading out around me. It seems the love of our divine source is flowing through me, filling my heart with an intoxicating concoction of sensations, which renders everything else irrelevant.

Last year, I experienced peace and love during meditation, but was unable to carry it through the whole day. Now, however, it stays with me, not with the same intensity, but it's definitely present.

On January 14, I'm meditating at the Center, and experience a presence moving through me, an unseen sculptor who pushes and molds my muscles and organs. Then I see Him, the grandfatherly figure I've witnessed on a few occasions who represents God, standing in the Center of my heart, arms outstretched. A more breathtaking sight is hard to imagine, as He stands in the middle of my inner temple, brilliant golden light streaming out of him in all directions like piercing searchlights. He expands until my inner space can no longer contain Him. Unlike other times, when my heart seems capable of infinite expansion during visions, the walls appear to be constricted, but this doesn't deter the Creator. As He continues to grow, He enters the walls of my heart room, into the cellular structure of my being, as if He is possessing me. God persists in His growth, until He saturates every component of my body, then bursts forth into the Universe through the top of my head.

The vision fades, only to be replaced by another scene. I'm in a huge white dome like a great cathedral, only devoid of internal decorations. At the other end of the room, a figure comes into focus. This time, He has taken on human form, the body of a wise old man, glowing with a silvery, white translucence. He looks at me the way a loving grandfather would look at his favorite grandchild, through eyes of love and compassion.

Filled with nothing other than deep peace, I'm aware of the intense emotions being played out through the inner being I'm observing as I see myself fall to my knees before Him and pray. Then I rise and walk towards Him. Suddenly the floor opens up and a ravine appears in front of me, growing to about 30 feet wide.

Walking to the edge of the ravine, I look down and see evil, black creatures inside it, held captive by the sheer walls of their prison. I immediately recognize them as my fears, anxieties and insecurities.

God speaks to me, "You can walk across it if you believe in Me strongly enough. You have to cross them to get to Me."

I know I'm going to do it. Standing on the opposite side from God, knowing that to reach Him, I must transcend my fears, I'm struck by the simplicity and clarity of the vision. I contemplate the treacherous walk across the chasm of my fears, trying to increase my light and strength, preparing to plunge into empty space, with only faith to support my feet, when a bridge of light suddenly materializes.

Floating across the bridge, I stop halfway across, and lean over the edge of the bridge to offer love to my fears. But the voice of wisdom immediately chastises me, "Do not offer them your love until you are safely on this side."

Suddenly, I can't move, cemented to the bridge of light, immoblized by indecision and doubt. An agonizing cry comes from deep within me, from someone in real pain. How can this be, I wonder. I feel so peaceful, but, yes, the crying is definitely coming from within me, torturing my peace with its piercing wails. I stop trying to blot out the sound of despair and allow myself to enter into it.

I'm in a large room that smells like the musty old dungeon of some long-ruined castle. Candles provide enough light for me to make out the source of tormented cries. In horror, I realize it's me, lying on a medieval bed of torture, writhing in pain and screaming.

God stands on one side and my fears, taking on a demonic appearance, loom on the other side. They're fighting over me and appear to be evenly matched, while tearing me apart, as I scream in agony, helpless as to the outcome of this deadly battle for my soul.

Suddenly I sit bolt upright and scream at the satanic figure, representing my inner fears. *"I love God. I want only to be with Him."*

With this, God grows in size and a powerful light comes blasting out of Him.

"My child, that is all I need. Your devotion gives me strength. Look, he cannot stand up to me now."

The demonic representation of my fears cowers, bent over in pain, unable to withstand the glare of God's light, and he turns and runs away. As the love I feel for God explodes in me, the vision slowly fades.

After meditation, I drive Robin home to the apartment he rented after he left my house, and I share the experience with him.

"Man, that's really intense."

"Yes, it was. I believe that the incredibly beautiful vision represents what's going on within me: a battle between my fears and God's light. To reach God's light, I have to overcome my fears, and yet a part of me is afraid to do that. A part of me that's afraid to fully commit to God. There's no doubt that this is the message of the vision."

"This is great, brother. Only a few weeks ago in Perth, you told me you were afraid to make a commitment to yourself, and now you get something like this. Clearly, it's time to move onward and upward." He slaps me gleefully on the knee.

"Yes, I guess so. I feel like I'm being really blessed, and I still find myself wondering why. It's like God took me by the hand a year ago and gently led me along a path. I didn't recognize, nor accept Him then, but He slowly revealed Himself to me in a more personal form. Like a loving father gently encouraging his son to reach greater heights."

"And now you're ready to move forward?"

"I don't really see it like that. I mean, we're both moving forward all the time. But perhaps I'm just getting a deeper understanding of how much doubt I have, of how my fears keep dragging me back to my old ways. Perhaps now it's time to consciously work to overcome these things, rather than letting it happen."

" Man, you amaze me at how you're able to analyze and understand everything that happens to you. What a gift! I just know stuff is going on inside me, but I can't always figure out what it is like you do."

"Maybe it's not a gift. Perhaps it's just my ego trying to understand so it can take the credit. Perhaps I'd be better off if I just offered everything to God and didn't worry about trying to understand?"

"I don't think so, but it doesn't matter. What *is* important is that we don't forget where the love comes from, that we remember to accept and love God, for only then can we really love others. You know, I can actually look at others now and see God breathing through them, and when I do, I feel a real love and oneness."

In the pause as we both reflect on the discussion, my mind drifts to the constant procession of challenges in my life. "You know, Robin, I've been thinking about how much God does and how much we do, and I think I'm finally getting it."

He turns to look at me, keen interest written all over his face. "Yeah?"

"Despite the guidance I'm being given, there are so many times when I've been faced with a decision point, and at each one, I must decide whether to confront my fears or retreat. It seems that no matter how powerful God is, He cannot, or perhaps chooses not to, force me to make a decision that I'm not prepared to make on my own. He presents me with the choice, but it's still up to me to accept the challenge. And it's always easy to take the comfortable option and run, rather than standing up to my fears."

"Give yourself a break. It seems to me that your running days are over."

After dropping Robin, I drive home reflecting on the conversation. Perhaps I've stopped running away. But if I have, why am I not prepared to tell anyone about the messages I've been getting regarding my life's purpose? I can't keep denying it.

Ashoka comes into my mind, and I make a pledge to find him and to tell him about the messages on my mission. I recall an earlier conversation with him, and I'm struck by how close what I just said to Robin was to something Ashoka told me several months ago about God presenting us with challenges that we can either accept or turn away from. Now I know what he meant back then.

Ashoka must be able to read my thoughts, for only three days later, he's waiting for me on the bank of the creek. His greeting is more jovial than usual. "Ah, young one, where have you been?"

Before I can answer, he continues, "Would you be so kind as to allow an old man to show off the contents of his world to you?"

"What do you mean?" I ask.

"It's time I showed you where I live."

What excitement! I've wondered where this mystery man lived, but more importantly, I'll know where to find him when I need to talk to him. He is deeply engrossed in his own thoughts and not inviting conversation, so we walk in silence about two kilometers into the suburb of Windsor Gardens. It's a Housing Trust neighborhood, the rents subsidized for those on social security, and many of them are run down.

Suddenly, Ashoka announces, "We are here," and leads me down a narrow driveway. To my surprise, he keeps walking to the back of the house. He opens a door and ushers me in, saying, "It's not much, but it's home."

"Not much" is one of the great understatements of all time: one room, about 25 feet by 10, a toilet and shower hidden behind a curtain next to a basic kitchen with a stove and a washbasin. The only furniture is a small table with one chair, and a thin, aging mattress.

Two strikingly different areas, however, point to a man no longer attached to human comfort, yet passionate about things close to his spirit. The first is a shrine, a small table draped with a beautiful, golden cloth and adorned with incense, candles, a red flower and pictures of spiritual masters, some of whom I recognize. A small statue of the Buddha rests peacefully on the floor next to the shrine, alongside a small pile of well-read books. The whole area is exquisite and immaculate.

The second telltale area is a section of wall above the mattress that's decorated with pictures of two boys at ages from about five years old to their early twenties. Clearly, I think, these are his sons. My heart breaks for him when I realize that he has received no photos of his children for over a decade or more, except for a few tattered newspaper clippings showing an obviously important man in a business suit. I can't even begin to imagine the pain this causes him, but I daren't ask any questions.

Ashoka offers me the only cushion in front of his shrine and sits down on the floor next to me. As I sit, I'm thankful that he is saving me embarrassment by not asking what I think of his home.

"So, young one, where has the journey taken you this fine Christmas period."

I tell him of the marathon, the trip to Perth and the story of Robin. As I finish, I say, "It seems that I have a real fundamental fear of commitment. I'm not even able to commit to God."

"Not even able to commit to God. What *is* wrong with you?" He laughs heartily and I'm taken by his jovial mood. "Listen, I've never met a man or woman yet who has gone on this journey who was not afraid to commit to God.

"I don't understand."

"What we are talking about here is pretty heavy stuff. Making a commitment to God means surrendering your will to His. This drives the ego crazy, terrifies it even. And I do not suppose you would tell me your ego is totally tamed?"

"Of course not."

"It is perfectly natural to be afraid to commit. This fear of commitment is deeply rooted in a lack of trust for oneself. This lack of trust is a tool of the ego. It stems from the fact that you think you must be responsible for your life, rather than letting God do the work. If you can accept that you are a spirit being, then you can trust yourself totally, for you realize that you have access to all the wisdom and power of the universe."

"Just like the water in the cup remembering that it has access to the power of the ocean?"

"Exactly."

His words comfort me and I'm relieved to discover I'm not alone in feeling fear at the thought of committing my life to God. This gives me the confidence to raise the issue of my purpose. "Ashoka, there are some things that I haven't shared with you before. I'm sorry, I just couldn't talk about them."

"It would amaze me if that were not the case. Do you want to talk about them now?"

"Yes." So I tell him about the messages in New York, and since my return, and the latest visions in Perth, including the one with Jesus. "What does it all mean?"

"Fascinating, absolutely fascinating. My boy, you are in for one mighty powerful ride. My suggestion is that you just hang on and enjoy it, for if you resist, it will torture you."

"But I don't understand how this can be happening."

"Let me try to explain it in the best way I can. The teachings I believe in say that each soul comes to Earth with a specific mission to carry out. When we are born, our soul knows what it is supposed to do, but the mind and body are not well enough developed to carry out the mission. During the infant months, the mission is forgotten, by most of us anyway, and we become initiated into the world of our parents and their belief system. At some time in the future, some of us realize that we are going in the wrong direction, that there must be more to life."

"Oh yes, I recognize that in me. That's exactly what happened."

"When this happens, we go searching. We are not sure what we are searching for, but we go on a journey anyway. The real purpose of the journey is to discover what our true mission is, here on Earth, and to pursue that mission. Many people search all their life and never find it, but you, my young friend, have discovered it in only a year or so. When you discover your mission, it takes hold of you, it becomes your passion, and it becomes your life."

"So what do I do with it."

He gives me a funny look as if to suggest I haven't been listening to him. "Nothing. You do nothing. You are blessed at being shown these things, but you are not ready yet. You will know when the time comes for you to move. It will feel right at the time."

"How do I do nothing with it?"

"That, my boy, is your ego talking. Remember, you are not responsible. God is. Your higher self is. They will let you know when you must act. For now, just follow their guidance."

"But why me? Why am I being given all this information? And why can't I yet buy into it?"

"That is because of your fear of commitment. It is the same underlying fear of not being able to trust yourself. I cannot give you any advice here. You will just have to learn how to trust yourself, and how to trust God."

"Ashoka, tell me, where does Jesus fit into all this?"

"Now that is an interesting question. I do not know. You will just have to wait and see how it all unfolds."

"But what does it mean for my relationship with my teacher?"

"Nothing. At your teacher's level, they are all one."

"I don't understand?"

"Both your teacher and Jesus have attained a state where they are fully conscious of the ocean. They no longer see themselves as the water in the cup, but as an integral part of the ocean. In this sense, they are the same. In the human, they are separate, but at the spiritual level, they have attained the highest understanding and as such, are the same. Your higher self must have a reason for introducing Jesus to you, one that we are not aware of, but it does not harm the relationship you have with your teacher. He is not attached to you, only to your soul's manifestation."

I still don't understand, but at least his words are comforting and, walking home, I marvel at the magical inner world unfolding in my life.

Part 6 • God Descends

I Stop Running

A T THE END of January, I'm due to fly to New Zealand on a business trip. A few days before I leave, Robin stops by to discuss an upcoming trip to Canberra, a drive of about 1200 kilometers each way. I plan to take my car and a few other people.

"There's a change in plan, Alistair. More people are coming so we're going to hire a mini-bus."

"You know, I've been thinking," I reply, "something's come up at work and I might not be able to go."

Robin looks at me with a funny smile on his face, and I burst out laughing as it hits me. "There I go again, looking for excuses not to do something because it's been taken out of my control."

Robin laughs with me, "Hey, brother, it was pretty obvious to me, but I didn't want to say anything."

"Why not? You're not supposed to let me get away with things like this remember."

We talk about my fears for a few minutes and then I say, "I'm definitely going to Canberra by whatever means is best for everyone. I'm not going to be controlled by my fears any more."

My need to be in control has come up again, and with the trip to New Zealand less than a week away, I sense it won't be long before I have to confront this fear head on. A country I've never been to, I know no one there, and for the most part, I'll be traveling alone—all the ingredients to bring out my worst anxieties.

A growing anticipation of the battle looms within me, tinged with excitement at the thought of confronting and defeating my fears, of not being in control.

I take the anticipation/anxiety cocktail into my evening meditation. I've come to recognize that I'm often blessed with wonderful
inner experiences just before a major challenge. I see it as God's
way of filling me with His light and love before going into battle
with my fears. This evening, my teacher appears and I stand before
him, asking for guidance, "Please help me overcome my problems
with control and anxiety."

Devoid of emotion, he says, "No! I will not let you tackle bits
of it. You must tackle the whole issue."

What does he mean by this, I wonder, as he walks away, playing
a sort of wind instrument, like a flute. Suddenly, a mountain of light
rises out of my heart calling me to climb it. I see my inner being
struggle up the mountain, the exertion taking its toll. The temptation
to slip back down to the safety of the ledge below grows, but fighting off the desire for security, my inner being climbs with renewed
vigor. A rocky outcrop, jutting out at an alarming angle, materializes, like a raging bull charging at a matador. As I climb around the
grim face of desolation, half upside down, I hear my teacher's voice,
"You must expose yourself if you are to move forward."

Driven by the knowledge of the finality of failure, I struggle
over the ledge to the next level, and am greeted by my teacher,
who stands calmly waiting for me, showing no signs of exertion.

Surprised, I ask, "How did you get here?"

"There is another way. What have I taught you before? You are
so busy fighting yourself that you forget that love is the way."

Love and relief sweep through me at the thought that perhaps it's
not going to be so hard. He carries on, "In the past, you had to keep
people away from your heart, mind and emotions. That was because
you were vulnerable and insecure. It was too threatening to let them
in, because you did not have God. You did not have me. You did not
have the light of your soul. So you did not know how to deal with life
through love. But now you know. Now you can accept yourself as
having been this way, and know that it is no longer necessary. No
one can harm you now that you have your soul's light. So tackle your
problem through love. You do not have to lose your joy."

I hear the message and want to embrace it, to become the
essence of my teacher's words, but I can't. When I leave the medi-
tative state and move back into my daily existence, doubt and fear
once more creep into my life.

Three days later, as I try to meditate, fears over my trip surface again, preying on my peace like a thirsty leech. As I grapple with the constricting chains of my fears, my angels appear, both the male and female, who first appeared in San Francisco and have visited me sparingly since. They beckon me, and lead the way down a path of light, to a place deep within myself. Appearing from the light, in the depth of my being is a beautiful young woman, emanating such love that she can only be the most precious representation of my inner self, my soul.

She is divine, her unparalleled beauty radiating from every pore, and as we stare at each other, a backdrop of purple and gold light mystically materializes. Unable to hold back my feelings, I cry to my inner female, asking for forgiveness for all the pain I've caused her.

"Stop whimpering," she commands. "You are simply indulging in the past and looking for pity. This does nothing for me. I do not need this, I always forgive you. What you should ask for is self-acceptance and self-forgiveness. Look positively forward and move onwards."

Once again, my inner being has exposed me by cutting through the shields of my fears, barriers of falsity erected to protect myself, in a time where I knew no love from within. I *am* indulging myself in self-pity, rather than accepting ownership of my fears and imperfections, and moving on from there.

The scene changes, and a silvery, gold ball emerges before me, brilliant light shining from apertures all around it. Then a bright beam of light radiates from the ball of light in my heart, and I watch in amazement as a huge being emerges from the ball, a being in human form, but with beautiful white wings, like a giant bird. As he flies out of my chest and soars gracefully into the sky, I feel as though my soul has left my body, my heart the aircraft hangar waiting patiently for its owner's return.

A deep voice, the Source itself booms out, "I exist in the silence of your heart."

With these words echoing through me, the meditation comes to a close, and my heart is inundated with a magic concoction of power and love, as the great man/bird returns from his flight of freedom. And I know that I'm ready to go to New Zealand.

I arrive in Wellington on Thursday and have two successful days. On Friday afternoon, I pick up the rental car for the weekend's drive from Wellington to Auckland, about 800km, through New Zealand's volcanic region. The clerk asks for my driver's license, and as she hands it back, I notice that it expired four weeks ago. Of course, she should check the expiry date, and should not give me the car without a current license, but she overlooks it and hands me the keys.

Returning to the hotel, I call my secretary. "Jessy, please call the Adelaide police department and work out the best way to get my driver's license fixed up. I imagine it will be a simple matter of letting them know and having them give me an extension, like you can with an insurance policy cover note."

"I hope so," she says, cautiously.

"Well, if you can't get me one, I don't want to know. Then, at least I can act in ignorance."

I go out for a jog and, on my return, there's no message yet from Jessy. Not wanting to hang around waiting, I call her.

"I didn't know what to do. You said you didn't want to know if there were problems."

Concern rising in my throat, I ask, "What do you mean? What did they say?"

"They can't give you an extension. You have to come in personally, have a new photograph taken and sign some forms explaining why it wasn't renewed on time."

"This is ridiculous. Surely it can't be that hard. What happens if I just drive?"

"You'll be driving without a license and won't be insured if there's an accident."

My God, I'd be crazy to risk it. How could I have let this happen? I never received a renewal notice. Then I realize what happened. I have a five-year license, and when I left Belinda, I had my mail redirected for a year, picking up all the annual mail. But that was three years ago, so my renewal notice went to the old address and would have been returned. I drive a company car so there's no car registration in my name. Damn. A three-day drive ahead and no license!

"Okay, thanks, Jessy. I'll call them myself and see what happens."

I get the same message. The person I speak to is apologetic, but the answer is the same. "Sorry, Mr. Smith, but there's absolutely no way I can help you."

Part of me wants to get mad at the system, but another, more rational part of me takes over and I somehow stay calm. I recall Nelson Mandela's words about his time in prison, when he was able to separate the system from the individuals working in it. So instead of getting angry at the system, I plead with the clerk.

"Please look into your heart and see if there's a way to overcome the system and help a fellow South Australian in an overseas country and in trouble."

After a brief silence, I hear a click. All government phone calls are routinely recorded to check on the quality of the staff, and I suspect that it's just been turned off. Then I hear, "Can you wait for a moment please, Mr. Smith."

After a moment she returns. "There may be a way, but I need to talk to my supervisor."

While she is gone, I offer the situation to God. I'm surprised to feel happy to accept whatever the outcome is as being the way it's meant to be. Perhaps I would have had a car accident on this trip and this is to prevent me from going? But I'm not giving up without a fight.

She comes back on the line. "There is a way, but you have to get someone to bring the renewal fee into our office in Adelaide and we'll exchange forms by fax."

Her voice has changed and I detect an edge of excitement in it. She seems to have taken up a personal challenge to beat the system and get this stranger his driver's license. But it's three o'clock on the Friday before a long weekend, so we have to work quickly.

After several phone and fax calls, my license arrives, the note on the fax cover sheet simply reading:

Mission accomplished. Have a great weekend.

What joy! The clerk had so many excuses not to do this, but took it as a personal goal to get a driver's license for a complete stranger. I'm obviously meant to go on this trip. Another aspect of this episode fills me with joy. In the past, I would have used this as an excuse not to head off into the unknown. I would have indulged in self-pity and stayed in Wellington, then caught a plane to Auckland. But I'm not running any more, I'm no longer indulging in excuses. The messages of the previous week are having an impact. But unknown to me, this was a molehill compared to the mountain that would soon challenge me.

Early Saturday morning, I start out energized with freedom, eager to explore. On approaching Wanganui, however, at the entrance to the National Park area, my mood changes. I had planned to arrive in Auckland on Sunday in time to meditate with friends. Since I've already told them I'll be there, to my mind, that's a commitment that I must keep. But now I'm on the road, it's obvious that to explore as I intend will take longer and I won't get to Auckland in time for meditation. Okay, so what does it matter if I'm not there? Surely I'm the only one who's worried about whether I make it or not? But it's not that simple. I created the expectation in others, so I'm responsible for meeting it. Oh God, I'm drowning in my own limitations.

As I drive, I detach from my emotions and observe how I'm reacting. Restricting my freedom for no good reason is ridiculous, but I can't do anything about it. And so the inner battle rages. A man liberated from his past through the discovery of an inner life, a man determined to cast off the bondage of fear that has shrouded his life battles a man caught in the grip of his own fears, and resisting at all costs the light increasingly pouring from his heart. *Who's gonna win, Alistair?*

I make a decision. No matter how negative my thoughts, no matter how much anxiety sweeps through me, I'm going to follow my heart and go wherever it takes me. I will not let my need to control, to meet others' expectations, to gain their approval interfere with a weekend in nature.

At the Tourist Bureau, I ask about places to find peace and harmony. The Tongario National Park captures my attention and pulls my heart towards it, so I head for the remote mountain park, a ski resort in winter, but a paradise for walkers in the summer month of January. As I drive up the mountain, rain sheets down in torrents, visibility about 100 yards, and I'm tempted to forget the whole idea. Ignoring the temptation to turn and run, I enter the park office and the ranger recommends walking to a nearby scenic waterfall.

The walk starts further down the mountain, beyond where the rain has cast its gloomy net, and I head out into the wilderness. I didn't come prepared for wilderness hiking but that's not going to stop me. Walking through the peaceful terrain, I sense God is with me. Just as I reach the waterfall, the rain starts in and my running shoes quickly soak through. Commonsense dictates turning back to avoid blisters, but I know I have to push on, that this waterfall, beautiful though it is, isn't why I'm here.

After 30 minutes of the mud trying to suck my shoes off my feet, a distinctive rocky outcrop draws me to it. I get chills when I see the eerie resemblance to the rock I sometimes see myself sitting on during meditation. It's well off the track and I have to scramble over wet, slippery rocks. By now, my clothing is soaked, but I am undeterred. The sight of the craggy rock emerging above the low, undulating hills takes my breath away. Distracted, I lose my footing, fall over in the mud, and slide several yards on my rear. Oh, what fun! I feel like a kid playing truant on a summer's day, escaping to the fun of the outdoors. As I look down at my bedraggled appearance, I roar with laughter.

The rock draws me ever stronger, like a moth to a flame, and I scrabble to a lofty perch from which I see the valley below unfolding in a rolling expanse of green through which a river gorge meanders like a giant snake.

Intuitively, I look at the sky and start to meditate, my gaze drawn to a bird wheeling majestically above the outcrop. It epitomizes freedom, simply drifting where the wind takes it, but at the same time able to turn and fly into the wind if it chooses. As I watch the bird, transfixed by its flight of freedom, I'm transported to another dimension, and a voice resounds in my mind, "You do not have to be bound by others' expectations. Indeed it is you, not others, who create these expectations. You can let go and be free, just like the bird. This freedom is not something you have to fight for, you just have to accept it. Your freedom is already within you. Nobody can take it away from you, nobody, that is, except yourself."

With a clarity matched only by the mountain air around me, I realize this is exactly what I've been doing for as long as I can remember—giving my freedom away.

A sudden squall signals that it's time to move on. The gift I came for has been received. With the blisters on my heels screaming for respite, I find the path, now a muddy rivulet, but I don't care; all that matters is that my heart guided me to my rightful destination this afternoon.

Filled with peace, I head to Taupo, hoping to find a quiet little cottage nestled in the bush somewhere, and stay for two nights. As I approach Taupo, however, I begin to panic, first a trickle, quickly becoming a flood, as anxiety consumes me. It's a long weekend. What if I can't find anywhere to stay? What if all the good places are booked? No reservation. My God, what am I doing? I must be crazy. My emotions twist in agonizing contortions, unwilling to join the adventure my heart so desperately seeks.

Far from the secluded holiday retreat I hoped for, Taupo is actually a busy lakeside resort, the main street lined with motels, all looking much the same. This is definitely not what I had in mind. My spirits crash in flames, leaving me a burnt out wreck. What happened? An hour ago, I was overflowing with peace after a wondrous adventure in the mountains, and now this.

At the Information Center, rather than ask about the rural retreat of my dreams, I grab a bundle of brochures and flee. I run, looking for a place to hide, unable to think with any independence or creativity. My confidence gone, I book into the first place with a vacancy, a box with a view of other boxes. I'm out of my safety zone, no control over my environment, inadequate, a lonely child lost in a strange land, with no familiar landmarks.

I'm famished, not having eaten since breakfast and it's now six o'clock. In the vegetarian restaurant next to the motel, I can't decide between take-out and eat-in, so I mumble something about coming back later and flee, confidence shot. Back in the seclusion and safety of my room, I think that even by my old standards, this is bad.

In the bathroom mirror, I tell myself, "My God, Alistair, you've got to do something! You have to overcome this! What are you achieving by running and hiding. Didn't you declare earlier you weren't going to run any more? What about your commitment to yourself to follow your heart and stand up to any negativity that throws itself your way? Well, you're not standing up to it very well!"

I throw myself on the bed and continue the tirade. "This is ridiculous. If I can create all this negativity all on my own, then I can also become positive, as well. Right?"

Suddenly, it's so clear that I roar with laughter. My God, you're testing me. The wonderful messages in the mountains, the emotional crash as I arrived in Taupo, and now the loss of confidence. If I declare to myself that I'm ready for anything, then of course my higher self will provide the opportunity to prove it. "Okay, I accept the challenge."

I leave the safety of the hotel room to walk along the shore of the lake. After breathing in the fresh lakeside air, I return to the hotel, shower, and stroll casually to the restaurant and a table for one. All traces of negativity have gone, cast out by a refusal to yield to my pre-programmed responses. I can't remember turning an attack of the 'negatives' around like this before, but it was easy once I accepted that I had the power to control my reactions.

Over a wonderful meal, I reflect on all the times I thought I'd overcome something, only for it resurface later at a deeper level. Why does that happen?

Next morning, I plan an early start. Despite all the positive talk and inner heroics, I still entertain the idea of getting to Auckland in time for meditation. The manager, outside sweeping the sidewalk, suggests I visit nearby Huka Falls. When he adds that I can get there via a pleasant running track, I forget my sore knees and the bandages on yesterday's blisters.

The falls are magnificent, an awesome combination of beauty and power. They sit at a point where the river narrows from about 300 feet to a channel about 30 feet wide, at the end of which are the falls, a drop of 15 feet. The narrowing causes the water to increase in depth and velocity, and it reaches the falls a mass of liquid fury. This spectacle of nature's wonder is inspiring, as if the power of the water has a message for me. Alone in the fresh morning air, I visualize the awesome strength of the raging water as the power of my soul, able to sweep away my worries and anxieties if only I can let them go.

The pain from the blister on my left heel has eased, so I decide to run further along the river. The track winds steeply upwards to a lookout point about 100 feet above the falls. The viewing platform protrudes about 10 feet out over the cliff face and as I lean over the railing, I recoil in horror. I'm afraid of heights but, in the spirit of challenge, I force myself to lean out over the railing and look down into the frothing white turbulence. Waves of fear roll through me, yet I force myself to look down until the fear is replaced by the exultation of success.

Elated, I continue running through a lightly wooded forest and emerge on a ledge with a 50 foot sheer drop to the water below.

The river is about 150 feet wide, the banks on both sides covered by evergreens. The river is crystal clear and I can see the rocky bottom, stones changing color as the sun reflects at different angles off the riverbed. In this heaven manifested on Earth by nature's hand, the presence of my spirit is strong, and I feel as if God has descended to the valley to bask with me in its glory. I feel myself letting go of the inner turmoil that's pursued me through New Zealand, as if the gentle warmth of Mother Nature is reaching out to caress my soul. I'm enjoying myself so much that the mere thought of getting back on the road appalls me, and so I resume my foray into the wilderness.

About 20 minutes later, the trail winds into a small pine forest, whose trees reach up like guardians, branches joining overhead to shut out the sun. Deep in the forest, the silence is absolute, musical in itself. A sharp pain shoots up the back of my neck where the neck spasms once tormented me and tension flows from my neck out into the forest, as if the trees are bending down to relieve me of my unwanted burden.

The blister on my left heel screams in protest but still I can't stop. Some inner command compels me to continue. Eventually the track becomes overgrown and narrows, so I have to slow down to avoid overhanging branches. Just as I'm about to turn back, the trail opens up to a grassy meadow alongside the river, now about 300 feet wide. I perch myself on the bank, about 10 feet above the river and look down into crystal clear water.

The peace and beauty is overpowering and once more I begin to meditate, drifting off to a world without care. A voice brings me back, not from within me, but from the outside, as if someone is sitting on the bank next to me.

"My child, look at the river. It is so beautiful. It has so much love. Yet it does not hide its beauty. It does not hide its love. No! It offers it to the world. It offers it to the fish that swim in it, to the birds that float gently on its surface, to the trees that hang their leaves in it and draw their sustenance from it through their roots. It even offers it to mankind to admire, to anyone who takes the time to look. But it does not thrust this beauty on the world. It does not thrust its love on anyone, but simply makes it available for all to see.

"Why can you not be like this, My child? Why do you have to hide your beauty, your love? Why do you cover it up? Deny it? Why are you afraid to let it be seen? Indeed how can you manifest the beauty and love that I have given you if you hide it from the world?

"So this is your challenge, My child. It is not enough to find beauty, peace and love for Me inside. You must manifest it and show the world that this is what I can give you. You must do this for Me."

Spoken by an unseen messenger of the Divine Creator, these words of truth reverberate through my mind, heart and beyond. I know my destination has been reached. This is what I came to hear.

After soaking in the atmosphere for a few more minutes, I head back. Reaching the pine forest, I slow to a walk and wander through the trees, touching their mossy bark. Their energy soothes me and calls me deeper into the forest. Retracing my steps, I come to the heart of the forest where the trees form an arch over the trail and shelter it from the penetrating sunlight. I sit in the middle of the trail and let the forest permeate me with its tenderness and love, washing away the fears and anxieties from my body.

I sense that it's time to depart the beauty and gentleness of the forest and am overcome with humility. Looking around at the trees, which seem more like friends, I instinctively bow to them and say out loud, " Thank you, thank you, forest, for letting me share this experience with you."

I finally leave the motel at about 11 a.m., and head for the volcanic region and its hot mud baths and sulfur formations. By 3 p.m., I've seen enough volcanic craters to last a lifetime, and my feet are telling me that more walking is definitely not a good idea. I could still make it to Auckland in time for meditation, but I haven't finished exploring yet. For a brief moment, the "should's" and "ought to's" resurface, but my driving need to satisfy the expectations of others has waned in the light of the morning's experience, so I head in the opposite direction, roll the window down, let the wind blow in my hair and follow my heart whence it takes me.

The next morning, I'm in a fine pickle. I arrived late the previous night from my tour around the north island of New Zealand and hoped to continue my exploration today, Monday. But my blisters have other ideas, the skin being completely worn away, exposing raw flesh on most of my left heel. I can't put my shoe on and the thought of driving all day without being able to explore on foot doesn't appeal. Still, it was worth it, I think, as I remember

Saturday's rain-soaked valley, and Sunday's river encounter. So, shortly before noon, confined to a motel room, I meditate.

I find myself walking though a dense tropical jungle. The sound of running water grows, and I emerge from the undergrowth to a breathtaking scene. A waterfall cascades over a rocky ledge, a 100-foot plunge to a turbulent pool below. Butterflies abound, skipping from flower to flower, and the sun beats down yet I feel no heat. At first, I don't see the old man sitting under a tree a few yards upstream from the falls, but he coughs gently to catch my attention.

As I approach, the old man who calls himself 'my wisdom,' says, "Hello, my boy, I thought you might need some help this day."

"What do you mean?" I ask, still trying to adjust to his intrusion of the peace of the waterfall.

"Do you mean to tell me you understand everything you have experienced over the past few days?"

"Er ... not really. It seems it's all about love, yet I still keep repeating the same lessons over and over."

"Yes, it is about love, but you are not living that. You are so used to fighting all your inner demons that you have difficulty changing that. But this will never get you to your goal."

"What do you mean?"

"When you fight your fears, you overcome them at one level, but they are not transformed. So they escape, go off to regroup and come at you on a more subtle level."

"So this is why I keep having to deal with the same issues, like my need to be in control?"

"Exactly. But there's another way, you know. Accept all of these things you consider negatively as being a part of you. Do not reject them, do not fight them. Offer them your love, embrace them and they lose their power. You cannot change something you do not accept as belonging to you. Embrace the darkness within you and you can transform it."

"Is it really that simple? How can I feel so much love within me and yet still react so negatively at times."

"Yes, in some ways, it is that simple but in other ways, it is not. What was it our Father told you at the river? Remember this well. Changes take place at an inner level, the transformation is ready to be revealed to the world, but you are not able to do it. You must bring the inner transformation into your outer life."

"But how do I do this?"

"Your reactions are being controlled by your mind. All your life, you have reacted in a certain way, and these reactions have become a pre-determined program that dictates how you respond. It is time for you to realize that you have the power to change these reactions. But it will not happen overnight. You must consciously bring the inner being, where the transformation has taken place, into your outer actions."

"But how?" I repeat.

"You did it this weekend. But I cannot tell you more, for you will not understand it. You must experience the process yourself so that you can become the reality, rather than hearing my empty words. But I will be with you all the time."

My wisdom stands and walks off along the riverbank, turning to look at me with great compassion. "Remember, there is only one way to truly overcome your fears, and that is through love. Love is more powerful than fear."

With this, he disappears, and the vision fades. What a message! Old man wisdom was right, I had done it on Saturday, when I was overcome with anxiety in Taupo, when my confidence deserted me, and I turned it around. So I can do it again. I have finally stopped running! I stood my ground and faced the truth about myself and I know I'm not going to run from myself any more.

A few days after returning from New Zealand, I'm sorting out some old paperwork and I come across the letter I wrote to my father three years earlier but never mailed on the pretext that he wasn't ready for it. As I re-read it, tears well up in my eyes and the reason I didn't send it is apparent. I used Dad as an excuse, but the truth was that I was scared to open up my heart to my own father, scared that perhaps he might want to open up as well.

So, three years late, I mail it to him with all the love in my heart. A few days later, he calls. My heart leaps into my throat at what he's about to say, but he doesn't mention the letter at all. Instead, we talk about sports, the weather, and other inconsequential things, but I know he read it because his voice is different, more open, a genuine warmth I can feel even over the phone. And after decades of distance, feeling the warmth of my father's love means more to me than I can even begin to describe.

Further Guidance

A T WORK, A new project puts me in the limelight, aggressively promoting my views. As a result, the old self-importance monster creeps up on me. At the same time, another personal conflict arises at the Center, and people seek me out, asking me to apply my managerial skills to the troubled waters.

In the now familiar dilemma, part of me wants to become involved and help the Center out, while another part holds back, afraid of my ego wanting to take responsibility for other people's problems? Is it just another way for me to express my self-importance? Whenever I promote my views more than necessary, a warning ache in my heart tells me that I'm behaving inappropriately. While I struggle with the growing conflict, I revisit the question of leadership and love. What does it mean to lead through love, as I was shown in Perth? And just how do I do this?

On February 10, I'm in Sydney on business, and in my morning meditation, I find myself on a beach looking out to sea at dusk, as the sun drops over the horizon. Behind me, a city is burning to the ground, flames raging out of control, fiery fingers reaching upwards in eerie salute to the darkening sky.

A strange heaviness clings to me, a numb detachment, even dejection. As the last of the sun slips from view, the sky opens up in front of me, and two angels emerge and glide silently towards me. A booming voice reverberates through the heavens and transfixes me to the spot. "My child, you must go back and finish your work."

"But what can I do?"

"You will know what to do! You must go back!" The authority renders disobedience unthinkable.

A gathering of ten or twelve people I don't recognize walks down the beach towards me, led by my teacher. Sparkles of brilliant glitter fall from the sky and into every cell of my being, and I know I'm being prepared for some task. My teacher disappears, leaving us alone on the beach. They gather round me and we embrace in oneness.

We begin meditating on the desolate beach while the fire rages in the background and smoke blots out the evening stars. A powerful love flows from my heart and from the hearts of the others and coalesces at the center of the group into a glowing mass of energy from which shoots a powerful beam of love light straight into the sky. Almost immediately, dark storm clouds form and rain begins to fall, increasing to a deluge that quickly extinguishes the fires ravaging the city. As we continue to meditate, the rain stops, the clouds clear, and even though it's still night, the sun shines through the sky and baths me in peace.

An hour later, sitting in the hotel room eating breakfast, I ponder how this latest vision relates to what's going on in my life. Does the city represent what's happening at the Center, or is it broader, planetary even, perhaps reflecting the state of man's inner life? Whatever it represents, the message is very clear. The way to overcome these problems is always the same, through love.

After breakfast, I check my answering machine and find a message from Sabrina, surprising since we've not spoken for nearly two months, after I curtailed my increasing emotional dependency on her. She ends her message with a cheerful, "Where have you been all my life?"

After our exchange of letters in December, communication has proved too difficult, and I have distanced myself, despite what I said about the importance of our friendship. I've thought about her, however, and she's appeared in several meditation visions, so I know I've not yet erased my attachment to her. This is a chance to test what turmoil reopening contact creates.

I quit work early, return to the hotel room, and call her. I psych myself up for the conversation, but nothing could have prepared me. Believing that my feelings for her are stronger than her's for me, I expect her to be cool and controlled. Wrong! She emotes at length over her pain at backing off from our relationship, at one point saying, "I feel as if you've taken a part of me, and that a part of my heart will always belong to you. I wish I could cut myself in two, so that one of me could be with you."

Ironically, I find myself being strong for her since I've already let go to an extent. Her confusion is evident as she cries for me yet pushes me away. We agree that I'll call her next time I'm in Sydney, on the basis of a friendship only, she is quick to reiterate, although I can tell a part of her wants much more.

A few nights later, after meditation at the Center, a few of us meet to discuss organization matters, but some personal wounds get opened up. I know I could step in and take charge, but I'm still the newest member so I keep a low profile. In the following morning's meditation, I ask God for guidance on the role He wants me to play. The next evening, while running, my mind is filled with a poem that just pops in, line by line:

Oh God! What Should I Do?

Aspiration, inspiration, love and delight.
Fear, obligation, control and fright.
Conflict rises where harmony is due.
Oh God, please tell me, what should I do?

Skills to apply, I have my share.
But am I supposed to bring them to bear?
Or let it go, and get on with my own?
Oh God, how do I use the seeds You have sown?

Caught in the middle with nowhere to move.
But surely things will have to improve.
Everyone's facing fears, doubts, too.
Oh God, please tell me, what should I do?

It perfectly captures my conflict. Since I started meditating, I've written a handful of poems, but I've never received one like this. Two mornings later, I'm running again and the same thing happens, only the second poem answers the first:

My Child This is What You Should Do!

My child, you asked Me, What should I do?
Yours is not to solve their problems.
They must reach out to Me on their own.
My child, I shall tell you what you should do.

Offer the love that flows from within you.
Speak from your heart when I inspire you.
Let your light shine whenever I guide you.
This, My child, is what you should do!

You have your own work I have given you.
Let Me inspire you and manifest through you.
Listen to your inner voice as I speak to you.
This, My child, is what you should do!

A week of being a mental pendulum is over and I now have my answer. Over the next week, 13 poems similarly appear as God reveals Himself in increasingly more personal ways, as a caring and loving guardian, all of them with a relevant message about love. The final poem arrives during meditation in a Canberra hotel room with such force that I stop meditating and write:

My Child

Like a glowing star from heaven you came.
Falling to Earth to play in My game.
To shine your light for others to see.
Showing to them what love could really be.

But you fell asleep along the way.
Your heart lost, your mind ruled the day.
Deep in darkness, you had no time for Me.
Without your faith, I could not set you free.

Your soul knew the truth of your life all along.
It longed to be free, to sing its own song.
Slowly, so slowly, you began to ask why,
Dark clouds always hung over your heart's sky.

So I sent you a message, time to wake up.
Time to start filling your heart's empty cup.
To do the things you came here to do,
And to your very self, your soul, be true.

Now your heart is open, love has started to flow.
You know what the truth is, I have shown you so.
To show the world what real love can be,
Love that can liberate, lead and set free.

The love that is sung of in songs this is not.
Love that binds and possesses, our hearts get so caught.
No! This is a love that can lead and inspire.
And with which we can soar ever higher and higher.

My child, for Me, I ask you go freely,
Now that your truth I have revealed so clearly.
Go deep in silence, I will be your guide.
In your greatest need, I'll be by your side.

So do not doubt, not for one moment long.
Let your heart sing its own blossoming song.
Go on, shine your light, like a star up in space.
I will flood you with compassion, love and My grace.

My child, we spoke not so very long ago,
About things that you wanted so dearly to know.
You asked me then, Father, what should I do?
And I wanted to recap my answer to you.

Open your heart, Oh please, do not hide it.
Let your love flow, Oh no, do not bind it.
Let your light shine, in the way I inspire you.
Listen to your inner voice, and know I will guide you.

The messages are unmistakable—the voice in the river in New Zealand; the growing feeling of love I experience towards God; the poems—clearly, I'm not to get embroiled in the Center's management. Once that clicks into place, any motivation to do so evaporates. Instead, it's clear to me that I'm to express the love I have received from God, to express it in writing and in words, and let His beauty show through my actions. This is a departure from my training, but it feels so comfortable that I make a conscious vow to keep out of Center management unless I'm guided inwardly. Instead, I'll actively reach out to people's hearts by speaking openly about my change in focus. Also, I plan to distribute the poems and encourage other people to contribute their poetry to an anthology.

I want to share the poetic messages of love with Ashoka and seek his wisdom on what they mean in the larger arena of my life, so one evening that's perfect for a walk, I decide to go to see him. As he answers the door, a huge grin breaks over his face. "Ho, young one, where have you been?"

"Where have I been? I haven't seen you on the trail lately."

"Oh," he says, his brow furrowing, "My knees are not so good at the moment, the old bones are playing up."

I hadn't realized he had difficulty walking, my question made in jest. He has a second cushion in front of his shrine so that we both sit in comfort. After I recount my inner adventures, he says, "Ah, the power of love. You see, young one, there really are only two states one can exist in. Fear and love." He pauses for a moment as if reminiscing.

"We have many names for these states. Fear gets called guilt, doubt, insecurity and anxiety, but in the end, they are all emotions that are invoked through an underlying fear. Similarly for love. When we express emotions of joy, beauty and peace, we are experiencing life through a state of love. We always operate out of one of these states, but never both at the same time."

"I'm not sure I see what you're saying, Ashoka. Many times, I don't feel I'm operating in either fear or love."

"Ah, yes, but that is because you are talking in the traditional definition, which is limited. So many of our actions are initiated in a state of fear. Unfortunately, it is the prevailing state in which our society operates. Of course, I do not mean the extreme case of fear, where we are scared for our physical or personal safety."

"I still don't get you."

"Let me give you an example. When you are faced with a choice of doing something different, or following the same routine, most people chose the same routine. In reality we have the choice of doing something different every day, but we follow a routine because it is safe. In this way, we are operating in the fear of the unknown. How many people go to the same boring job every day because they know they can do it without being extended? Again this is a subtle example of how much our lives are controlled by fear. Fear of facing challenges, fear of failure, and so on. It is fear that keeps us in our established paradigms, and allows us to be controlled and manipulated.

"Now, if we operate in love, we can offer love to everyone around us. Life takes on a whole new meaning. We experience spontaneous joy and life becomes an adventure, where there are no boundaries.

"Importantly, it is not only ourselves we impact in the choice of our state of existence. Every person we come in contact with experiences, to some extent, the state in which we are existing at the time."

His face glows with excitement as he talks and I ask, "Ashoka, do you always live in a state of love?"

"Now remember, my boy, I am the teacher here, so it is not about me," he gently rebukes, and then laughs from deep in his belly, "Oh yes, I know the truth of what I say, but I never really got there. I still have things that hold me back, fears that stop me living in love. I have tasted it, held it in my hand, but then it slipped away again."

A wistful look steals his radiant face and he turns to look at the photos of his boys. Silently, I curse myself for bringing him down, but he quickly gathers himself and continues, "But you, young one, God is clearly telling you that it is time to move out of fear, that you are ready to move to a state of love, no doubt."

"But how do I do this?"

"Ha! Only you can work that out. But I know from my own experience that when fear of any type exists, love will not flow. I failed to face all my fears. I met a hurdle too big and it stopped me in my tracks, it blocked my path to a life in love. You must not let this happen, my son."

He leans across, puts his hand on my knee and looks at me with imploring eyes, pleading with me not to make the same mistakes he did.

"Young one, your visions are so powerful they all but over-whelm me. The message is clear and you must not turn your back on His call. You must never let a hurdle stop you in your tracks. And be sure that you will be asked to face some big hurdles."

Walking home, I feel uneasy, fearful even, that Ashoka seems to be overwhelmed by what's happening. He's always been so con-fident, but this evening, I pushed him out of his comfort zone. The vision of the burning city hit him hard, and in retrospect, he was struggling to understand where I'm being called to go. The fact that my trusted counselor is baffled bothers me. And I know I don't understand what I'm getting myself into, but then, what choice do I have? As Ashoka said, "You must not turn your back on His call."

So I continue struggling with how to live in love. I feel I should already be able to do it, yet I've just been introduced to the idea and have much to learn and experience before I fully understand what it all means.

My Spiritual Pride

T's THE FIRST week in March and I'm meditating at the Center. The inner atmosphere is serene, entry into the silent spaces coming easily. After about ten minutes, an inner cry calls out to God and an image appears in my heart of a monk in an ancient monastery. Intuitively, I know it's me. After several minutes, during which I strive unsuccessfully to see what he's doing, the image changes. Now I'm on a train rattling and swaying through rural Southeast Asia. Then I'm standing on the balcony of a secluded beach house overlooking the sea, using the solitude that this house offers to write. Are these scenes from past lives or future possibilities? I don't know. A woman puts her arms around me from behind, and I know she's helping me with my work. Sabrina? No! I must vanquish those thoughts, yet after our recent phone call ....

Now I'm one of a group of chanting monks, calling for God, intently engaged in some serious endeavor. Moving on, I descend even deeper into my heart. Suddenly, a great explosion of light ignites the serenity, and light floods out of me into the candle-lit room, my hands and arms tingling with energy. I dissolve into particles of light dispersed across the universe, with no focal point to call "me." I lose track of how long I remain in this blissful state of dispersed energy.

A waterfall appears, a towering cascade of light, and I sense that I am the light flowing over the cataract and being carried downstream to a silent pool, out of which emerge two figures. I am one; the other is the wise old man who represents God. He says, "My child, you are doing very well and now you are ready for your next challenge: to learn not to anticipate the reactions of other people to what you do and say. You limit yourself by thinking that others will react negatively. This simply feeds negative thoughts about your work.

"When you are inspired to do something, do it for the inspiration alone, unconcerned over the reaction of others. This is the secret. Always speak with humility and sincerity. And never speak badly of another. If you do this, you need not worry about how others react."

Message delivered, He disappears. Of course, I think, He is absolutely right. I *have* been worrying about what people will think if I read out a poem or if I speak from my heart. Yes, I'm taking responsibility for my actions in love, but I place a veil of fear over my love, preventing it from flowing naturally.

My love for God, my faith in Him, reaches new levels. I feel like surrendering to the light within, and flying free in the sky of golden delight till I arrive at His feet, where He can cradle me in His loving arms and flood me with His intoxicating love, a love I've never known in the past on the human level. I know that this love, God's love, is not going to disappear, that I'm not going to lose it. No, on the contrary, I've only tasted the very tip of His love, and it's only going to grow more and more beautiful.

March brings a hectic pace at work, with a major acquisition being targeted that distracts me from my constant ruminations over my spiritual direction. I wake up on March 16, my son's birthday, feeling like a young child myself, caught in a raging river in full flood.

As I'm about to come out of meditation, a vivid image forms, and I'm caught in a rowdy mob, jostled and elbowed by the unruly crowd. Suddenly I realize what's happening. We are watching Jesus carry his cross through a narrow street. As the scene finishes, I recoil from the power of the images, still floating through my vision, and am crushed under an immense sadness, puzzled as to what this means.

As I say my closing prayer, a mournful cry rises from the silent depth of my inner sanctuary, a cry I did not start and cannot stop. I hear myself pleading with God, "Father, my Father, please show Yourself to me. Father, please take my mind so that it will not stop me seeing You."

Powerful ripples flow through my body, as if some inner aspect of me is exerting itself. After a bright flash, an image appears in which Jesus sits on the ground in the desert and calls to me. Sad and desperate for His forgiveness, I approach Him, my tortured words pleading, "How could I have stood back and watched you die?"

His compassionate answer soothes me, "Many rejoiced at my death, but you were saddened."

He smiles, and suddenly, he's gone.

"Please don't go," I implore.

Another flash of light almost blinds me, and Jesus says, "See, I did not die. You need not worry."

Tears flow down my physical face, my body flooded with humility and wonderment so powerful, yet sweet, ballooning up from a fathomless depth, and at the same time descending from somewhere far beyond the limits of the Universe.

My teacher appears next to Jesus and as they embrace, one of them says, "You do not need to say the words any more. You do not need to hear every word. Just intuit the meaning."

A collage of messages flashes across my mind, each striking me with a mixture of fear and excitement as its meaning permeates every cell of my being: "You are a very old soul, one of the older ones on Earth. You have a very important responsibility to carry out but one that will give you unlimited joy."

Jesus and my teacher merge before me, walk towards me and merge with me, engulfing me in bliss. "Can you tell me what my mission is," I ask.

"When you are ready, it will be revealed to you in more detail. Right now it is about love."

As their love flows into me, they continue with a warning, "But you must be absolutely careful about Sabrina. You are to have no emotional or romantic attachments."

They are gone. I should feel wonderful, but don't. "It's all an illusion," my mind carps, but, deep down, I know it's not.

Later, at work, I can't focus on anything, so in desperation, I call Robin. "I don't understand why I feel so flat."

"Hey, brother, it sounds like your mind is freaking out. The same thing happens to me sometimes."

"What do you mean?"

"Well, your mind has accepted a certain level of spiritual experience, but this morning pushed it way beyond its comfort zone. And it's fighting back."

"Yeah, that's exactly what it feels like."

"Your mind sets limits on you all the time and you've pushed it past those limits. Now it's trying to restrict your concept of reality to what it's comfortable with by saying your experience was an illusion. Hey, don't let it do it."

"I get it. My mind is like a big elastic band wrapped tightly around my perception of truth. When I enlarge my truth, it will stretch a little, but if I push too far, the tension becomes too great and it wants to spring back to its original size."

"That's one cool analogy."

"My God, Robin, it's hard to imagine just how much control our minds have over us. I mean, even though I'm aware of this, I seem powerless to stop its games."

"Yeah, well, just think. Before you had this awareness, it had total control over you. How much does it limit our life and what we think we're capable of."

"Yes, but let's turn it around. Imagine the wonderful capacity we can have if we're able to use our mind to project only positive thoughts. What a transformation would this make to our lives?"

"You got it, brother. Onwards and upwards."

"You're a marvel, my dear friend. Thanks for being there for me."

On Sunday morning, I settle into a long meditation. After about an hour of peace and light, I feel myself rising into the heavens and I see a familiar sight on my inner movie screen. Robin and I, as beings of light, are rising high into the Universe. Eventually, we arrive at a place shrouded in beautiful silvery light. Other souls and angels casually drift above what appears to be a soft, fluffy, white cloud. As we follow the path of light, Robin speaks quietly to me, so as not to disturb the tranquility of the scene, "This is as far as I can go for now."

Knowing I haven't yet reached my destination, I continue alone and soon come upon a large temple. Unseen hands usher me through the imposing entrance, and the wise old grandfather figure sits in the center of a huge, domed room. As usual, He glows in golden light and smiles when He sees me. Many other divine beings flank

Him, some I recognize—my teacher, Jesus, Krishna, Buddha and Mohammed—and some I don't know.

Unconditional love pours through the room, immersing me in a concoction of ecstasy and security that makes my knees wobble. Jesus rises and approaches me, looking younger and more playful than I've seen Him in other visions. He embraces me and takes me by the hand. I look across at my teacher who nods in reassurance. Jesus says, "You are mine! Your teacher is looking after you for me. My people are in trouble. They have lost their way. I am putting together an army of people to help, and I need you."

He takes me by the hand and we travel a great distance in a short time, until we come upon a mountain and ascend to a perch near the summit. He quells my multitude of questions with, "Meditate with me. That will give you all the answers you need."

It's been ten days since my last meeting with Ashoka, and I feel an urge to see him again. I don't want to become dependent on him, but I rationalize that since he, too, is opening up, he will be interested in my experiences. I arrive close to sunset, and he warmly invites me in, happy to have company. After recounting my two latest experiences with Jesus, I voice the concern that continues to grow within me, "Ashoka, I'm concerned that I feel special, that I will feel superior. I sense it creeping up on me at times."

"But you *are* special, my boy. We are all special in God's eyes."

"That doesn't exactly help me."

"Okay, spiritual superiority can be a great challenge for the seeker of God. I have met many spiritual people who consider themselves better than those less enlightened. But that is not the case. Indeed, we should feel ourselves fortunate to have received such grace."

"I know that, but it doesn't stop my ego wanting to take the credit."

"I cannot stop your ego playing its little games. But it seems to me that you are being hard on yourself, perhaps even indulging yourself and using your ego as an excuse."

"What do you mean by that?" I retort, taken aback by the suggestion that I'm using my ego as an excuse.

"You are so aware of your ego that I do not think it has a chance. You jump on it so quickly. But I get the impression you do not want to accept the blessings you are being given. Could it be that you are using the fear of your ego to provide you with an excuse not to move forward into the light? Young one, is your fear of your ego really only an excuse to stop you making a deeper commitment to God?"

Ashoka bellows this last sentence, which shakes the very foundation of my reality. Once more exposed for what I am, pretence stripped away by the penetrating insight of a wise old man, I see that my fear of committing to God looms from horizon to horizon, like the Great Wall of China.

Voice once again gentle and soothing, Ashoka continues, "You must remember that we are all equal in God's eyes. Your journey to enlightenment is happening now because He chose to wake you up and you accepted the challenge. God is having an experience through each soul on Earth, and each experience plays out in a different way. It does not make you any better than anyone else. Remember that."

"I know what you say about looking for excuses is true. But it's just that I'm afraid of going back to where I was. I feel such a difference and the thought of going back is terrifying."

"It is good to be aware of the grace you have received, but do not get caught in the trap of looking back. Accept the past as having provided you with valuable lessons but then turn your attention forward. You must always look forward, for the direction in which you look is the direction in which you will travel."

Ashoka pauses, allowing the wisdom of his words to sink in, and I am drawn to the concept of oneness. Part of me knows that we are all part of a great chain, not separate links, but I struggle with this, so used am I to seeing myself as a separate entity. "Ashoka, I hear what you say, but I still struggle with the concept of oneness. I guess I've always seen myself as separate, but are you saying that we're all links in a great chain, that as an individual link we're useless, but as a chain, working together, we're powerful?"

"Well, well, who's coming up with the analogies now?" he chuckles. "It is not a bad analogy, but I prefer a different way of looking at it. You see, the concept of the chain implies we are all exactly the same and that each link is interchangeable. I prefer to think that we are all unique, like pieces in a jigsaw puzzle, and we all have a special role to play in God's game."

"Yes, I like that."

"I like to look at mankind like a great mansion in which God lives here on Earth. Some of the rooms in the mansion have the lights turned on and some are in darkness. Just because your room has the light on it does not mean it is more beautiful or important than a room with the light off. The rooms with the lights on represent people who have undertaken their spiritual awakening, and the rooms in darkness are those who have not yet commenced their journey. It is easy for the spiritual person to feel superior because his light is on, but this is a great mistake.

"Your light is on simply because God, the owner of the mansion, has chosen to turn it on. But just because the light in the toilet is turned on, does this make the toilet a better room than the beautiful library or the grand ballroom, where God has not yet turned on the light? Clearly not! Each room in the house is as important as the next. It is just that each serves a different purpose. So, too, with people. We all have a different purpose to carry out for God, and we are all equally important."

"You make it so clear. What would I do without you?"

He laughs again, a hearty laugh, the type reserved for intimate times with a close friend. "Young one, you do not need me, you only think you do. There will come a time when you will teach this old man."

The conversation finds a natural pause and we both meditate for a few minutes, simultaneously coming back to resume our exploration of the truth. "Ashoka, the experiences with Jesus are really pushing the limits of my beliefs and understanding. I mean, I've always shunned Christianity and everything it stood for, and now I feel this overwhelming love for him."

"Jesus and Christianity are two different things. The love you feel is coming from the great spirit of the Christ embodied by Jesus. We have talked about this before. The Christ energy is not unique to Jesus. It is the same energy embodied by all the true spiritual masters. I do not claim to fully understand the relationship between the great masters. How could I? But essentially they are all of the one consciousness. And they all have the same message of love."

"The Christians I know would never agree with you."

"No, I am sure they would not, and they are entirely entitled to believe their truth, just as much as I am mine. But you see, we humans have a tendency to separate ourselves and erect barriers. You did that at the individual level. Established religion has just done it on a collective level. People have separated themselves from their brothers and sisters out of ignorance and fear."

"Yes, well, I certainly feel a relationship between Jesus and my teacher, who comes from a Hindu background. But it's strange, I feel a great love for Jesus, but there's something stopping the same love flowing to my teacher."

"That could be for many reasons. It seems as if Jesus is calling you to him, that is for sure, but there may be a more human explanation. Perhaps you have trouble accepting your teacher in the same way because you see him in the human form. Our mind has real trouble with this one. But because Jesus has left the physical plane, you see him as a spirit. It is often easier to surrender to a spiritual figure than it is to a spirit in a human body."

"Wow, you could be right. I really felt that conflict when I was in New York."

"Whatever the case, you should not be swayed by what others believe. You must believe what your inner self tells you. It knows the truth, and just look at the last vision you had—Jesus, Krishna, Buddha, all the great teachers of the past, standing side-by-side next to God. What more do you want? This is the truth. My boy, one day you will have to share these experiences with the world."

"No one would believe me. I mean, I struggle to believe it myself."

"Young one, do not fool yourself. The world is desperately in need of hope. Our only salvation is to realize that we are all one people, that we are all one spirit. Do not delude yourself or belittle yourself. One day, you will realize that it is your responsibility to share these things with the world."

As we sit in silence, I question Ashoka's words. Surely I can't tell the world of my visions. And yet, why did Jesus tell me, "My people are in trouble. They have lost their way. You need to help them."

When I can override my fear of feeling superior, of slipping back to my old ways, the messages are so clear. But I'm not yet ready to accept them.

Caught In Attachment's Web

I N SYDNEY FOR three days this week, I arrange to meet Sabrina for lunch on Thursday. Our greeting is cautious as we both gauge the other, but in minutes, it's as it's always been. After eating, we seek out our favorite corner in the park and continue our conversation. As time rolls effortlessly by, the magic increases and my spirit soars in the bliss of the afternoon sun. We talk of our love for God, we open our hearts to each other, and we let our souls sing a duet and dance with the angels in the beauty of the occasion. We hold each other gently in moments of tenderness and openly speak of how right it feels to be together.

After several hours of bliss and beauty, overlain with respect and understanding, Sabrina becomes very serious. "Today wasn't supposed to be like this. It's been the most perfect day."

I nuzzle her hair, and she nestles in my arms before continuing. "Part of me hoped that today wouldn't be like this. I didn't think it was possible for us to have another day like the last one. I guess that part of me was hoping it would be just ordinary, and then I could put my feelings down to one euphoric day, a one-off fluke. But today's been even better."

I hold her gently in my arms, not daring to move or speak, hardly daring to breathe for fear that I may upset the intimacy of the moment. "It's not fair. It feels so perfect being with you, yet I know that we can't be together. I really don't know if I can see you again because it's just too hard."

An inner warning looms up, and I remain silent no longer. "Sabrina, it *is* fair. God has given us this experience, and we do

220

have a choice. You and I can be together tomorrow if we choose to be, but we're both making the conscious decision that we're not going to be. We can't go on feeling like this is something we have no choice in. That'll only cause us more pain."

"I can't accept that, Alistair. It may be okay for you, but to me, it's impossible to contemplate damaging my family. It's not something I can even consider. So what choice do I have in the matter?" she snaps back.

There's nothing else to say. All we can do is to melt into each other's arms one more time before heading off from what may well be our last meeting. Not even a kiss has passed between us, yet the depth of feelings we evoke in each other is far beyond what I've experienced in previous relationships. I say goodbye to Sabrina with a promise that we'll both try to continue our friendship, but in the knowledge that, on some level, our emotions have a different agenda.

The next few days are turmoil. Despite all the warnings I've received about Sabrina and emotional attachment ringing in my ears, there's nothing I can do about it, and I feel myself sliding. I survive a little over a week before I finally yield and call her. In the heat of our emotions, an hour slips by unnoticed until she just falls apart, stripped naked by the honesty of the conversation and the desperate need of the moment. "Part of me wants to be with you so badly," she admits.

I just feel as if I love her so much that I don't think of myself, but rather I let my concern and compassion for her take priority. I tell her that I just want her to be happy, and to my surprise, she spits back dejectedly, "Happy? Sure! How can I be happy without you?"

Every warning bell in me rings. This is exactly the level of pain we have to feel if we're to let go of our emotional dependency and move to a new level of love. But how can I explain this to her? How can I explain something I don't even understand myself?

As she cries, the tendrils of pain creep out of the telephone and wrap themselves around my heart like an icy talon. Then without warning, she switches into professional control mode, a courtroom technique developed to catch opposing counsel off guard.

"I love the way you can switch just like that."

"Alistair, I can't afford not to be in control. I can't afford to fall apart. I have to take my feelings for you and bury them deep inside. I have no choice."

My God, how difficult it must it be for her. I'm in complete turmoil, but at least I can go home and be on my own. And I can share my feelings with Robin and Karen, but she doesn't have such a luxury, and must go home to her family, wearing a happy face as though everything's wonderful.

"There's always a choice," I remind her, a lifeline to catch her plunge into despair.

"No! There's no choice. I have no choice. I just have to bury this and get on with my life," she screams.

"Oh God," I pray silently, "please protect her from me, from herself, from whatever."

The next day, I couldn't feel flatter if a road-roller had run over me, and my mood worsens as the day progresses. I'm worried for Sabrina, but to be honest, I know I'm indulging in self-pity over the mess we've gotten ourselves into. On top of that, I'm missing her like crazy. Yet if I really loved her in a divine way, I reason, I would do whatever I must to stop all of this.

But there's just so much stuff I haven't yet worked through in terms of relationships and I'm really stuck straddling a ravine, one foot in the world of emotional attachment and the other planted in the freedom of the love that comes from my spirit. As my weight shifts from one foot to the other, I'm being torn apart inside. And, yes, I know this is a test, and there'll never be a better opportunity to transcend my past dependencies, so I must keep moving forward, but it's so hard.

The next week, I'm in Sydney again. Being so close to Sabrina unleashes a flood of emotions, and that night over dinner with Karen, I let it all out. As I complete the story, Karen frowns and says, "Something doesn't sound right to me."

"What do you mean?"

"Well, your attachment to Sabrina feels too extreme. I mean, you've had some pretty powerful visions telling you to let her go, and you know you have to, but still you can't."

"I love her. I've never felt this way with anyone."

"Yes, I can see that, but is this all it is? If you weren't on your spiritual path, if you weren't celibate, were meeting other women who were available, would your feelings towards Sabrina be so strong?"

"What are you getting at?" I ask warily, sensing that Karen is going into places I don't want to follow, and is about to reveal a hidden truth that I've been refusing to see.

"Maybe Sabrina represents much more than just Sabrina. Suppose she embodies the choice between your spiritual path and an intimate relationship. It seems to me that you feel that by letting go of Sabrina, you are saying goodbye to any and all future relationships. That this relationship is really about the choice between either a life of service to God, or a life where there is room for a woman, and that there's no middle ground."

She puts it so clearly that I sit in stunned silence as the truth of it washes over me. "Perhaps you're right."

Karen remains silent and I'm carried back to Christmas in Perth, when Jesus appeared in the ocean of peace, calling me to leave Sabrina behind. I felt the turmoil then of having to choose between Jesus, representing the spiritual path, and a relationship with a woman, representing the worldly path. "But I don't get it. I've had so many messages about a divine relationship, and I feel my spirit so alive when I am with her."

"But a divine love is free of attachment, is it not?"

"Yes."

"Well, you certainly aren't there with Sabrina, are you?"

"No, I'm not," I admit with resignation. I slump back in my chair, and Karen continues, "Alistair, perhaps you're meant to have a divine relationship with a woman, but it seems to me that, if this is the case, maybe you have to walk away from both Sabrina and your spiritual path, and find a new path for yourself."

"What!"

"Maybe you're attached to both Sabrina and the Center, or at least what they represent. You seem to have bound your future hopes in both of them, and in this way bound yourself. Perhaps it's time for you to cut these ties and let go of your dependencies, so that you can move forward in your life, trusting your own guidance."

"I can't even consider the thought of leaving the Center," I protest.

"I think you need to ask yourself why that is. Why is your spiritual growth so dependent on you continuing to be a member of the Center. It seems to me your passion for God is so strong that nothing will stop you pursuing Him."

As April rolls in, I'm at the bottom of a deep hole. On top of the Sabrina confusion, the takeover battle at work is escalating, and I'm working about 60 hours a week. In addition, I help out at meditation classes nearly every evening, and am still trying to write the book in my spare time, not to mention spending time with my children. My life is a carousel that's spinning out of control. Deadlines on all fronts and I can't take it any more. The neck spasms are back, which frustrates me. My accustomed light and joy have taken a vacation, and I'm struggling in their absence.

In the first week of April, I go to the Geelong center, an eight-hour drive, for their weekend event. Robin is with me, plus Chris, another young man from our Center who reminds me of a Buddhist monk, not just because of his shaved head, but also his witty, insightful wisdom. At the halfway mark, I fall into self-imposed isolation, refraining from conversation, preferring the comfort of my own thoughts as I indulge in the sorry situation I find myself in.

"Hey, what's the matter with you, man," Robin inquires.

"Nothing!" I stonewall, unwilling to talk about it. I haven't shared the Sabrina story with the Center since my first attempt with Robin, sure that they'll misinterpret my motives and judge me for being trapped in emotional attachment. Of course, they'd be right, and that's why I won't share it with them.

Robin persists, "Okay, brother, you don't have to talk about it."

I hate shunning my best friend, and I know talking about my feelings would help. I don't *have* to bring up Sabrina. "I'm just totally overwhelmed. I'm under enormous pressure at work, I have to write the book, and my neck's really painful. You know I haven't had a sore neck like this since I started meditating."

Chris chips in. "Sounds pretty clear to me, man. You're taking responsibility for everything. Just listen to yourself. I have to do this, I have to do that."

"Well, it's okay for you guys, you don't have a job like mine."

"Well, excuse me," Chris retorts sarcastically.

Shame bubbles up for suggesting my job somehow makes me more important than them. I felt so close to God a few weeks ago, with all the experiences with Jesus, but now I feel so far away that I simply can't see the light.

Robin interrupts my thoughts. "Chris is right, brother. You've got to give all that responsibility to God. If you take all the responsibility yourself, you're going to burn out. Give it to God."

"Yeah, easy to say, but I've real deadlines to meet."

"Hey, come on now," Chris lends his support to Robin, "You know we're not saying you should be irresponsible, just that you shouldn't take responsibility for the outcome. The more you let go of responsibility, the more you free yourself from the burden and the more you'll be able to achieve. We've all been down this path before."

My God, they're right, I *have* been here before. And it's so obvious that for the last month, I *have* been trying to take responsibility for everything. I've spent so much energy worrying about the end result and playing martyr that I've nothing left to give. Yet if I accept that I can only do what I can, and take responsibility for my willingness rather than the result, then I'll produce my best without the stress.

I lean forward from the back seat and put a hand on each of their shoulders. "Thanks, guys, you've shown me how blind I've been."

And as the miles roll by, I lie back in the seat, close my eyes, and hand my responsibilities to God. By the time we arrive in Geelong, my neck pains have eased significantly, and by Sunday morning are completely gone, with me back to my newfound self.

This weekend is important to me for another reason in that, despite being in a strange environment over which I have no control, I feel completely at ease, able to let someone else do the controlling. Being able to sit back and go with the flow is a major step forward for me.

Chris stays in Geelong, and Robin and I drive back together. We stop at the Grampian Mountains, home to many wonderful walking trails. Needing a break from driving, we find a lonely trail and climb a rocky outcrop overlooking the low-lying plains.

"You know, Robin, it's like magic. When I really offered my problems to God, really gave up responsibility for them, they just disappeared."

"Yeah, it's great, isn't it. I noticed the change in you."

"It's as if God is like the old Grandfather Tree that I tell my children about, the one you can offer all your worries to and he takes care of them. This works for children because they believe it, they have faith. They don't let suspicion and doubt enter into them. And now it's actually working for me."

Back in Adelaide, the light returns. The realization of just how quickly God would respond to my call for help further enhances my relationship with the Divine Source. And I feel like I'm floating in a sea of love, drifting in clouds of gentle caresses, of radiant embraces. Yet at the same time, I'm able to focus totally. Oh, to be able to carry this feeling of love I'm receiving from God into the world with me, to swim in the sea of intoxicating love while going about my daily life.

It doesn't last, however. Like the Grim Reaper's scythe, the feelings I have for Sabrina cut me off at the ankles and drag me back to the reality of my limitations. She calls me mid-April, just to say hello, and we end up once more in a deeply emotional discussion that tells both of us that operating on a level of friendship is not going to be easy. We start off so well, but then I forget the warnings and let my fantasies of a life with her derail the locomotive pulling me towards my destiny.

In my next meditation, my teacher appears, smiling, but when he sees me, he turns serious and stares at me with gravity and bewilderment on his face. Then he turns and walks away. Almost immediately, Jesus appears looking sad. "My people are lost."

"I feel sad for you," I respond.

"Do not be sad. You need to help me."

A stream of light floods from my heart to my mind, and then out like a searchlight from my third eye, casting its glow to the Universe. Slow and deliberate, God's voice calls to me, "My child, My child, I have a message for you, but I am not going to deliver it because you are expecting it."

As I'm about to say my closing prayer and finish, I feel inspired to go back in, and soon the searchlight is back. The booming voice rebukes me sternly with ultimate authority, "My child, Get back in here."

A sharp pain like claws scrapes across my back, and as I try to enter into the pain, His voice booms once more, deliberate and clear. "You are special, very special and you have to accept that."

"But, I'm scared of my ego."

I start to cry, and the Divine Father speaks again, "Being special inwardly does not mean you will act with superiority. It does not mean that it will translate to arrogance. That is the old view you hold. Change it!"

The words are spoken as a command, no longer a gentle caressing voice, but one that demands compliance. He continues, "Very few people can receive Me like you do. You must let your heart's light shine for Me. Free yourself from the false humility of the ego, accept who you are, and you will find that real humility comes."

After a short pause, He adds, "Doubt is your real enemy. Let it go."

I spontaneously cry out, "Go! Go!" and as I do, I feel my Divine Father swoop down and flood me with His love. As I come out of meditation, my first question is, What do I do with this one? How do I cope with a message like this?

Tired and listless all day at work, I leave early and go home to bed. There, I hear crying in my heart and I know my inner self is calling to God. I feel like a little child snuggling in its mother's arms. I drift off in the surrender of a baby nestled in the security of its mother's bosom, yet my mind is furiously rooting for answers. I desperately crave a humility that would stand up to the prowling creatures of pride that are intent on their reign of fear.

A great wave of softness, yet with the force of a tsunami, enters through the crown of my head and spreads relentlessly through my body, sweeping any resistance aside. As I bask in the majesty of the unseen force, a voice announces, "Your cry has been heard. Open your heart to the power of humility."

As the voice fades, I know it's my wake-up call, time to move to a new level and let go of my excuses. And I know why I've been so flat all day. My resistances, fears, limitations, and excuses are old friends, and help me define who I am. I've let some of them go in small pieces, but this is more profound and I am grieving. Part of me doesn't want to let go of them, as if I'm saying goodbye to old friends at the airport and know that I'll never see them again.

I also sense trepidation. My days of wonderful yet passive meditation experiences are over. Now I'm being called to action. My draft papers have been served, and I must report for duty. It's time to integrate my inner and outer lives, I only wish I knew what that means, but I'm learning not to predict which way the journey will take me.

A few days later, I'm meditating to access my heart, but the entrance is blocked by a black, gluey mass, its arms extending across my inner sanctuary like the tentacles of a giant octopus. I know this black mass represents my attachment for Sabrina, and remembering the messages from my teacher and my inner wisdom, I resist the temptation to fight the black intruder, and rather offer it love. As I consciously evoke and focus love on the black gooey creature, it dissolves.

Suddenly, I'm in a river, flowing downstream past a magnificent tropical forest. I'm a part of the river itself, moving onwards as it delivers its precious cargo of nature's blood to the great ocean. An island emerges out of the water in front of me, and on reaching the shore, I notice Sabrina, crying.

I know that she's crying because she senses my attachment for her, the need I transmit continuously. She reaches out to attach herself to me with tendrils of energy, but I don't let her. The message clear, we're in a tug-of-war, both being sucked down into the murky depths of dependency as we fight to the surface to breathe the air of freedom. As I pour unconditional love into her, light cascades from the sky and over us in a sensuous display of heaven's unseen beauty. An empty boat beaches itself on the shore and as I move to get in, a voice commands, "No, do not get in. Put your attachments in here. It is going over the waterfall."

We both comply and a great peace sweeps through me, a heightening of love as I let go of my need. Another boat arrives carrying my teacher, and as I try to get in, bringing Sabrina with me, he smiles lovingly and says gently, but firmly, "No, she cannot come. She is not ready. You must go on alone."

I get in the boat, which moves off, leaving Sabrina behind. Freedom and love pour through me, billowing out a spinnaker in a blustery sea breeze, and I feel flooded with God's presence. Ahead, a large opening of light appears over the ocean, as if God's heart is opening up to allow me to enter into it, and as we sail through the opening, the Creator wraps me in His arms and caresses my heart in hands of velvet compassion.

This vision is clearly telling me that when I throw away my attachment, I will be blessed with unimaginable love. But equally obviously, Sabrina is not coming on the journey with me. My higher self is applying increasing pressure on me to pursue my calling, and is now commanding me to end the relationship with Sabrina. It really is that cut and dried, but the power of my emotional need and my fear of sailing into the uncharted waters of God's love are such that a slight crack remains, offering me hope that the vision meant Sabrina is not *yet* ready, leaving room for me to come back for her later.

A third meaningful message arrives a few days later, when I eavesdrop on a conversation between God and my higher self. They agree that I'm ready to move forward, that the next step is to go through the door to "nothing." This requires great faith and sincerity because the conscious part of me cannot see anything through this door. It's a huge, silent void, and part of me is afraid of extinction in the absolute "nothing."

Suddenly, I'm in a vast, white dome growing inside my heart. A door appears at one end of my heart, and opens to a place with no boundaries. I know it's the door to "nothing," and anxiety engulfs me. When I try to pass through, I'm paralyzed, lacking the trust necessary to pass through.

My attachments and lower desires, including sexual desires, parade before me, and I offer them to God. Despite the cleansing, I'm still not pure enough to go through the door. I look longingly out into the "nothing" for a long time, then try again, but still a fear of the unknown holds me back. After several failed attempts, a voice emanates from deep within me, resounding across the great dome, "I am coming to get you."

I'm back at the door, only now, it no longer opens on nothingness but a room in which stands a beautiful woman waiting for me, radiating golden light from her entire body. Suddenly I'm a small child basking in the warmth emanating from the woman. I intuit that the golden light is the same that I see when facing the representation of the Divine Father aspect of God, and I know this beautiful woman represents the Divine Mother aspect. This tells me that I'm ready to see different aspects of God, and in particular the Mother's compassion, not just the Father's love. Or is it that I *need* to see God in this way before I can move forward on the journey?

The following day, I travel to Canberra on business, and spend the night in the hotel room writing poems. I lie on the bed with the lights out and just let everything go, opening my heart to the freedom of inspiration. After a while, a poem forms in my mind, the words materializing, my only role being to provide the hand to write them down. Four poems come through, each of about 40 – 50 lines.

I awake the next morning with another poem forming in my head, and despite my efforts to ignore it and fall asleep again, it won't go away. Eventually, I succumb and still half asleep, write a poem with 88 lines about Sabrina and myself. It seems to be written for both of us and I feel I should send it to her, yet it will evoke intense emotions and challenge her spiritual views. But, who am I to decide what she can and can't read, and surely it's been written for both of us, so I send it. Several of the lines really capture my heart, and each time I read them, I see a different interpretation.

> *Trust that I am guiding you,*
> *Seek not to understand.*
> *Just listen to your spirits' voice,*
> *Reach out for My loving hand.*
>
> *But in this love you have for her,*
> *Your love for me must prevail.*
> *I must come first and always so,*
> *In My arms your heart must sail.*
>
> *Yes, I know it causes pain,*
> *The way you do not know.*
> *But trust in Me to love you all,*
> *And the way know I will show.*

In the wake of these powerful messages, I decide to share them with Ashoka. His door opens to reveal a haggard, tear-soaked face, tears hastily wiped away, and I'm shocked by how old he looks.

His greeting is polite rather than the jovial one I've come to expect. We sit in our usual positions on the cushions. I recount my continuing journey, the three visions and the poem I've sent to Sabrina, and the growing acceptance I have that there will be a time for us.

With an agility that belies his years, he leaps from his cushion and, towering over me, delivers a vehement tirade. "You young fool! Can't you see what you are doing. You are jeopardizing everything."

Stunned by his outburst, I'm rooted to the cushion, my mouth hanging open. "Don't you see what the messages are saying. You have a very important mission to carry out and you have woken up to it. You are being clearly told to put your attachment for this woman away and send it tumbling over the waterfall, so you can move forward to find God. But you do not listen, you fool. Do you want to throw everything away?"

His barrage spent, he slumps to his cushion, tears in his eyes. His face looking even older, he quietly asks, "Please forgive this old man. It is my youngest boy's birthday today. He would be forty, and I wish he were with me."

Putting aside my own confusion, I wrap my arms around him as the pain of years are unleashed from a fragile heart. His body surrenders to wracking, convulsing sobs borne in the desperation of a man who lost his son, and blames himself. As the agony within this dear old man flows down my arm, my own eyes fill with tears as I wonder about my relationship with my children.

Ashoka slowly gathers himself and rises to pace around the room. He returns to his cushion and tells me his story.

"I lost my real chance, you know. I was called to India. My Guru wanted me there by his side. I could have gone. My ex-wife had remarried, the boys were seven and eleven. They would have been fine.

"But my need to be responsible for them would not let me go. I could not trust another man with my boys, so I stayed. I stayed and I resented giving up the pursuit of God. So I turned my resentment on them. Oh, I did not see it at the time, but it is what I did. I became so focused on making them see the way they should live their life, in some forlorn attempt to live my truncated life through them.

"Oh, I would have taught them so much more by leaving, and learning the lessons of love I was called to learn. Then I could have helped them, guided them like a gentle beacon away from the traps of the needle and the corporation. Instead, I pushed them away from me."

"But you did go."

"Yes, but only after they turned away from me, only after they rejected me, only when I had no choice."

"But you still went."

"Ah, but my time had passed."

"You say that, but you have such wisdom."

"It is easy for an old man to have wisdom in hindsight. It is easy to give someone else advice. But the real measure of progress, the real learning, is in being able to apply the wisdom to your own life. I missed that chance."

"Ashoka, you have to stop blaming yourself."

A flicker of a smile expresses his appreciation at my concern. "Yes, I know that. But I also know that God calls us when He wants us as part of His game. And it is at that time we must go to Him. Do not miss your time, young one. Do not miss your time."

We fall silent, there being nothing more to be said. All I can do is stay with him, a poor substitute for a son he never knew as a man. After an hour, I feel his energy shift and sense it is time for him to be alone. We rise together and he hugs me, burying his head into my chest. Through a voice muffled by the fabric of my shirt, he says, "You may think that I have imparted wisdom into you. Perhaps you will never really appreciate how much you helped me by letting me share your journey."

A ripple of fear runs through me when I realize that his words are spoken in the past tense, as if he's saying goodbye. As I walk out the door, the last words I hear are, "Don't miss your chance, young one. Don't let your calling slip past you."

Part 7 • Trusting Myself

The Crash

ON THE WEDNESDAY following the tearful meeting with Ashoka, I'm at the Center, and am surprised when Robin doesn't arrive. He never misses a meeting. After meditation, Daphnie speaks to us in a very serious voice, "I'm sorry to let you know that Robin has been asked to leave the Center."

What! Not again. No reason why, no questions allowed, so I leave in confusion and call him. "What's going on, Robin?"

"Hey, brother, I don't really know. It seems there are some things I'm just not learning. But I trust our teacher, and I know it's for the best."

Though confused, he sounds relatively peaceful and once more, I'm taken by his faith. He continues, "You know, it's rare for someone to be asked to leave, and it never happens without a good reason. I just have to accept that it's for my own good."

"Yes," I agree, "we so often think that something's not right, but I'm learning that I simply don't have the full picture, and so how can I determine what's right?"

From what I know, it's very rare for our teacher to ask someone to leave a Center, and knowing the love he has for all his students, his decision to ask Robin to leave must surely be based on compassion. And, yes, I can see that Robin is stuck overcoming some fears that are likely to hold him back, so I figure this must be what he needs to help him move forward. I accept the decision and decide to honor the rule about not initiating contact with him.

The next day I fly to Melbourne for the day and, in the airport lounge, pick up a newspaper that's reporting about the riots in Indonesia that have been going on for several days. Since I don't have a television or read the newspaper, I was unaware of them. Then I remember that Karen is in Djakarta, so I call her secretary and discover that Karen is stuck there, trying to get a flight out.

The four people with whom I'm most intimate with are Robin, Karen, Sabrina and Ashoka. I have a very different relationship with each of them, but they all play an important role in my life, and now, I'm cut off from Robin and Karen.

A knot of fear forms in my stomach when I think of Sabrina. By now, she'll have received the poem and I wonder how she reacted to it. I call her from my cell phone in the cab on my way back to the airport and find that she's decidedly unhappy, angry even, about the poem. "The words cut into me like a knife. Such an outpouring of love from you is so unfair. I'm only human. How could you subject me to such conflict. If I could cut myself in half, I'd be with you in a flash, but you know where I'm at, you know about my feelings for my family. I just don't think I can cope with any more intensity from you."

I sit in the cab, ripped to shreds, my desires exposed for what they are, realizing that, despite all my promises to the contrary, despite all my words of inner strength and sincerity, my emotions have zapped my commonsense to the point of jeopardizing our friendship. The poem pushed her to the edge, the exact opposite of what I planned. I just want to sink into the cab's back seat and die, unable to bear the thought that I've deeply hurt this most precious and wonderful being.

"Look, perhaps I should just walk away and out of your life," I suggest.

In the long pause, I hold my heart in my hands, waiting for her to agree with the suggestion, but when she speaks, her tiny voice conveys such sorrow that my heart explodes in agony, "Don't go too far away."

Undoubtedly, Sabrina feels for me as I do for her, but the difference is that she has the will power to control her emotions, whereas I cannot. While I profess strength and the capacity to do the right things, the simple truth is that my emotions are wild animals, running where they wish. I still can't make the hard decisions and do the really difficult things, whereas Sabrina can call upon a deep strength to help her through. And how I love and respect her for it. But this time, I've pushed her to the absolute edge. Or have I? Who brought this to a head anyway? Who really composed the words of the poem that precipitated this situation?

In my own game plan, I try to work things out for myself, but at the same time, I'm just reacting to cues from the players in an even bigger game, a puppet being operated by my beloved Father. With increasing clarity, I see the two game plans playing out in my life. The divine plan, orchestrated by a higher force, by God, is evident in countless ways, and I wonder if I really have any say in what goes on in the smaller plan, driven by my ego and my desires. And as I wallow in the ruins of yet another relationship, I despair over whether my own little plan has one iota of significance within the divine plan.

Whatever the situation, the message is clear. I've been given enough messages, and have yet to act on them. But now, I can no longer let my emotions run unchecked, I can no longer indulge my emotional needs at Sabrina's expense. I've unfairly exposed her to an emotional outpouring that challenges her commitment to her family, the cornerstone of her life, and she's deeply hurt. But maybe I'm being too hard on myself for taking all the blame. Perhaps she, too, needs to learn a few things.

My failure to demonstrate the inner strength and faith in God necessary for the spiritual path plunges me into despair, and knocks me into the swamp of self-indulgence, into the darkness of my own ignorance. With no one else to turn to, I visit Ashoka, aware that he's far from sympathetic about my attachment, but deeply in need of someone talk to, someone to provide me with perspective and wisdom.

That's odd. His place is dark, but the door's ajar, so I push it open and enter. I'm horrified. It's empty. He's gone! A half-burned incense stick lies on the otherwise bare kitchen table. My God, where has he gone? Dazed at the disappearance of my friend, I leave the deserted room and walk along the side of the house to the front.

"Lookin' for som 'un, young fella," a craggy voice calls to me. Its owner stands at the front door, presumably Ashoka's landlady and well into her sixties with a tough weathered appearance.

"I just came to see Ashoka."

"He's gone."

"Yes, I can see that. Do you know where he's gone?"

"Nup. Din't leave no forwarding address. All he said was 'is boys needed 'im."

His boys needed him? One of them was dead. I walk out of the front gate consumed in my own thoughts, barely aware of the landlady's continuing prattle. "Strange old coot, don't ya think?"

No, not strange at all, I think. Just a wise, gentle, enlightened man caught in the strangling clutches of a fear he was never able to confront. I hope he's gone to confront it now. "Goodbye, old friend, I owe you a lot, and may you find what you're looking for. It's never too late to tackle your fears."

In just three days, I've lost perhaps the three most influential people in my life, and a fourth one is still out of reach. If God is playing a game on me, then He's really testing me now, but I know He's not about to desert me. He's blessed me with unimaginably wonderful experiences in the weeks leading up to this, and given me something to hold on to, something to help me climb back out of the swamp. By taking away from me at the same time three people on whom I've come to depend, He's clearly signaling that I need to rely on Him, and Him alone. Having the difference between His light and the darkness of emotional attachment so dramatically highlighted, I feel the attachment seep through every cell of my body, every corner of my being, and I hurt.

There's no way I want to live with the emotional attachment I've endured throughout my life, yet at the same time, it's familiar and safe in a way. Clearly, I'm being called higher, to rise up and cast off my human limitations, but exactly where this will end up, I have no idea, so a part of me remains afraid of the beauty, afraid of the potential, afraid to believe, resisting the move towards the light. I sense that part, a dark cloud roiling in my belly, stretching its claw-like hands up to clutch my heart, stalking out from the depth of my being to smother the light shining from my heart. It drags me down into a net of emotional need. I stew in it, indulge in it.

Sabrina constantly occupies my thoughts, and I'm unable to function at anywhere near my normal level. And yet, at the same time, I realize this is not so much about Sabrina as it is about my need for emotional dependency. Karen was right. And I know that I'm never going to have a better opportunity to deal with this life-long plague than right now. If I'm ever to have a fulfilling relationship, it has to be free of emotional codependence, in which I smother my partner in my own needs and drain her feminine energy to slake my own thirst.

I spend the next week challenging my faith in God, my spiritual path, and everything else in my life. Somehow, I find the strength within, the determination to climb out of the mire and back onto the path of light. And I try to do it on my own, even though I know the only way is to cry to God to set my heart free.

As I emerge from the wilderness, I look back on the words of the poem I sent to Sabrina:

> *"But in this love you have for her,*
> *Your love for Me must prevail.*
> *I must come first and always so,*
> *In My arms your heart must sail."*

For a while, I failed to put God first and it was necessary for me to experience, once again, the emotional trauma this produced within me. Having glimpsed what the love for another being could be like if based on spirit, on divinity, I was still unable to prevent my emotions from taking control and crushing it like a fragile flower. I've been unable to put God's love first even though I've glimpsed it, touched its beauty, felt its breath against my cheek, and seen it ascend like a beautiful sunrise. But somehow I feel I've been given a taste of what's possible, at a deeper and sustainable level for a time when I'm ready to receive it. God has shown me just how much work is required, and I also know that something is still missing. I'm not ready yet.

And so I let Sabrina go. I never had her in any sense, but I sought to bind her on an emotional level, and in doing so, I bound myself. As I free her from the chains of my illusion, I marvel at how much sweeter and purer my love for her feels. The more I'm able to let her go, the more I'm able to experience love.

So the mystery of love continues to unfold, and I once more find myself a captive on the journey to unravel it.

Paradigms Challenged

I N SYDNEY ONCE again, and I meet Karen for dinner. Finished with my work report, I update her on the Sabrina situation and what I've learned from the experience. I give her a copy of the poem that precipitated my conflict with Sabrina. As she reads, tears roll down her cheeks. "This is beautiful. You say you wrote it in fifteen minutes?"

"Yes, and when I rewrote it neatly, I couldn't even remember writing it. I'm sure it was given to me."

"Yes, I can see that. It looks like you've been set up, my friend."

"What do you mean?"

"You've been given so many messages about ending your relationship with Sabrina, but you didn't or couldn't listen to your inner voice. So it seems that a higher aspect of you gave you the poem, knowing it would force you and Sabrina to a decision point."

I laugh at the clarity of her thinking. She's so right. The Divine Creator is a master planner. Undoubtedly, He placed the poem in my mind and inspired me to send it to Sabrina, knowing that it would precipitate a crisis that would push me to face my dependency. Karen continues, "So you've finally let her go?"

"Yes, and I'm accepting that I need to listen to my inner voice. Every time I don't, I end up in turmoil."

Probing and to the point, Karen asks, "So what's stopping you from following it when you first hear it?"

"Increasingly the messages seem to be sending me in a direction contrary to everything I've known from the past."

"Why do you have to be constrained by the past?"

"Well, I guess I'm afraid. It comes down to faith. My mind wants to understand everything, and to just accept my inner messages, to ignore my mind, requires real faith. To be honest, my faith is strong as long as what the inner guidance tells me sits comfortably with what my mind, or should I say my ego, can accept as being good for me."

"But from what you tell me, when you do trust your inner messages, you experience joy. And when you don't, you get turmoil. Seems to be a message there."

"Yes, I know, but it's not that easy."

"Are you sure you're not just making excuses?"

I'll need a little time to reflect on this, and fall silent, so Karen opens up a new topic. "So what does all this mean for your future at work?"

"I really don't know. I'm happy with the environment and wouldn't want to be anywhere else. But I must admit, I'm struggling to get motivated these days. I feel the need for a change."

"That doesn't surprise me. What do you think you'd like to do?"

"I'm not sure. I believe there's a radically new way of looking at the business world, taking in the concepts of spirituality. I'm not sure how, but I sense that I'd like to try to implement something along these lines."

"Interesting. Let's talk about it some more soon."

Next morning, meditating in my hotel room, I'm taken to new heights. A brightly lit globe appears, light radiating outwards, yet at the same time shining inwards. I feel everything being sucked into the globe. My body, emotions and mind are all being drawn into the sphere of light in my heart. It's small and well defined on the outside but, as I enter into it, I realize that inside, it's vast. My whole life, my whole existence, my work, the house, my children, everything are being drawn into this light, as if everything is just one big universal reality.

Inside the globe, I'm in awe of its dimensions, and spellbound, I witness exploding stars and catch a glimpse of what appears to be the entire universe. Now it changes and I transform into a light grid that spans the Universe with no real form. I'm so vast that my presence stretches forever, and the music playing on a tape seems to be a part of me rather that some external sound I'm listening to.

The notes dance on the nerves of my heart, enticing them to a new height of awareness.

Suddenly, the scene changes once more and the nine planets appear. Bolts of lightning flash across the solar system and explosions of light cascade over the stars. Watching as the Universe plays games within me leaves me with a sense of our unlimited capacity.

With my heart still full of wonder, I take a run along the Sydney Harbor waterfront. In the lush greenery of the Botanic Gardens, a voice calls me, the words clearly spoken from within me, "You are doing well, but changes lie ahead. You have yet to meet the people you will move forward with spiritually."

What does this mean? The words stir up something I've been trying to ignore—a discomfort at the Center. At first I put this down to Robin's departure, but to my surprise, I soon accepted that as the best thing for his development. No, it's nothing to do with Robin, so what is it? For a year, it's literally been the center of my life, and I've loved going there, but now I feel reluctant, resentful even, and prefer to meditate on my own.

What's happening? Last night, Karen and I talked about my motivation at work, and this morning, my continued association with the Center is under the spotlight. Perhaps I just need a rest. Work is very intense at the moment and I need some alone time. I've arranged a retreat, a period of seclusion for myself, south of Perth next week, and hopefully, in the quiet of nature, I can receive some guidance. I recall the conversation with Karen over a month ago when she said, "Maybe you'll have to walk away from both Sabrina and your spiritual path and find a new path for yourself." Could she be right?

Tuesday morning, in mid June, and I arrive at the Stirling Ranges, a four-hour drive south of Perth, where I've rented one of two isolated cabins. Following my heart, I take a scenic route and come to a walking trail, straight up the steep slopes of Mount Talyberup. Halfway up, I'm exhausted but determined to reach the top. Higher up, a westerly wind howls ferociously and I'm happy to find shelter in a cave near the peak.

Looking out over the landscape, I notice the sky light up at one point on the horizon. A hole actually appears in the sky, from which stream bolts of lightning. As the light intensifies, I rub my eyes to make sure it's not a mirage. Without doubt, there really is a hole in the sky, and as I watch, the sky goes berserk with a light show that's so bright and powerful that it reminds me of a nuclear explosion.

In the past, I've seen energy coming from trees, but this is different, not a vision I'm seeing in my heart, but out in the sky and far away. Neither is it a reflection of the sun since the sky is socked in thick cloud. Slowly, the effect diminishes, and as I climb down the mountain, I sense that Mother Nature has a few surprises for me this week.

Further down the road, I arrive at Bluff Knoll, the biggest mountain in the park, which I intend to climb. The early winter weather is fierce, the wind screaming treacherously as the trail snakes its way around the mountain, and I'm in danger of being blown over the sheer drop on one side. The absence of other cars in the parking lot tells me that I'm alone on the mountain, the only one in the area crazy enough to venture up the rocky peak on such a dismal day. This only heightens my excitement, and yet underlying that is fear of some nameless fate awaiting me.

About half way up, I round a corner and become fully exposed to the howling gale. To prevent being ripped off the mountain and cast several hundred feet straight down on to the rocks below, I quickly sit down and grab on to a well-anchored boulder. Terror sets in, saying, "I'm crazy to be up here. I should turn around. Even seasoned climbers aren't daring to risk it, and I'm just a city boy in running shoes."

I'm about stand up, ready to go back, when the wind eases off enough for me to hear the soft, but firm words, "My child, you have to go on. You have not come here by mistake. No, I have brought you here to learn some lessons. You cannot think that, just because you have climbed one mountain, you need not climb the next. This outer challenge, in the face of the howling wind and chilling cold is symbolic of the inner mountains you must climb. In the inner world, you cannot just avoid a challenge just because you have already vanquished an earlier one. So go on, My child, overcome this one and see it as a symbol of your inner life."

Inspiration bubbles up within me, banishing all fear, and I stand up, face to the gale force buffeting, and head for the summit. The wind shrieks past me as ferociously as ever and I realize it never abated. I had simply become unaware of it.

At the summit, with no protection at all, I brace myself into the wind and let the magnificent forces of nature empower me as I exult in my success. The onset of dusk signals time to go back down, and the wind is even stronger and colder, but I feel no fear as I literally dance down the mountain.

I spend the next day by the ocean, walking over the rugged coastline, thinking about purity, and the relationship between this precious commodity and love. The weather has improved considerably, but it's still winter, and I have the beaches to myself. Solitary walking helps me turn inward in search of answers, but instead of answers, I find only more questions. What is love really, anyway? If I listen to the songs of lament, it is constant struggle, pain, and reliance on finding the right person to make you happy. Where are the songs about self-love and being whole?

Back at the cabin, I lie down and gaze out the window at the leaves of a nearby tree, and the backdrop of more trees and a grassy meadow. I have the entire place to myself, and can't remember ever feeling as peaceful and comfortable in my own solitude.

It's dark when I come downstairs to meditate, and about 15 minutes in, five gunshots ring out, close by. I'm shaken and scared, really scared because the other cabin is empty and there's no other house for miles. With meditation out of the question, I take a cautious look around outside, but apart from a cow in the next field, I sense no presence. I lock the doors, anyway.

After a jumpy evening, I retire early hoping to wake in the morning with my peace restored, but I'm woken in the early hours by geese honking and agitation among the other animals. Unable to get back to sleep, I shower and sit down to meditate. The meditation is filled with dark images, and a strong urge to leave the chalet. As I try to push my disquiet away, a voice clearly instructs me, "Go back to the coast this morning. Go to the blowholes and meditate there. Be there before the sun comes up."

Since I can't identify the source of the voice, and no vision accompanied it, I ignore it and make breakfast. As I'm eating, a wave of terror grips my throat and moves stealthily down to my heart. Something or someone is intent on my not being in that cabin, so close to panic, I grab my gear, pack the car and leave. I've never experienced such total and instant panic before and wonder whether the gunshots rattled me more than I realized, or is there something else?

I arrive at the blowholes at first light, with sunrise some time away. The blowholes are odd pipe-like rock configurations that direct incoming waves vertically in spectacular spouts, especially at high tide on stormy days. I find a sheltered place overlooking an outcropping that takes the brunt of the ocean's ferocity, and meditate to the soundtrack of booming and crashing waves. This close to nature, I quickly enter a deep meditation, and the soundtrack drifts away, unable to follow me within.

A voice, soft yet commanding, gently rebukes me, " My child, you must forge your own way in life. You must carve your own journey, not bound by any restrictions others place on you, or that you place on yourself. But always, always remember, maintain your love for Me and your loyal service to Me at all times in everything you do."

Netting appears across my heart and the voice directs, "Cut it, my child, cut it away – be free."

More instructions follow. "Look at the ocean below you."

Through half-open eyes, I gaze on the rocks about 50 feet below my lofty perch, being pounded by the fury of the ocean waves.

"Heed the lessons of nature, My child. In the face of nature's fury, they stand and absorb it all. They symbolize patience, courage and relentless faith. Like the rocks, you, too, must bring these qualities into your life if you are to withstand the challenges that await you."

I linger to enjoy the play of energies a little longer, and then make my way back to the car. It's already 8.30, and I've been there for nearly two hours, lost in meditation.

I head west in search of an isolated forest and, at the small town of Wallpool, I inquire about wilderness trails. "Go to Shannon," I'm told so, armed with a map, I head for the Shannon National Park, some 50 miles away.

While driving, I reflect on my two days of solitude and the lessons nature has taught me about inner strength, the courage and the determination needed to stand firm in the storm. These messages must be coming now because I'm going to need them, I reason, and shudder at the implications.

As I head out on the 5-mile trail, the rain starts, but unperturbed I march on, singing as I go, and soon reach the end of the trail, pleased at having the forest to myself. I turn round, and a mile back, I look for the perfect place to meditate. In front of me, the trees are glowing with light. This is the place.

Sitting down on the damp ground in the middle of the trail, I close my eyes and marvel at the absolute silence around me. I could be the only human on the planet, the solitude of the remote forest penetrated only by the chirping of birds and the wind sighing in the tree tops far above. My inner sanctuary comes easily, and I drift into a peaceful state of heightened awareness, experiencing a deep peace yet totally conscious of my inner workings.

I'm soon in my heart and watch the scene unfold. I've been here before, the colorful jungle scene, where my wisdom sits on the rock overlooking the towering waterfall. Today, my younger inner self joins him and I eavesdrop on their conversation.

"Have you come to talk about love?" my wisdom inquires.

"I'm not sure. What have you got to tell me? You're the one with the knowledge."

"Ha, ha, so true," he jokes, and continues, "Discovering love is like anything else. To change, you must take a journey, and this journey involves three steps. First you must let go of your old ways, dissolving the way you relate to love emotionally as well as intellectually. Only then can you move to the second stage, to rediscover love in a different context, to redefine the way you view love, the way you feel love, and the way you respond to it. When you have redefined the way you see love, you can start to live in this new way, and only then can embark on the third stage, which involves helping others go on their own journey of discovery."

He tosses a leaf into the water and watches it tumble over the falls. I wait intrigued to hear what he has to say next, but he surprises me with a question. "So where do you think you are on this journey?"

I'm intrigued at two aspects of myself conversing, with me not only the observer, but also contained within the younger of my two inner aspects. I'm participating in the discussion as the representation of my self, while receiving the wisdom of my older, higher aspect. I'm both a player in the scene and the audience, unable to influence what the player says.

The young seeker answers, "I feel I'm close to the transition of steps two and three. I've let go of my old ways and I'm learning a new way of love through God."

My wisdom looks bemused and smiles compassionately. "I'm sorry, my young friend, but you will have to think again. You have not yet completed step one. You still hold onto some old emotional views that must be discarded. You are just about ready to move to stage two, to redefine the way you look at love."

Taken aback that I still haven't shaken off my old emotional patterns after what I've been through with Sabrina, I flounder, and my wisdom poses another pertinent question. "What does love mean to you? How would you define it?"

"I don't know, I really don't know. I don't understand the relationship between the love for God growing within me and the love for other humans."

"Oh well, it doesn't matter. No one else does either."

I fall silent, and the older man speaks again, as a butterfly glides gently past his nose. "What do you think your mission is?"

Finally a question I can answer, thanks to the many visions on the subject. "To establish a bridge between the materialistic, intellectual population and true spirituality, and in doing so inspire the current generation to redefine the nature of love and human relations."

"Pretty good. So if you are to play even a tiny part in helping to redefine the nature of love, don't you think that you need to understand it first?"

"Yes, of course."

The older aspect of me continues, "Love! What a misleading word it has become in the world. Most people restrict it to the person they have a sexual relationship with, or to their immediate family, but it is much more encompassing than this. It is the key to unlocking the fear within each of us, the fear that must be released if we are to move forward in this world. But more than this, it is a state of consciousness that we enter into when we allow our spirit to come to the fore, thereby unleashing the full potential that exists within us."

"What a captivating definition. I love it," I retort, and we both laugh.

"Yes, it is. As you can see, real love has nothing to do with anyone else. It is not a feeling, but a state of consciousness. But to live in this state of consciousness, we must realize that we are spiritual beings, beings of pure love and light, here to have a human experience, not the other way around. Only with this understanding can we overcome the fear which prevents us living in love."

"How do I achieve this state?"

"Give it time. You must first rediscover the essence of your true self, and in the process you will discover the secrets of love. Someone will come into your life soon who will help you move down this path."

With that intriguing prediction, the vision fades.

As the miles roll by on the four-hour drive back to Perth, my thoughts are captured by the appearance of my inner wisdom. Since I've lost the people on whom I relied outwardly for support, my inner wisdom had appeared with greater frequency and is delivering longer messages than in the past, as if to fill the gaps left by Ashoka and, to a lesser extent, Robin.

Is this why Ashoka was so reluctant to let me visit him more often, I wonder, particularly in the early days of our relationship? Did he know how important it is to learn to seek the advice of my own inner wisdom, rather than relying on others?

A Testing Time

WITH THE EXPERIENCES of the wilderness still fresh, I feel as though I've been picked up, shaken, and put down in a different place, with the pieces in a new order, but with a body not yet capable of maintaining the balance of this new order. The trip to nature and solitude brought much to the fore, such as the feeling that I'm to leave the Center and follow a different path to God. I can no longer push from my mind the messages, for in the forests south of Perth, they spoke with a strident voice, creating great conflict, for I'm not ready to leave and don't want to leave. I love the people there as family, and I'm scared that leaving will cost me everything I've gained on the spiritual path and my only real contact with spirituality and God. Ironically, while I hear the messages in my heart, the fear of losing my connection with God strangles the tenuous thread through which these very messages flow.

Beneath the turmoil, however, I sense an inner strength and serenity looking for an opportunity to emerge. I know the goal and can achieve it, but must endure pain to get there. It's as though I'm looking across a ravine only a hundred feet wide, but must hack my way through the dense, steamy jungle below to get to the other side. I'd be crazy to leave the relative safety of the high ground to cross the crocodile-infested swamp below, but I know I must.

For about the last six months, Robin has suggested I contact Gerard, an Aikido teacher, massage therapist, and all round spiritual man. I haven't felt moved to follow his advice, but I sense that it's now time to pay him a visit. Tall and slender, with graying hair but a youngish face, he's nothing like I imagined. His soft, gentle manner puts me immediately at ease, and I pour out my life story, focusing on Sabrina and my conflict over leaving the Center. "I don't understand why I feel I need to leave. I love everyone there and it's given me so much."

He replies in a slow, gentle voice. "Sometimes we just have to accept our inner guidance, let go of the need to understand, and flow with the messages of our spirit."

"But I'm afraid to leave. Joining the spiritual path has given me so much. It's returned my life to me and I'm afraid that if I leave, then somehow I may lose everything and slip back to where I was."

"I understand how you feel. I had to go through a similar test years ago. But in reality, your connection with God belongs to you. It doesn't depend on the people at your Center. You will not lose it if you keep moving towards the light."

"But everyone at the Center seems terrified at the thought of ever leaving, or being asked to leave. They seem to feel their life would come to an end. I'd hate to feel like that, but I guess it rubs off on me."

"That view only exists because of their own fear. You see, God is steering each one of us according to our unique needs and our soul's mission here. Part of the problem with any organized group is that they develop a collective understanding that it's only their group that knows the truth. This generates a fear of losing what they have, as well as a feeling of superiority. We have to let go of the thought that our path is somehow separate, or better, and embrace the concept of oneness."

"That's what my teacher talks about. He never talks about his path being better or higher, but many of his students do."

Gerard starts the massage and I feel myself melting under his fingers. He continues, "You see, there is really only one path. I have a teacher in India, and I had one earlier, before he left the body. The messages of all the great masters are the same. It all comes down to opening up to love."

While he's working the muscles of my back, he adds, "It's all about letting go of where we are, and just accepting whatever comes from within, letting go and opening up to love."

"But what if I can't do that? What if I lose my connection?"

Gerard is not about to be fazed. "Look, God is the doer. The connection you have is with the Divine source, and no one can take that away except you. If your teacher is a genuine master, he will love you no matter what, and he'll understand whatever you do. You have nothing to fear from him. It's really up to you whether you keep moving forward, or slip back."

As he moves to my legs, he asks, "How comfortable have you been at leaving in the past?"

"What do you mean?"

"Well, have you been able to walk away from a relationship or a job without somewhere else to go?"

I review my life and gasp at his perspicacity. "You're right. I've never done it. To be honest, every time I've left someone or somewhere, I had someone or somewhere else to go."

"So, perhaps that's your real fear. Perhaps you're afraid of walking away with nowhere to go, and are looking for excuses to disguise the real issue. It's scary going into nothing, it takes real faith."

Panic floods me as I admit that Gerard has exposed one of my great fears. I'm afraid to walk away from something, with nothing to go to, like a circus trapeze artist worried that when he lets go of one trapeze, the next one won't be there, and he's left in mid-air.

"Sometimes," Gerard continues gently, "we just have to go deep into our hearts, ask the question and act on the first message we hear without giving our mind a chance to analyze it."

The massage over, I leave Gerard, feeling wonderful, flooded with light and peace, and with a new challenge to overcome. At home that evening, I open a book by Deepak Chopra, and a statement on the first page stops me in dead my tracks:

> *You are not going to follow a path that doesn't feel natural for very long, nor will it bring the growth you need, no matter how well intentioned you are.*

I read no further, the message delivered and I know what I must do. I know I must leave the Center, and face my fear of having nowhere to go, of stepping into a void. I know I must trust that God is guiding me, and will guide me where to go next. I must trust my own inner messages. But knowing this doesn't make it any easier.

It's the weekend and I'm enjoying the bi-weekly visits with my two beautiful children. Out at dinner on the Sunday night, my son insists I go to the ice cream machine with him. On the way back he says, "Dad, there are two reasons why I wanted you to come with me. One was to show you where the ice cream was, and the other was because I just like being with you."

Such a simple and honest statement from a young boy, but said with such love and affection, melts me. He sits on my knee and just cuddles in, and I feel so much love for both of them.

The next day, Belinda, my ex-wife, calls to tell me she is engaged to be married in November. I'm genuinely happy for her and for the children. It will be wonderful for them to have a "father" home every night. At the same time, I'm not naïve enough to think my children calling another man "Daddy" will be easy for me.

A few days later, I'm back in Sydney. Sabrina and I have talked only once since the poem incident and it was a pretty cool conversation. A distance has formed between us and I really feel as though I've let her go, yet I'm still bothered by the message I received in the forest on my Perth retreat telling me I'm at a junction regarding the way I view love. If I'm to truly move forward on the path of a divine love, I must be able to see Sabrina without becoming emotional. So I call her and suggest lunch. At first, she's reluctant, but she agrees to meet me later in the week.

Ten minutes after our agreed rendezvous time, I'm wondering if she hasn't changed her mind and is standing me up. She arrives a few minutes later and I'm expecting a relatively cool and uncomplicated encounter, more like two old friends catching up on each other's lives. After some small talk about our respective jobs, she starts to cry, and just falls apart.

Between sobs, she admits, "I'm really struggling just being with you. I'm finding it so hard to keep myself together."

Taken totally by surprise, I just sit while she sobs into her handkerchief. Then, as gently as possible, I ask, "How are you feeling now? I mean, how are you feeling being with me right now?"

"That's the real problem. It feels so right, so perfect. I'm not supposed to feel this good being with you. My marriage is really suffering as a result of my feelings for you, and I'm really struggling to keep it all together."

I'm lost for words. I've worked so hard to let her go, and now accept that a relationship is not right for us, not now at least. But I love her so much and feel so much pain for her that I want to wrap my arms around her and comfort her. But that just wouldn't be right. I search my feelings for something to say that would be appropriate, but the right words don't come.

Suddenly, she gets up, " I'm sorry, I have to go. I shouldn't even be here with you. The longer I stay, the harder it is. I thought that it would be okay this time, that maybe I was over you, but it just feels too right. I can't take it any more."

As she turns and flees the café, every fiber in me wants to run after her, wrap my arms around her and tell her how I feel about her. A month ago, I'd have done just that, but now I know it wouldn't be right. And besides, everything has already been said. We both know how we feel and that the relationship has nowhere to go. So, I sit in the booth alone and let my heart break in silence.

I realize that once I let her go, she felt safer in letting her true feelings surface, and they simply overwhelmed her. I saw so much love in her eyes and in her heart, but also so much pain. She is asking me to let her go yet, at the same time, to rescue her. I'm worried that she'll suppress her feelings to such an extent that she'll lose the essence of who she is and become a slave to the expectations she has of her duty to others. Ironically, she'll end up where I was several years ago.

Can I sit back and let her do that? On the one hand, she needs space to sort her life out, but on the other, I want to challenge her to do what's right for herself, and to listen to her spirit when it says it feels so right being with me. But I'm probably the last person who should do that. Not being impartial, what right do I have to do that? And maybe it's just my own desires talking anyway, trying to create another opportunity to talk to her.

I've worked so hard to let my attachment to Sabrina go, and now I'm plunged into a new emotional quagmire. All I know is that this is not the love I'm supposed to pursue, but merely a challenge to work through. It's also a challenge Sabrina has to work through, and I must resist the temptation to take responsibility for her pain. So, once more, I bury my pain and resign myself to walking out of her life for good, since we obviously can't see each other even just as friends.

Back in my hotel room, I'm drained and fall asleep for a couple of hours. Waking up refreshed, I go into meditation. A point of light appears on my blank screen, and suddenly things start flying past me in all directions. Trying to grab hold of them, I'm pulled in different directions by an unseen force. I stop trying to grab them and just let them go by. Once I surrender, the unseen force releases me and tranquility descends. What a wonderful reflection of my life, I think. Just as Gerard said, I must let go of everything and follow my spirit, and I'm sure it's urging me to let go of Sabrina for good.

Letting Go

S ATURDAY EVENING, AND I'm home alone when the phone rings, breaking my reverie. I'm surprised to hear Sabrina's voice. "Wow, I didn't expect to hear from you."

"Yes, I understand," she says, her voice calm and peaceful. "I just had to call and tell you that I'm all right. After the way I left you, I didn't know what you'd think."

"Well, it did take me by surprise, that's for sure."

"Look, Alistair, you know how I feel about you. I thought I was ready to deal with you face-to-face, but clearly I wasn't. I still had more work to do. I've been through hell in the last few days, but I'm through it now. I've climbed back up the mountain and I'm out of the darkness."

"Are you sure? You don't have to pretend to me."

"No, honestly, I've got my marriage back on track. I know what my priorities are, and I've been able to put you in the place in my life that you should be in. And now I feel a lot better about myself."

I can sense a deep peace in her that I've not heard in her previous attempts to convince me she's doing well, and I tell her, "Well, I'm really pleased for you. It's time for us both to let each other go."

"Yes, but you know, you'll always have a place in my heart."

"Yes, I know. And you'll always have a place in mine, too."

So, it's over. At first, I feel positive, knowing in my heart that she's doing the right thing, and respecting her courage and strength. But ironically, her display of strength only serves to further fuel my love for her, and my sense of loss is magnified. I've worked so hard to let her go over the months, and now I have to do it all over again, and it still hurts like crazy. But there's no turning back, only the opportunity to understand more deeply how easily my emotions can become so traumatized in the name of love.

The following Thursday, during my second appointment with Gerard, I tell him about the meeting with Sabrina and the subsequent phone call. Then he starts work on me. He works with energy, and he lets the feelings he receives through his hands guide him as to what to do. As he works on my stomach, he asks me to do an exercise on my abdomen. "I want you imagine you are breathing in through your heart and abdomen at the same time."

As I do, I can clearly visualize the two spots. My heart is full of light, but my abdomen looks like one of the hot mud pools I saw in the volcanic regions of New Zealand, full of black, smelly ooze. As I breathe through it, slowly it lightens in color, eventually becoming clear, sparkling spring water. My legs tingle as I feel a flow of energy moving through them and a sense of peace radiates from my abdomen.

Next, he moves his hands to the upper part of my chest, and resumes the discussion. "You have a blockage of energy in your heart. This could be stopping your love from really flowing. It seems to be associated with the left side, which is related to the mother."

"This is all new to me. I know nothing about energy flow."

"Well, we all contain male and female energy within us. In most men, the male energy is dominant. To be in balance, we need to have both the male and female energy."

His next question sparks my interest. "How do you relate to God?"

"Mainly as a divine old Grandfather figure, or as infinite light and power."

"So, you would say you see God more in the masculine form?"

"Oh, yes, most definitely. Recently, I've been seeing a divine female form, but usually it's always male."

"Then perhaps it's time to reach out for the Divine Mother aspect of God."

"What do you mean?"

"Well, God has many aspects. In the West, we tend to relate to the Father, due to our Christian upbringing, but in the East, they relate to many aspects of God including the Divine Mother and Divine Lover. I have a feeling that the difficulties you experience in intimate relationships are because you have a very well developed male energy but your female energy is underdeveloped. This makes you want to attach to the female in your life in order to tap into her energy."

Gerard continues talking but I'm no longer listening. My mind is back in the forest with a wise inner being sitting by a waterfall talking about discovering love, "Someone will come into your life soon who will help you move down this path."

Well, this someone is massaging me at this very moment, and he's just given me the clue I need. It's time to go searching for my inner female, and for the Divine Mother.

In the next morning's meditation, I'm walking along a path through the jungle. A strong impulse urges me to leave the path and strike off in another direction, but the jungle is a dense wall of vegetation and I can't see which way to go. Just then, I see my teacher sitting at a big junction in the path ahead with a bag of provisions and a map for the next leg of my journey. Down on the ground, the "me" in the vision can't see him, but observing the scene from above, I can. The vision fades from view, and the message is clear: that I'm to head off into the unknown jungle of life, trusting that I will be guided. In the vision, a clear trail headed off from where my teacher sat, suggesting that the way forward will be clear.

I could write to my teacher, asking him what the vision means, but I dismiss the urge because he has literally thousands of students who have been with him for many years, and I've been on his path for just over a year. I've never spoken to him personally and I don't know him at all as a person, even though I feel he knows me intimately on an inner level.

I could talk to the older members at the Center, but I honestly don't trust their judgement on this one. They are so focussed on the path that they can see no other, and I know what they'll say, so there's no point turning to them. And deep down, I'm afraid that if I ask my teacher for advice, he'll tell me to stay when I feel I should go. Oh brother, now I don't even trust my teacher to tell me openly what's right.

I recall Ashoka's words: "Remember, you each have your own unique path to follow to manifest your soul on Earth, so his words will not mean the same to everyone. It is what he says to you inwardly, what he communicates to you through your inner self during meditation, that is important."

He was right. I must listen to what I receive during meditation. And clearly the messages tell me I've to go, but when? In six weeks, I have another opportunity to go to New York, but I've been putting off the decision because of my conflict. Perhaps this vision is showing me that I should commit to going, that I need to go there to get my next set of instructions.

Jessy, my secretary, has already found out the best airfare deals, so that morning I ask, "Jessy, can you please book my flight to New York."

"Sure, Alistair, the best deal is one where you have to pay within 72 hours and you can't change it without a cancellation fee."

"Okay, book it."

"Are you sure you're really going?"

"Yes."

That evening, I get really sick, throwing up for the first time in over 20 years. The children are staying with me, but I have to go to bed at 6 pm and I stay there for 14 hours, except for a few brief spells to put the children to bed, and throw up some more. I'm wiped out, and wonder how I can be so sick. Is it associated with the black stuff I saw in my stomach the previous day with Gerard?

I promised the children that we'd go for a long day trip the next day, and despite still feeling fragile in the morning, I don't want to let them down, so we head off, me hoping that my condition will improve. My son chatters away, enjoying his turn in the front passenger seat. Out of the blue he says, "Dad, you're dad, but Mark (Belinda's future husband) is an awesome cool dad."

Like a pointed spear, a father's worst fear pierces my heart, ripping through the thin defenses protecting my deepest vulnerability. It's not jealousy since I'm genuinely happy for the children, because now they'll have what they always wanted, a dad who'll be home for them every night. No, the hurt is much deeper, a father's realization that he cannot give his children what they need most, that for a whole lot of reasons, I've failed them. And also, at another level, they'll no longer need me. Sure I'll always be their dad but they won't need me in the same way any more.

As the painful realization invoked by a six-year-old's innocent comment twists and turns in my tormented mind, I'm hit by a crisis of unimaginable proportions. A man once ruled by duty and responsibility, his self-worth determined solely by how much others needed him, is brought crashing to the painful realization that this is false. I know it, I've known it for a year now, but never before have I been forced to face it so blatantly.

As the children play in the sand, I sit on the beach, alone and empty. Everyone who ever needed me and on whom I relied for support has gone; first, Robin, then Ashoka, Sabrina, and now most painful of all, my own children. As I plunge to the bottom of an abyss, my heart crying in desolate emptiness, I suddenly realize how much I need to be loved, how I covet someone to love me. But even the thought of Sabrina, if she were free to come to my arms, doesn't console me. The thought of the woman I once felt such love for is powerless to assuage the pain. The emptiness I feel is far vaster than any human could fill. So I cry inwardly and keep smiling on the outside so that the children won't see how badly their dad hurts.

My desolation is absolute. Deserted by everything and everyone, even God, I'm scared. And at the very time I'm being guided to leave the Center. How can I risk losing everything the Center has given me? How can I walk away to nothing at a time when my need is so great, when everything else in my life seems to be falling apart?

But I've grown more than I give myself credit for. Yes, my emotions are running rampant, trying to take charge, to engulf me in the swamp of self-indulgence as they have in the past. But as the tentacles of darkness rise up to smother my freedom, a newfound strength emerges within me. And while the tears continue to fall inside my heart, I recall the recent messages from the wilderness in which God warned me that a time would come when I'd be challenged to the very core of my faith. He also identified the qualities I'd need to withstand the howling storms of my life. Armed with this knowledge, I detach myself from my emotions and watch them play their self-indulgent games, aware that they are not who I really am. In His wisdom, God has prepared me for this challenge and is testing me once again.

Although my relationship with God has grown to where I see Him as a Father figure of power, light and guidance, I still cannot reach the compassionate female aspects of God that I've tried to find in others for so long because I couldn't find them within myself. As I reflect on this, I find myself drifting into a state of half asleep, yet still half conscious. Suddenly, a swirling light appears in my heart, rotating like a distant galaxy, moving closer, growing and opening to emanate graceful streaks of purple, reaching out like loving fingers, beckoning me. Then a voice, musical, soft, and so filled with love that the tears of a lifetime dissolve at their caress, says, "Come to me, My child. Let Me love you."

I have no idea how long I stay in this state of bliss until my children wake me with, "Dad, dad, come and look at the sand castle we've built."

After being suitably impressed by their accomplishment, I drive us to another seaside town, where the children find an old ruin to keep them busy, giving me time to reflect on the experience at the beach. There's no doubt that I was touched by the Divine Mother calling me to see God in a more universal way yet, at the same time, to search for the love I need within me. Now I know why the love of a woman couldn't satisfy me, not until I first find what's missing within myself—the female aspect of me, dormant for four decades.

With this understanding, I would have expected the torment of my crippled emotions to abate, but not so. Even though I now understand why I'm feeling such loss, it seems that I still have to go through the pain.

The next day, I drop the children off at Mark's house. When we arrive, they leap out of the car and jump all over him, lost in their own world, too busy to even give their dad a goodbye hug. It's more than I can take and have to get out of there, fast. As I drive away, I cry tears of pain as my heart wracks in sorrow and loss. Yet the pain is tinged with hope because I know I'm finally leaving behind my old dependency relationships. It's been a long, hard journey, but finally She knows I'm ready to move on.

That evening, at Sunday meditation, I hope my decision to fly to New York will alleviate the turmoil and allow me to enjoy myself once more, but it doesn't. I'm still torn, part of me enjoying the camaraderie of the Center, yet the other part acutely aware of the message, "Leave, leave now!" But can I cope with two challenges at once?

As I drive home, my thoughts drift to Sabrina and I sense that closure is incomplete. Arriving home, I know I must write her one final letter telling her that in calling me to set herself free, she gave me another set of shackles from which I must free myself. Her call took me by surprise and I was unprepared to say the things I need to say to be able to draw to a close this part of my life, so I write from my heart:

> *"How my admiration, my love and my respect for you have grown even deeper than they were before. I'm so proud of you for fighting through your conflict and reaching the right decision, and I heard a peace in your voice the other night that I've not heard before. I also want to thank you for opening up your heart to me when we last spoke. You know you have been trying to hide it somewhere, but that is not possible. I know you just didn't feel safe letting it out, but it's so beautiful to see you let out your loving, caring, tender inner self. Please do not stop doing that.*
>
> *I reacted strongly to our conversation. I must say that it took me by surprise. Come to think of it, that's not a surprise, because so often you've taken me by surprise. First, I felt a relief and happiness for you – a feeling that everything was right. But I also felt a sense of loss. I know I've no right to feel a loss, but I did. I had worked so hard to let you go before we met this last time and I guess it was all a bit too much for my emotions. So, while deep within me I know it's right, my emotions are not always at one with what my spirit knows to be correct, and I must sit quietly and watch them do their dance.*
>
> *You know we have both been to the valley of despair at times in our relationship, but on our own, with God's guiding hand, and with, dare I say it, each other's help (we could have made it so much harder for each other), we have made it back to the top of the mountain. And I thank you for showing me the courage and the strength necessary for me to continue on my spiritual journey.*
>
> *I know you said how you were torn apart, and I feel for you in that. But I also have to tell you how badly I hurt*

at times, because I do not want to leave any secrets unsaid. I've not told you before just how much pain the last nine months have caused me, because it would not have been right, but now I feel that we've moved on to a new plane, and it's important for me that you know I've suffered too.

There have been times when I've been torn apart by inner conflict just as you have, torn by desperately wanting to do what was right by you and your family, and, of course, by God. Wanting to die before I would put you through the sort of pain that I eventually did, and yet driven also by such intense feelings that moved through me like a misty cloud, smothering my spirit's vision and clouding my heart. But I would do it all over again, endure it all over again, rather than having turned my back and walked away from the love we shared, albeit only briefly and from a distance.

So, my friend, I will always remember you, and you will always remain so very dear in my heart. You have taught me things, and shared things with me that I've never experienced before. But you are right, it's time to put your life back in order, time for me to continue on my journey, and time to appreciate the things that we had and to be thankful for the choices we made in the end.

And so, my dear Sabrina, I hope in writing this letter that I'm setting you free, in the same way that I'm setting myself free. I will always love you for who you are, and I hope you find true happiness in your life.

And so it ends. In closing the book on the story of Sabrina, I can now redirect my search for love from a woman to the Divine Mother, wherever that may take me.

The next day at work, Jessy reminds me, "Don't forget, you have to pay for your airline ticket today."

"Can you put it on my Visa card for me?"

"Yes, but are you sure you want to pay for it?"

"Why do you ask that?"

"Oh, I just have a feeling you won't go."

"Pay for the ticket."

Where did she get that idea from, I wonder. I haven't said anything to her about my conflict over the Center. Once I'm in New
York, then I'll know what to do.

At the Wednesday evening meditation, I struggle for answers
but none come. I can't even get into the discussion afterwards. In
fact, I'm not present in any form other than physically and I just
don't want to be there. I feel as if everyone can see through my
pretence, negative energy oozing out of every pore in my body,
and eventually I just have to get out, crying to God, to my teacher,
to tell me what's going on. "My dear God, I just can't stay here any
longer. I love all these people as my brothers and sisters, but I can't
be here any more."

As I slip out of the Center before any one else that night, I
know I'm leaving for the last time, and my heart bleeds in desperation and my mind screams, still reeling from the pain of the weekend, but I must accept the truth. It's time to move on, but knowing
this doesn't make leaving any easier. The path I'm on is intense
and beautiful. When you join, you're accepted as part of a larger
family and treated warmly by everyone as a brother or sister. So
it's no easy thing to leave, as in a way, I'm leaving what has become my new family. And so I walk out the door with a heavy
heart, but also knowing that whatever lies ahead is exactly what I
must face, and that I must find the courage to go out on my own.

Driving home, I sense a new direction, a new adventure in my
life. For the first time, I've followed my inner voice when it's in
direct conflict with my mind, which is telling me all the reasons to
stay. For the first time, I've found the courage, the faith, to trust the
messages from within. I'm walking into the unknown, leaving somewhere simply because it's no longer right to stay. There is nowhere
else to go, but I have a faith in the guidance I receive, and I've
come to see this as the most powerful gift one can ever be given.
Because with this faith, I need never again be afraid of where life
will take me.

I can't just walk away without officially resigning from the
Center, and I need to test my feelings before taking that step. I
decide to talk to Ivan, whom I trust completely. He's a little older
than me, married with four children. His wife is also a member and
they embody, in my eyes, what love in a marriage should be.

On Friday, I drive over to see Ivan to tell him about my decision. He's taken aback but listens patiently as I relate my story. We meditate together and afterwards we just sit, old friends saying farewell. I look into his eyes and see nothing but love, total unconditional love, as I've never before seen in another man. "I don't understand it, my friend, but it feels right. I feel a real peace in you."

"Thanks, Ivan." In the circumstances, he couldn't have uttered more consoling words.

As I get up to leave, we hug and he says, "I don't know where you're going, but I know you're on a journey."

I've already written out a departure letter, and the next morning, I deliver it to the Center leader. Her reaction is quite different, and in shock, she protests, "No, Alistair, not you."

Tears come to her eyes and I feel like I'm going through another divorce. After composing herself, she continues, "Do you know what you're doing? Do you know what you're giving up?"

"Perhaps not, but I don't have a choice. If I can't trust my inner voice, then what else is there? I've got to go."

How ironic, I think, that I find myself consoling her. Driving home, I feel a newfound freedom, much as one does when a failed relationship finally comes to an end and the turmoil of living in falsity is over.

As Sunday evening arrives, the time I should be at the Center, all my fears surface with a vengeance. I've made a commitment to myself to continue meditating, knowing how important it is to reach for a deeper connection with God. I sit down alone, doubt raging in my mind. What if I can't meditate any more? What if all my light is gone?

My worst fears are confirmed. The meditation is terrible, unable to move past the constant thoughts flooding through my brain. Soon my head is splitting open with a headache as an excruciating pain shoots up the center of my back. After half an hour, which seems like two, I'm close to giving up, when I remember the messages from my trip to nature. I realize that, once more, I've fallen into the trap of thinking I can fight my fear, rather than embrace it and offer it love. So I visualize love shooting up out of my heart into my mind, comforting it in a time of crisis.

Almost immediately, a blazing light sweeps into me from above, through the top of my head, spreading out through my heart and flooding the room. A voice comes to me from within, "Come in here, young one."

Out of the light materializes the familiar scene of an old man sitting at a waterfall. My inner wisdom speaks again. "Well boy, you really have done it. You have trusted your heart and walked away, with nowhere to go."

"Yes, but I'm afraid. What if I've done the wrong thing?"

"There is no such thing."

"What do you mean?"

"Providing you act sincerely in the belief that you are following your inner guidance, there are no right or wrong decisions, only choices made out of a series of possibilities."

"I don't understand."

"You must learn to trust your inner guidance and not be influenced by the reactions of others. This is an important decision for you. Even if you look back in hindsight with regret, you have to follow your inner voice."

"But I'm afraid of losing my connection with God."

"Oh, how little faith we have, eh. Do you think God is going to abandon you?"

"Well, no," I reply, more in hope than certainty.

He sits back and closes his eyes, a relaxed look on his face, but apparently deep in concentration, as if deciding what to say next. Eventually he turns to me and continues. "You cannot approach God through fear. God can only be reached through a state of love. If you stay at the Center out of fear, you cannot operate out of love. God will not judge your decision. To Him, past decisions are exactly those, past. What is important is your willingness to serve Him right now.

"People get so caught up over which great teacher is right, which one has the most influence and which one can take you further. There is so much conflict in the world because humans try to separate everything and put a structure around it. The truth is that the messages of all the great masters, both past and present are the same. They all talk about love and the need to approach God through love."

"So what happened to all the religions?"

"When groups of people get together, they place their own interpretations on the teacher's words. They start to erect their own structures, their own constraints and their own limitations. As this continues, fear starts to creep in and, as the constraints grow, it becomes increasingly difficult to maintain a state of love and hence to approach God through love."

"I can see the constraints in Christianity."

"We should not single out Christianity, because it happens to them all. Every religion starts in the same foundation of love, of approaching God through love, but over time the structures built around the teachings of the great masters become more established, and it becomes increasingly difficult to approach God through a state of love within the confines of these structures. So in essence, there is little difference between the teachings of all the great masters past and present, only a difference in the structures that have been erected around these teachings."

"So are you saying that the traditional religions are driven out of fear?"

"Well, yes, although it is changing in some areas. But it is not just the traditional religions. Your Center was the same."

"But my teacher talks only of love."

"Yes, he does. But was love practiced in the Center you belonged in, or are we already seeing the establishment of the structures that impose a condition of fear?"

His words strike a chord. That's exactly what was happening there.

He continues, "When we get to the stage that the structure takes over, rather than unconditional surrender to the Creator, then we are driven not out of love, but out of fear, out of a need to conform to the collective judgements of others. In placing constraints on God, when we place Him within the confines of a structured teaching, with strict guidelines established for the masses, then one feels confusion, tension, and inner turmoil. When our own inner voice is sending messages that do not fit exactly within the confines of the structure, then this inner turmoil is inevitable, and in this state of turmoil, fear sweeps in to replace love."

"So how do we attain a state of love so we can approach God in this state?"

"The only way to remain in a state of love, where love is the prevailing consciousness, is to establish your own personal connection with God."

I reflect on his words, and another question strikes me, "But some of the people I see on the spiritual path seem very happy and I would have thought they were in a state of love."

"Indeed, many are. Some are extremely happy and making wonderful progress."

"But doesn't that contradict everything you've just told me?"

"No, not at all. Those people have seen beyond the structures that inevitably must be established to maintain an organization the size of your teacher's. They clearly see your teacher as being separate from the other students they mix with. In this way, they go beyond the confines of the structures and approach the teacher through an individual connection, through love. And this allows them to enter into a state of love in which they can approach God."

"I wasn't able to do that."

"No, it seems you were not able to. Perhaps you were never meant to."

My inner wisdom seems to have completed his lesson, and leans back against a tree to watch the water cascade over the rocks. What lessons in nature! Isn't life just like the river? Sometimes we have to go through periods of turbulence and upheaval to get to a new level, but if we try to resist, we can be caught in a stagnant lagoon in the quiet corners of the river.

My thoughts are disturbed as I hear my wisdom continues my education. "Ah, but talking of love, what a fascinating subject. Do you recall the conversation we had in the forest a while back?"

"Yes, of course."

"I told you then that the pursuit of love was a three-step process."

"Yes, I recall well."

"The first part is over. You have let go of Sabrina, and there is no going back."

"Yes, I know."

"You have realized that the second part of the journey is all about seeking out the female within you, and to do that, you must pursue the Mother aspect of God. Throw off the limited view you have of God and cry to Her in all Her splendor."

"How do I do that?"

"You will know. You are ready."

"Am I to have another relationship?"

"Ah, my boy, that is up to you. But first you must become whole enough. You must bring to the fore your inner female so that you no longer need to take another's energy. You must seek the feminine love from within, and from God, for only then can you pursue true love in a relationship."

After a short pause, he continues, "Do not go looking for another relationship. She will come when you are ready, but she will not come *until you no longer need her*. Remember those words."

My wisdom gets up as if to leave, but then turns back to me. "Oh, there is one more thing which is important. Now listen very carefully. Just because you have left his Center, do not turn your back on your teacher. He is a very great soul, and despite what others may try to tell you, he will never desert you. He has taken you on as a student, and made a commitment to you at the level of your soul. His love for you is greater than you can ever imagine.

"You have been guided to go off in another direction, but do not think that means you can do it on your own. It is more important than ever to maintain your spiritual practice. And you can, in fact, you *must*, nurture the inner connection with your teacher."

As he turns to leave, I call out, "How can I find you?"

"I'm always here within you. I will appear when you need me. Enjoy the journey."

About the Author

Alistair Smith is an ordinary man who was taken on a remarkable journey. As a qualified engineer, he enjoyed a successful career in the construction industry. In 1992, he joined an Australian energy utility based out of Adelaide, his home city, where a series of promotions took him to head up the Mergers and Acquisitions Division.

Following a divorce and a reassessment of his life, he started meditating and his journey of discovery began. Soon after, a series of messages from a higher source directed him to turn his back on his career and dedicate his life to communicating the journey to love.

While grappling with the significance of this challenge, he traveled to Assisi, Italy, where he met Janine, his twin flame. Their spiritual merging provided the final impetus to follow the inner messages and commit to a life of service. He has dedicated his life to bringing a message of hope to people also on the journey to love, through sharing his own experiences in a way that leaves nothing hidden.

Alistair now lives with his wife Janine in Hull, Quebec. His two wonderful children remain in Australia with their mother, and he visits them at every opportunity. He is currently working on his next two books: *Coming Home to ...* and *Adventure into Innocence*.

For information about his workshop schedule, email him at:
alistair.smith@sympatico.ca